Small Doses

Amanda Seales

Editor: Samantha Weiner
Designer: Sebit Min
Production Manager: Michael Kaserkie

Library of Congress Control Number: 2018958836

ISBN: 978-1-4197-3450-2
eISBN: 978-1-68335-494-9

Printed and bound in the U.S.A.
10 9 8 7 6 5 4 3 2

Abrams Image books are available at special discounts
when purchased in quantity for premiums and
promotions as well as fundraising or educational use.
Special editions can also be created to specification.
For details, contact specialsales@abramsbooks.com
or the address below.

Abrams Image® is a registered trademark
of Harry N. Abrams, Inc.

ABRAMS The Art of Books
195 Broadway, New York, NY 10007
abramsbooks.com

Small Doses

Amanda Seales

ABRAMS IMAGE, NEW YORK

FOR NETS

These words come from experience, hope, and faith. You may not agree with all of them, but know they're born from a pure place.

CHAPTER 1

Ladies First

In a Woman's Best Interest &
Slaying in Spite of Sexism

WOMANHOOD IS BY NO MEANS EASY. I mean, it's def got its perks, but the whole period thing is a drag, and we could all do without that pesky patriarchy and its pal, misogyny. Women are the shit! It has to be said. We've made an entire existence out of proving that on a regular basis, in arenas welcoming or not, and I see no signs of stopping any time soon. We can't.

> One thing I became aware of in my traveling recently through Africa and the Middle East is in every country that you go to usually the degree of progress can never be separated from the woman. If you're in the country that's progressive, the woman is progressive. If you're in a country that reflects the consciousness of the importance of education, it's because the woman is aware of the importance of education. But in every backward country you'll find the women are backward and in every country where education is not stressed, it's because the women don't have education.
>
> —Malcolm X

As Malcolm states above, when women flourish, the community flourishes. Everybody wins. Why do you think the Black Eyed Peas added Fergie? Ruff Ryders brought in Eve? The Roots tossed around the possibility of making me a member because women have a way of elevating any previously predominantly male space. Some might say it's the estrogen, or the natural nurturing, but I liken it to a different perspective being added that extends the vision beyond its previous horizon.

Full of life, figuratively, and in some cases, literally, we are vitality in human form. Even in the stories of religion, whether Eve with the apple or Durga with her trishul or Isis spreading her wings, women are simply not the falsehood that has been told throughout history, depicting us as weak, unable, and unworthy of education. Unfortunately, instead of this making more spaces for women, it fuels the fear-driven insecurities of those propping up the pillars of patriarchy, freeaakkss weak men out, and they then resort to acts of oppression and suppression in an attempt to dull our glow. The world over, women have been underutilized, disrespected, and battered in unique ways that intersect at the site of our gender, yet we have continued to rise.

Now, we find ourselves at a turning point in history, where, particularly in the west, though our rights to our bodies continue to be decided upon by rooms of soulless, melanin-less men in expensive muted suits and Fantastic Sams haircuts, we lean in, and grow our numbers, pushing the narrative to finally hold the pen in writing herstory. Daily we defy the degradation of being considered only for a reproductive purpose, or objectified for sexual pleasure, or vilified for independent thought. We actively disembowel proponents of body shaming, reclaiming our many shapes and sizes in their natural forms. We are raising the volume on having zero tolerance for abuse and mistreatment. We are educating the masses on rape culture and holding predators accountable. We are a movement.

That said, we are not a monolith. Once upon a time womanhood was measured simply by being born with a certain set of reproductive organs. Over time, as we have expanded beyond just our sexuality and gender assignments, we have come to see the broadness of its beauty, and the complexity in its actuality. No matter what type of woman you identify as, be it cisgender, trans, lesbian, queer, another label, or without a label at all, to speak about being a woman is to speak about all of these things from various points of marginalized society while being fully aware of your inner sanctum of "supa." The most privileged women to the most forgotten have all been relegated to the back in one way or another to stand behind as patriarchy impedes their progress. For that you would think intersectionality would be a natural part of feminism—the fight for women's equality. However, feminism is still navigating its way through other obstacles of difference to truly be effective for the various types of women it should be speaking for. In the meantime, we must continue to speak for ourselves, and when that ain't enough, join with others in bringing the noise!

Body and Beauty BS

Bras, Brows,
and Bics

Tummies,
Tanks, and Tits

Our bodies,
and faces,

Are glorious,
even when graceless.

ASSETS

I was on a red carpet once and an interviewer asked me, "What do you consider your best body part." I could have said, "My booty." I've been told it's nice and booties are all the rage. I could have said, "My eyes." That always sounds poetic and like you're deep and whatnot. I could have said, "My feet," then launched into the tale of overcoming my high-school-born "caveman-feet" complex. All would have been perfectly acceptable and somewhat predictable. To be honest, none of those occurred to me. I replied, "My brain." She looked at me as if she had never considered that the answer could be something outside of a body part typically objectified, whether in adoration or with disdain. I watched as her face contorted from confused to intrigued to impressed. She high-fived me, and I was glad that it seemed like not only had she been presented with a new perspective on her question, but also a new perspective on how we women should view our bodies.

"CLASSIC BEAUTY"

To some, when a woman is considered a "classic beauty," it is based on Greek art. She is the modern-day example of what the artisans of classic visual art considered beautiful. To others, it refers to a certain symmetry of the features and how they align. To others it's a reference to simplicity and timelessness. I get that, but at this point, in our neocolonial post-implant media-soaked society when I hear "classic beauty" it's code for describing the features of women that the white guys with the most money think are pretty. They are driving the dollars to the companies that drive the media which drives the masses in how they are influenced to spend their dollars. If the Fortune 500 CEOs thought red hair and freckles were the cat's meow, blond and blue-eyed would be demoted from the "classic beauty" standard to "meh." My point is that beauty can be observed by men, but it is not and should not be determined by them. It has all kinds of definitions and truly is determined by each of us individually.

PLEASE TELL OTHER WOMEN:

- When they have food in their teeth.
- If their tag is sticking out.
- If they have lipstick on their teeth.
- If their thong is showing.
- If their fly is down.
- If you like their outfit.
- If you've been cautioned about a creep.
- If their significant other is being shady.

In other words, let's look out for each other. Society has created multiple ways for us to be self-conscious about things that naturally happen if you're simply moving in the world. So, let's at least help to alleviate the feeling of embarrassment by normalizing this stuff with basic acts of attentiveness to your fellow gals!

BROWS, BRAS, AND BICS

I was a late bloomer. So beauty stuff really wasn't my speed. Sure, I obsessed over supermodels like Naomi Campbell and Christy Turlington, and yes, I absolutely tried on my mom's Fashion Fair lipstick when she wasn't home, and I had an overabundance of Lip Smackers lip gloss pouring out of my Spice Girls, Lisa Frank, 5-7-9 existence, but still, I was 4'9" junior year of high school, so I never really delved into the glam of it all till much, much later. So imagine my shock and dismay when one day at lunch my BFF, Tara, turned to me and said, "I'm sorry but we can't be best friends anymore. You don't even pluck your eyebrows." The horror. I'm not sure I can blame her—my eyebrows resembled two very voluminous caterpillars hoisted above my eyes; pair that with my Gap Kids wardrobe and I really wasn't what you would consider a "cool kid." Three years later, I would eventually get my eyebrows plucked on a hotel bed at National Foundation for Advancement in the Arts week (now YoungArts) by Alex, a fellow actor, in full acceptance of his homosexuality and sporting a flare for the dramatic. That flare had my eyebrows diminished from hungry hungry caterpillars to skinny skinny snakes. My driver's license photo looked like I was surprised I passed. These days eyebrows are a movement! I had no idea that something so seemingly mundane could be the source of entire product lines, careers, and stores! Folks are getting their brows tattooed, threaded, implanted—it's big business! Maybe my eleventh grade BFF was ahead of the pack and knew the brow game was going to be poppin'. Alex sure did!

Does anyone else's titties audibly sigh when they take off their bra at the end of the day? It truly doesn't matter the size of your set, bras can feel like straightjackets. You get home and that clasp comes off and you gotta just let 'em hang free, run with the wind, embrace the indigenous ways, and let 'em breathe. Dance to Fela Kuti in your living room.

I was so scared to ask my mom if I could shave my legs that I created a game of hangman and had her play with me at the kitchen table revealing, "I want to shave my legs." In true Caribbean mother fashion she just waved her hand and said, "So shave your legs . . . don't get cut!" That was my teaching. The first time, I created a lather that was cartoon worthy, and blindly sunk the Bic razor deep in like when you fall backward into a snowbank, until I felt it make contact with my skin. I tried my best to mimic the relaxed wrist movements I saw in the commercials in order to avoid any nicks. It was so far, so good until I caught one little piece of shin skin. When the water hit it, I thought I was overreacting but no, THAT SHIT STUNG LIKE HELL. It hurt so bad I contemplated if this was the life for me or if I could be a woman liberated from the pressures of hair removal. I remembered that I had two more years of middle school and at that very second boys were cooking up a slew of insults tailor-made for the prepubescent posse. I was already flat-chested. I refused to provide any more ammunition. Next time I'd just have to use clippers.

MAKEUP IS A FRONT

Makeup serves many purposes. None of them are to fool men. That's all I have to say about that.

FAT SHAMING

Our bodies are not up for discussion.

So many of women's decisions on how we manage our bodies are based on influences that are outside of our best interests. This business of expecting women to have a bald nether region is just foolish. To each their own! I, for one, don't feel comfortable rocking the pubic high-top fade, but at the same time, I'm not with feeling like I have to have a hairless cat, either.

AND NOW, A LIST OF ALTERNATIVE NAMES FOR YOUR VAGINA

- Shang-ri-lina
- The Magic Middle
- Vajayjay
- Your Sanctuary
- Pinkville
- *La + whatever your middle name is* Mine would be: La *Ingrid*
- Dulcevita
- Moonriver
- Ambrosia
- Yes Man's Land

Pretty
vs. Gorgeous

YOU KNOW WHAT? EVERY WOMAN IS PRETTY, gorgeous, fly, sexy, cute, bangin', fine, bad, stacked, pretty hot and tempting (or PHAT), etc., etc., etc., in their own way. Learn and love what YOU consider to be pretty, gorgeous, fly, sexy, cute, bangin', fine, bad, stacked, pretty hot and tempting (or PHAT) about you, and don't base that on what anyone else thinks. And that's all I have to say about that!

Styles Upon Styles Is What I Wear

Style is personal and speaks for you without you having to say a word. Super flared jeans, a Pepto-pink Old Navy bubble coat, and Kangols . . . SO. Many. Kangols! I look back at some of my style choices and just SMH at what they were attempting to say "Sexy?" "B-girl steez?" "I'M DIFFERENT!" "New New Yorker in college that doesn't live with my mom so I can wear what I want?" For a long time my style was speaking for me and how I wanted people to see me. Eventually I'd be lucky enough to have the opportunity to work with a number of dope stylists on different projects who helped me to get closer to my own voice. I'd learn different tips and tricks along the way, like the hair look is a part of the whole look, and that I can pretty much never go wrong in green, or my own rule, the "I'm giving you _____" principle of color blocking. For instance, if I'm wearing two different versions of pink, I feel like I'm not matching. However, if I hit you with three versions, it ain't that I'm not matching, I'm just "giving you pink." I live by this to this day, LOL.

Another rule is that a label doesn't make it fly. Too often, I see folks in a look that is not flattering and wonder why they wore that, then it all becomes clear: It's by some designer. Money don't make it fly. When you see celebrities in brands that are considered luxury, sure they may be better quality fabric, or construction, but at the end of the day it's about what looks good on you. Don't let that be determined by what comes out of your wallet. Instead let it be determined by how it makes you feel. I clown my Kangols now, but back then they really made me feel like myself. I was a true B-girl and hip-hop head at heart, and it was a key component to my uniform.

When I first got on MTV2 I had peers who told me I needed to start dressing differently now that I was on my way to being a celebrity. They told me I had to stop wearing sneakers all the time and start rocking stilettos. I needed to cut out rockin my natural curl, press my hair, and wear it straight. There were all these rules and none of them felt right for me. So where did I end up? Right back in my Chucks and Kangols, gold bangles, door knockers, and I was a showstopper!

Still, so much about knowing your style is knowing yourself, and that is an ever-changing process. Every time you leave the house to go somewhere of note, you want to have the confidence of knowing you're at your best. You want to walk into a room as if upon leaving your house you took one last look in the mirror and a masterfully stylish black gay man named La'Travius popped up and said, "Yassssssssss biiiiiiiiiiiiiihhhhhhhhhhh," then sent you on your way. After a certain point my Kangols were no longer feeling La'Travius-approved when I looked in the mirror, and I went through that awkward stage we all go through in grade school, but as a full-on adult in my late twenties. Even though I always know how to identify and articulate my point of view about seemingly everything, when it came to fashion, I could never find my own words. I didn't have them because in my constant quest to define myself, and my work, and my brand, and yada yada yada, I became more concerned about how my look spoke to others than how it spoke to me. It was designer Sharufa Rashied-Walker of JINAKI that changed that.

In 2012 we were introduced via a mutual acquaintance who felt we'd work well together. Sharufa began dressing me in her designs for events but would add pieces from my closet to bring the look together. I would always be amazed at how she'd uncover gems from my drawers and put them in looks in ways that I *never* would have imagined. Finally, one afternoon when we were doing a fitting, I asked her, "How do you do it? How do you turn these particles in my closet into pieces? How do you give these typically inane items identity?" She told me I needed to change my perspective. "You're a painter. In your work you do all this dope stuff with color on the canvas. You gotta dress yourself with the same vision. Think of yourself as the canvas. Create art with your clothes." A lightbulb went on. It was like I'd successfully completed Rosetta Stone for the unstylish. The sky opened up and rained down ideas. I know that may sound like some existential BS to some, but how I was viewing myself truly changed and redefined how I approached style, and how it represented me.

I no longer dress based on how I want folks to see me, but how I want to see myself—as art that elevates the vibrance in a room. That doesn't mean with just colors or prints, it's also in the confidence of how I feel in my fashion, the distinctiveness of the pieces, and how they're paired. I do my best (and sometimes I'm lucky enough to work with bomb-ass stylists, like Shiona Turini, Mecca, and Bryan) to create/wear looks that, like my artwork, are abstract yet defined, bold and black, eclectic but not eccentric. Fashion, clothes, and style do not define you. It may not be your thing. Don't let it get in the way of you being you and loving you. For me, fashion is art. The same way you walk into a room and marvel at a masterpiece crafted by an artisan of creative vision, that's how I want my style to be seen when I walk in a room! My style, like my voice, is developing every day to emphatically encourage folks to challenge the status quo, comfortably live their truth, and be the light on their own path to joy. Now, when my style speaks for me, it says what I truly am: "This woman is vitality . . . and won't take no shit!"

Rape Culture

"Boys will be boys" they say
to excuse the violence,
but let's call it what it is
and break the silence.

EVERYDAY FORMS OF SEXISM

There are phrases that are so ingrained in our society that we don't even realize just how problematic they are until we take a closer look at what's truly behind the words.

- **"...like a girl" really means:** "I believe women are capable of a lesser standard of skill/strength than men, so I'm using them as a synonym for addressing your less than stellar performance."
- **"...for a girl" really means:** "I believe women are capable of a lesser standard of skill/strength than men, however, you, a girl, seem to defy my blanket, uneducated assumption, and I am attempting to give you a compliment while completely disrespecting your entire gender group."
- **"...unladylike" really means:** "I believe women are supposed to behave a certain way that makes me feel safe in my toxic masculinity, and your ability to casually demonstrate your freedom by moving your backside like that is making me VERY uncomfortable!"

Let's be clear, #metoo was never just about (white) women in Hollywood finally addressing their abusers and opening the vault on the centuries' old practice of men in power wielding it to satisfy their desires. Tarana Burke started #metoo as a movement to encourage women to feel safe in sharing their stories of assault in order to empower others to do so. The idea being that when you say #metoo it helps to deflect the shame, loneliness, and stigma of being a victim. It is great that it has extended to the entertainment and music industries—however, to be clear, #metoo is not about bringing down men, it is about lifting victims up.

WAS THAT RAPE?

I remember being so drunk that I went home with someone who, though we'd spoken on email for a while, I had never met in person before that night. He hit me up to say that he was in New York City and we met at a club and danced the night away. He was attractive. And the more drinks I had, the more bold I got. However, at a certain point, I was so drunk I couldn't even stand on my own. He didn't put me in a cab, he took me to his hotel room. All I remember is being on the bed, my clothes being taken off, and falling asleep. I don't even know what his dick looked like. I only know it was in me because, well, when you wake up the next morning, you know when a dick's been in you. Not a hand. Not a dildo. A dick. Let's just say there are "dickstinct" differences. We had a brief convo. He said he'd keep in touch. He got in a cab. I didn't hear from him for two weeks. I texted him that I was shocked to have not heard from him and that that wasn't the behavior of a stand-up dude. He called me, yelling into my phone that I had no right to tell him how to be a man. That was the end of that. Now, was that rape? A large part of me says yes. A smaller part of me says no. The bottom line, however, is that if you have to ask, at the very least, it wasn't right. #metoo

Hip-hop really did a number on us. Y'all know I love hip-hop 'til the day I die, but like calling out your problematic uncle who is being a bit too out of pocket with the young ladies in the family, we must check our own. More on this on page 20 . . .

CATCALLING

The reality is catcalling is simply rooted in men who think all or at least one of the below:

1. Women don't deserve basic respect.
2. Women are waiting for men to acknowledge them so they could walk right up and offer up their bodies like cookies for Santa on Christmas.
3. Women are deaf.

These are the only explanations I can drum up for why any adult would think it's okay to say sexual, body-objectifying, degrading things to women on the street and consider it a "compliment." Furthermore, a man offering up his dick IS NOT A COMPLIMENT.

WHAT IS CONSENT?

Consent is a RESOUNDING YES! It is the verbal equivalent to joining the electric slide. It's jumping in with both feet! It is being an EQUAL partici-pant! It is *continuing* to say YES! It is important to know that if at some point YES turns to NO!, THE TRAIN STOPS. Consent does not have to continue. It is not a blood oath or an unbreakable contract. Whether you arrive in some-one's hotel room with the intent to have sex—whether you begin messing around and there is intent to have sex—whether you are IN THE MIDDLE OF SEX—if the circumstances change and you are no longer:

Cognizant	Conscious	In the mood
Enjoying it	Awake	

You DO NOT HAVE TO CONTINUE. And no one should force you to.

SLUT-SHAMING

This practice of judging a woman's character based on her sexual inter-actions is tired and baseless. It is rooted in a desire to limit sexual inde-pendence and continue the patriarchal narrative that women are sexual objects and, as they are men's possessions, have no right to their own sexual agency. Your Vagenda ain't nobody's business but your own!

Sexual Harassment
vs. Hollering

IN 2018 A COUP OF SORTS HAPPENED IN HOLLYWOOD when major players Harvey Weinstein, Russell Simmons, Louis C.K., and more were outed for their inappropriate, and in many cases predatory, behaviors toward women in or seeking to be in their employ.* Though the #metoo movement had begun in 2006, started by educator Tarana Burke to help survivors of sexual violence, particularly young women of color from low-income communities, find pathways to healing, it crossed over to Hollywood and became the rally cry for an industry of women fed up with patriarchy and surprise penises finding their way into their career paths. This started a new dialogue that included inquiry from so many men on what the distinction is between sexual harassment and hollering. The confusion was shocking really (not really). The common discourse was, "How am I supposed to approach women if anything I say in the romantic direction is considered sexual harassment?!" Well, first off, calm your balls. As with most things, there is a spectrum and when you put the two on either end, what's in the middle is mainly about courtesy and consideration.

Remember that commercial that came out in the '80s on the heels of the Anita Hill/Clarence Thomas hearing? A scene in a workplace shows a woman being groped by her boss and she looks him square in the eye and says, "This is sexual harassment and I don't have to take it!" It seems cheesy now, but that was an effective ad because that clear and direct way of thinking has stuck with me on my path through various entertainment industries. Although the ad took place in a work setting, sexual harassment can take place anywhere.

---

* To be clear there are women who are also operating below the standard of ethics, as it relates to sexual harassment, by abusing their authority.

It's simply the concept of harassing someone by making unsolicited sexual advances/comments. That dude at your job who keeps making little comments about your ass when you're just trying to make a latte? Sexual harassment. That guy on the train who's looking you dead in the eye while he gropes himself? That's sexual harassment. That time Russell Simmons asked me in a business meeting, "Hey Amanda, have we ever fucked?" YUP! That was sexual harassment, too. The thing is, even though we know we don't have to take it, so many of us get stuck doing exactly that because it is typically administered by individuals in positions of power who can affect our livelihood. These individuals know that, and they use it as their shield in order to harass people without consequence. This stems from the old guard patriarchal platform that views women as objects. It's no wonder so many men feel disarmed at the revelation of what sexual harassment involves and how present it is in their daily interactions. Once aware, it forces them to have to consider new modes of approach and levels of respect that previously had not been expected of them. Get over it and get into it. Women are on the rise. We are taking ownership of our agency, our talents, and our voices. We are moving forward with momentum and focus that is toppling previously conceived notions of gender roles and the like. In this new direction, the hyper masculinity that supports sexual harassment as a practice has no place.

Fear not homeboys, there is a way to holler that does not resemble sexual harassment. For instance, I was walking down the street in LA to my car, and I heard a brotha's voice behind me saying, "Excuse me, miss, excuse me." My New Yorker self was doing the quick walk ingrained in our being and I did not slow my roll. He persisted. Finally, I turned around and asked, "Wassup?" The six-footish homie, in cargo shorts and a button-up, gathered himself and said, "First and foremost you are an incredible specimen of femininity." I was pleasantly surprised at the word choice and after thanking him, he continued. "I was wondering if there was a possibility that maybe perhaps at a later date, we could possibly get dinner sometime." Though I appreciated his mode of advancement, I wasn't interested, and he was still a stranger. I gave him the universal woman go-to for a nice no, "I'm sorry, I have a man" (this is often responded to with, "You can't have friends?!") but he simply replied, "He's a lucky dude. Have a nice day" and walked away. That's it!!! Nothing mean. Nothing imposing. Nothing sexual. He shot his shot and kept it moving, head held high! Now, we all know there are MANY ways men approach women. I think most women agree with me that far too often, when approached in the street, it's done aggressively and without any real consideration for them. There is also very often sexual innuendo included. None of this is necessary or okay. You can "holler" at a woman without doing any of this. This young man in

LA demonstrated it perfectly. His approach was polite. His intro was without sexual reference, and at no point did I feel unsafe. If more dudes considered women as *individuals* in their holleration tactics rather than simply as *sexual objects*, they would have a way better outcome and more positive responses.

The key to hollering in a way that does not encroach upon sexual harassment is simply that: leave the sex out. The reality, though, is too many dudes approach women for their bodies, not their minds, and when we respond using our minds they are put off. If you're in a workplace, it's even MORE imperative. Especially if you are the superior to the person of interest. In that case, you should chill. You don't want to put someone in a position where they feel like they if they reject your advancement it would create an awkward work environment. Love is a beautiful thing, and there's nothing wrong with going after it, but being mindful of when and how is something everyone needs to consider before they step into a person's space.

In 2013, I was asked to come on CNN to discuss a video that had gone viral of a young woman walking through New York City and being catcalled along the way. The woman, ambiguous in ethnicity (read: you can tell she wasn't white but you don't know how not white she was) was wearing leggings and a T-shirt. Nothing crazy. And as she walked, she got the attention of men who said/yelled a bevy of verbiage her way, ranging from compliments on her beauty, to acknowledgment of her booty, and of course how both make them feel. The panel I was on quickly devolved from a discussion to a debate when the white man on the panel of three (which also included the host, Fredricka Whitfield) piped up IN DEFENSE of catcalling, and proceeding to tell a nation of women that, "If it had been handsome men doing the yelling they would be alright with it because all women love getting compliments." I do not support the notion that says if a dude approaches you, outside of work, in a respectful way, with a romantic advancement (note: I did not say a sexual advancement) that it is sexual harassment. I also don't support the notion that says, if a stranger on the street says, "You look nice," or any other compliment, that that it is sexual harassment. The key is in noting what is a compliment and that even though the dude may have given a compliment or approached, IT DOESN'T MEAN THE WOMAN MUST RESPOND.

There have been many advancements in the world, but there is still a long way to go before "stranger danger" ain't a thing, and many women simply don't feel comfortable conversing, even to simply say "Thank you" to men they don't know who are commenting on their appearance. Unfortunately, this failure to respond has too many times led to a hurt ego that in turn caused a man to respond with hurtful words. We've all heard, "That's why you an ugly bitch!" or the remix of that. In some cases, the man/men has sought to hurt or even kill the woman. Until violence against women stops or is at the very least aggressively challenged by the justice system, there will be a certain reserve for safety that sometimes simply means silence. Sexual harassment has been ingrained in our society for so long that it can be difficult to discern its difference from hollering. That said, the bottom line is you should never be made to feel uncomfortable in any environment, be it work or otherwise, by someone's pursuit of your attention. Even if they're your boss, even if they're a friend, even if they're a stranger, always remember, you have agency, so you DON'T have to take it.

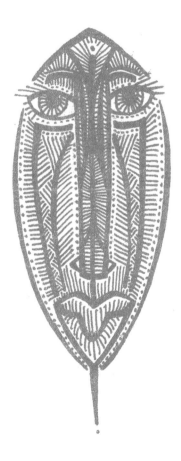

A woman being disrespected in hip-hop is nothing new. As much as I love hip-hop, I think we can all pretty much agree it hasn't been the best about requiting that love to us ladies. We all sing along to songs like "Bitches Ain't Shit" and "Ain't No Fun," brushing aside the wildly misogynistic lyrics because, well, it's hip-hop and we've made it "okay." We conjure up all kinds of explanations to cushion our cognitive dissonance; "It's self-expression!" "The beat is really what I'm dancing to!" and the all-time classic, "Well, he ain't talking 'bout ME!" Be real, we've all said all of these at one point or another to excuse ourselves from basically willingly taking part in the marring of our own femininity at the hands of a male MC. So the beat goes on, along with the beat-down of our worth, as disrespect gets packaged as entertainment. It's just the way it is. I wish it stopped there. However, unfortunately, it doesn't.

See the thing about art is it often imitates life, and vice versa, creating somewhat of a conundrum of cause and effect. Now, I don't know which came first, the chicken or the egg, or in this case the chickenhead or the MC, but somehow the disrespect that was being put on wax began being put in the mix. Many of the men on the mic who were disrespecting and objectifying women in their songs began doing that in reality. Which then trickled down to their crews, to behind-the-scenes professionals, and to fans, until it became a known part of the culture.

I'm not saying it was embraced by all, but few challenged it. I've always said that hip-hop is a cockfest and women simply don't have any party favors. Meaning the culture, as much as women were a vital part of building it and are a vital part of living, sustaining, and nurturing it, is a man's world. Therefore women, by nature of being, well, women, will never get an equal shake. So when faced with that all-too-common less-than treatment, many of us women of the hip-hop guard are put in the predicament of having to put up or shut up. We want to be taken seriously as members of this rhythmic realm, so even though the instinct may be, "Wait this doesn't feel right. I shouldn't let this rock," the common reaction chosen is to just "be cool."

Nothing gets checked or challenged. Like I said, hip-hop is a man's world, and by crying foul you easily get ostracized, labeled a "bitch" or, dare I say, a "diva," or even worse, "weak." "Can't handle the heat, stay out the studio." We allow ourselves to become "one of the guys" in order to fit in and prosper, letting countless infractions of disrespect go down. (Have *you* ever heard of someone claiming "sexual harassment" in hip-hop? Me neither.) Thus, the behavior continues, and with the anonymity of the internet it has only worsened.

When I was hosting the Fifth Annual Roots Picnic in Philly, during a performance by the rapper Wale, I tweeted:

This ni99a Wale just moonwalked on stage.
I'm always amazed at the love women have for him
Lol He be rappin tho

The Wale I had come to know was an underground emcee who appealed to a mostly male audience and spit about Nike boots and Seinfeld. So to see him dancing onto the stage, to women screaming for him à la Marvin in his heyday, and doing so without forfeiting his lyricism, tickled me to type. Back on his bus he saw the tweet, inquired about where I was, and brazenly approached me while I sat on stage taking in De La Soul's amazing set. Furiously, he demanded an explanation for the tweet, yelling, "So if I tweeted that I'm amazed at how men like you, you wouldn't be upset?"

I tried to brush him off telling him to "Leave it alone and lemme enjoy the show!" Still he was bothered, yelling over the music, "You tryna diss me?!"

Frustrated with the topic and his accusatory tone I yelled back sarcastically, "Yes, okay, yes I was trying to diss you. You happy now? Leave me alone!"

He stormed off. Now, I won't discount that the loud music and setting added to the heightened energy, but it was his actions when he then came back on stage and thereafter that transgressed beyond the lines of acceptability. Five minutes later, in a rage, he approached me head on, nose-to-nose, his hand in the well-known "two fingered gun" formation pointing threateningly as he demanded, "YOU NEED TO WATCH WHAT YOU SAY."

Fed up, I raised my hand to forcefully remove his hand from my face, so to speak, when my significant other stepped in and plucked Wale from in front of me and ushered him off the stage joined by Wale's bodyguard. Wale exclaimed, "She'd never get away with that in DC," to which my man replied, "But we in Philly this evening, Wale." That evening, Wale took to Twitter, calling me a #bumjoint and attempting to diminish my career saying, "You're irrelevant . . . you're broke . . . a charity case. You couldn't buy relevancy."

After hearing of the incident, several people told me things like "Don't sweat it," "It is what it is," or "Just brush it off, it ain't worth starting nothing."

In the past I would have taken their advice, and another instance of out-of-pocket behavior by a man in hip-hop to a woman in hip-hop would have gone down without any accountability being taken. But this time I chose to speak about it. Not because, as some suggest, I "want press,"* or as others suggest, I "like drama," but because I am NOT one of the guys. I'm a woman, a proud woman in and of hip-hop. I should be able to speak my mind freely without the threat of being, as one said on Twitter, "hoed down" by a peer.

I love this music and love this culture, but like any relationship, I feel that I deserve in return what I'm giving out. I'll admit, in that instance I wasn't afraid, not because I shouldn't have been but because I'd become so desensitized to the rampant mistreatment that it didn't even faze me that here was this grown man exuding hostility, in my face, in full view of an entire audience, while his security guard looked on. Had my boyfriend not stepped in, it would have gotten physical, and to consider that that could have even been a possibility is no dice. I know plenty of women in hip-hop who have been in situations where they didn't feel safe and chalked it up to simply being part of the game. Well, I have been out of hip-hop for a while now, so I hope it has changed. Because it is high time we as a culture take accountability for the environment of misogyny we've created and that we as women of the boom-bap demand our just due.

* Cut the shit. I have yet to see significant examples of women calling out by-products of toxic masculinity and gaining any level of uptick in their career to understand why there continues to be suggestion that "press" is an underlying motive for them speaking up about a male counterpart being problematic.

I AM HIP-HOP

Being a Black Woman

Brown girl,

look in the
mirror.

See your face and
smile.

Brown girl,

the picture

couldn't be clearer.

Let your dreams

run wild.

SHADES OF SISTAHOOD

There are all kinds of black women. All of our stories are relevant to the unique experience of what it is to be a sista. Whether you are from the 'hood or the high horse, ebony or beige, bald or "rockin' inches," you are us. Yes, you are your own woman and thus possess the right to preserve your own well-being, success, and survival. However, although we are each on our own path, we are of a shared community, in that our existence alone is resistance. So when you're moving and thriving and riding or dying, Respect that, Honor that, Consider that we are an US.

HAIR

Our hair is of a different ilk than what mainstream society puts so much money into presenting as beautiful. So much so, that it has its own culture and community. Not just because of its difference in texture, upkeep, and styles, but also because of its politicization. It is no secret that to this day black natural hair is still challenged in many workplace and school settings. At the same time, the cultural appropriation of black hair is rampant. From white people in locs (stop this) to major fashion mags using "Afro" to describe a woman of the white race with a big messy down-do, black hair in the mainstream space has been regarded as both alien and as a resource when convenient. That said, as I understand it, the original necessity to press and perm our hair straight was more about creating entrance and access into a white world. Sure, many may have bought into the concept that the European standard of beauty that was being sold to us was the premier standard, but I'm really over the notion that any black woman who doesn't wear her hair in its natural form is buying into the concept of European beauty as the supreme. Hair, for black women worldwide, can represent so many things: magic, confidence, style, your mother's strength, history, identity, and art.

ANGRY BLACK WOMAN, MAMMY, JEZEBEL

Sometimes I wonder if they've given us so many names out of envy that we are able to be so many things. The "Angry Black Woman" trope seeks to silence. The "Mammy" motif seeks to disarm. The "Jezebel" moniker seeks to shame. However, we are angry because we are aware. We are caregivers, but not a boundless resource. We are sexual because we are free. These stereotypes, though relics of a time before we breached the barriers of bondage, still permeate the social landscape very close to the surface. Daily we find ourselves facing them and having to step over, around, and sometimes right on through just to get to our point. Call us what you want, because we are all of the above and more; redefining the misconceptions assigned to us by people who know not of what they speak.

COLORISM

The realities of colorism:
- Its root is in white supremacy.
- It seeks to divide.
- It still exists.

HAIR *PART 2*

There is no such thing as good hair, only bad weaves.

TONE POLICING

Though there is a constant attempt by non-black folks to police our passion, we must acknowledge that it happens within our community as well. There are entire sects of folks who think if a black woman expresses distaste for problematic black male behavior, she hates black men. There are black women who, though wanting their own freedom of expression to air grievances, take offense to other black women doing the same when done in their direction. This is unproductive. In the pursuit of our best selves, we may not only be told hard truths but also told in harsh tones. Respect each other's intentions and passions. Not everything is personal.

NUDE COLORED ANYTHING?

All this time, black women have been wearing the bras, panties, and nylons of white women. I know someone just read this and is confused. "Nude" has forever and a day solely been based on the skin tones of white women! From Band-Aids to ballet shoes to lipstick. "Nude" was never about the fact that there are all different types of skin tones. Finally that is changing. The spectrum is broadening to acknowledge the fact that black women may also want to wear undergarments that are flesh-toned! We may also want to wear dance shoes that elongate our lines by continuing our hue to the toe! We may also want to wear a Band-Aid that attempts to be inconspicuous! When you are not a black woman, it is so easy to over-look these simple everyday things because they have always been at the ready for you. I don't even know how they cooked up twenty-five shades of no-melanin pantyhose! The time has come for a shift in that paradigm. Black women are out here. We're fly. And we want our Spanx to match our skin tone just like everybody else!

WELLNESS

This world will beat you black and blue and tell you that it is your duty as a black woman to grit your teeth and take it. Fuck that. Take care of yourself.

- Take breaks
- Travel
- Meditate
- Masturbate
- Go to therapy
- Clap back
- Indulge in your hobby
- Treat yo'self
- Say NO.
- Say YES!
- Cry
- Read
- Allow for excitement

Suffering and struggle are circumstantial and not to be accepted as a bottom line upon which to define your strength as a sista.

COMPLIMENTS

I love how black women extend compliments to each other. The format is "what you see is what you get." So if you're wearing a polka dot skirt what you'll get is, "OK, POLKA DOTS!" If you have a fly hairstyle, it might just be, "COME THRU, HAIR!" Or it may not even be verbal—an eyebrow raise with puckered lips and a point says so much without saying a word. With this ease we have in acknowledging each other's dopeness we should make it a point to do it as often as possible. It does not diminish you to big another sista up.

SIDEKICKS AND SAVIORS

I remember people saying, "Amanda it's time for you to be in a movie." As if this was some great revelation and up until that point I had been turning down roles in favor of staying home with my cat and making pro bono Instagram videos. The reality is that as a black, female comedian and actress in Hollywood, I find myself, on a regular basis, faced with roles that are simply dumb, lacking authenticity, or no roles at all. Making movies with black women leads is not "a thing." No, we are reserved for the position of "sidekick" and "savior." We are the "no-nonsense conscience" to the careless white girl. We are the "save the day in silence" to the hapless white girl. We are the "sassy truth teller" to the tyrannical white boss. We are a resource, not an equal. This is not *always* the case, and there are changes afoot, simply by hook or by crook. Black women have begun to lean in in ways that demand and declare our voices be heard and our talent be considered. We are writing our own stories (per usual) that give us dimension and individuality and creating spaces for them to be told. Our equality cannot be measured solely by inclusion but by the elevation of our own spaces as equal in merit, visibility, and value. Representation is key.

DEAR BROTHAS

We love you.

DEAR BROTHAS *PART 2*

Protect black girls. Protect black women.

DEAR BROTHAS *PART 3*

- We are not your enemy when we challenge you to be your own champion.
- We are not your enemy when we aspire to be our own champions.
- We are both the subject of centuries of trauma and division and must begin to see the value in each other as equal parts change agents, thought leaders, and movement makers.

"SO STRONG"

If you are not a black woman, please stop telling black women that they inspire you to be a "strong black woman." The reality is we've become strong out of necessity, not by choice. Our resolve and resilience has been toughened not because of a desire to ascend but because of a demand to do so in spite of the constraints surrounding us. We have never been widely regarded, protected, or preserved. We have consistently been admonished, abused, and appropriated. We have had to design our own shields, form our own foundations, and be each other's fortitude. So, yes, our strength is noble, and honorable, and commendable, however, it is far too often recognized but not received.

Hostile
vs. Passionate

TO BE A BLACK WOMAN is to be judged on tone before you even open your mouth. The way we hold our faces. The way our bodies are designed. The way we live in our skin. All of the above has been poked, prodded, and politicized for centuries by individuals who did so to oppress. Here we are now, in a world where although black women are no longer in the chains of slavery or relegated only to careers of service, we are still far too often diminished to monolithic stereotypes not based on who we are as individuals or even accurate cultural commonalities. These stereotypes often affect our effectiveness in the workplace and social sphere. In other words, folks try to say that we're ratchet and angry in order to undermine the real shit we are often voicing. This deterrent is incredibly problematic. Though black men are often misconstrued as thugs and dangerous, black women are by no means excluded from the blanket assumptions. Simply by asserting one's opinion, or even a fact, black women are often seen as confrontational and hostile, as opposed to being seen as intentional and passionate. In order to make the distinction, we gonna start at the real.

They didn't want us to read. It was literally a criminal act to educate one's self. To simply know how to write your name. So, I do not find it surprising that when a black woman speaks intelligently and with conviction she is often misnomered as hostile. She is in direct violation of the original American standard of thinking that considered her intellect to be a threat to democracy and peace! THEY DIDN'T WANT YOU TO READ! That concept was in place longer than black people have been out of the bonds of slavery and living under Jim Crow laws. It is in the DNA of this nation. Especially in the places where we were/are least visible. Hostile is a label reserved for individuals who seek to cause conflict and disrupt for antagonistic purposes. When you approach a conversation with an attitude of attack, it is hostile. The absence of compassion or fact replaced with indifference and assumption creates animosity that once inserted into any exchange creates an obstacle to finding a solution. You can't have a dialogue with a hostile person. They are not interested in discussion. They are only interested in defeat. They are not approaching the conversation with any level of deference or understanding. Nor are they willing to agree to disagree. The key, however, is that their indignance is not supported by truth. The tactic of calling individuals hostile simply because their argument doesn't align with yours is not only inaccurate, it's corny. You're the one on the court who keeps calling fouls because your shots can't make it past a strong defense. Black women are constantly mislabeled as hostile for expressing their thoughts, no matter how cordial or fact-based, because the stereotype of the angry black woman is so pervasive that it often speaks for us whether we like it or not. It's to the point where folks are often afraid of black women, and black women, themselves, are afraid to speak for fear of being misunderstood or dismissed based on the continued flawed application of hostility to our ability to communicate intellectually. We are constantly having to negotiate with ourselves on how to simply express our point without it being rendered pointless, by having hostility attached to it.

Passion comes from deep. It is supported. Like an opera singer's voice on a full breath. Its foundation comes from confidence in your cause and arguments, which resonate not because of volume but because of content. In a climate where sensitivity is at an all-time high, passionate discourse can often be misnomered as hostile when it is not. Some conversations are simply not effective in dulcet tones. The fact is that some truths can feel like hostility when spoken because they are so inconvenient to the other person. Which is the reason the phrase "the truth hurts" exists. It is important to always consider that passion does not relay acrimony. The discomfort you may feel when someone is speaking passionately, volume and momentum pushing the words from their consciousness to yours, is less about a feeling of disrespect and more about your displeasure at receiving information that is more often than not unsupportive of you or your cause. Passion is self-powered. To someone seeking to diminish another's voice or devalue their argument, passion can feel threatening. It shouldn't. It is passion that so many are lacking. Whether due to misdirection, lack of direction, or simply being tired after constantly moving with direction, passion is the flame within us all that can only be lit by oneself. Sure, there are people and things and occurrences and experiences that can inspire it, but at the end of the day you have to have the desire within you to not only light the candle, but to keep it lit. Passion is what gives you the will to fight for and challenge obstacles that seek to impede your desires or your principles. When you find yourself in a dialogue that ignites your passion, your heart rate increases, your brain synapses become more rapid, and you feel like it is emotion overtaking you. It is simply your truth rising to the surface. The work is on how to be in control of its release and avoid allowing attempts at considering it hostile to derail your directive.

So often I have black women ask me, "How can I get my point across, and be myself, without being labeled 'The Angry Black Woman'?" The problem is that the trend of misinterpreting a black woman's passion as hostility is so ingrained in society it can sometimes be unavoidable, especially in corporate spaces where the culture is passive aggression over direct dialogue. Let me be clear: Black women are passionate, yes, but I am not suggesting that women from other cultures are less passionate. I am, however, acknowledging that black women are continuously subjected to the specific microaggression of having their passion weaponized against them! As black women continue to navigate and achieve in spaces where our independent thought and assertion were once forbidden to us, whether it be the classroom, the boardroom, or the bedroom, we will continue to face the uphill battle of attempted dismissal of our passion as hostility as a means of silencing us. My suggestion to those who ask me the above question is that you have two choices, either decide that certain spaces are only for giving as much of you as is necessary for you to get your check and go on to the spaces that do receive you in your full Nubian dopeness, or simply be you and deal with it as it comes, knowing that you are standing on the shoulders of so many sistas who came before you with just as much to say and even less room to say it. To be a black woman in America carries with it unique burdens that force us to hone skills of navigation that at one time utilized the guidance of the stars and still require the guidance of intuition in order to chart our own course to freedom. In other words, feel the room, then fill the room. Knowing the facts and delivering them in a clear and direct fashion without wavering is not a hindrance, but a gift. Don't let anyone tell you otherwise.

Black Girl Magic

First of all
We make this look easy
Us black girls with all kindsa curls
Smellin' a' cocoa butter
Out here every damn day savin' the world.

Time and time again
We find the ways and means
Between packing lunches, planning launches,
    and *act out* patting weaves
To get information
And stay in FORMATION,
"Girl you heard what they're sayin'?"
"Ain't no games to be playin'."

So we show up
And show out
And turn up
And "turn this motha out"
And flip it
And Yasssss biiihhhh
Throw side-eyes
Gather
Get folks all the way together
With edges still in place
Skin defying time and space
They call it magic cuz ain't no way to explain our
    "Amazing Grace"

How sweet the sound
Of a black girl's point of a view
Knowing that nobody does it like we do, boo
Pride in our power
Strength in our strides
You can attempt to imitate
But soul you cannot buy
We work twice as hard

And must be twice as perfect,
Purveyors of potent truths
We deliver in small doses
Cuz folks is shook when she's movin'
"OH NO, IT'S ANOTHER
    ANGRY BLACK WOMAN!"
Bump that
We're not hostile,
We're passionate;
Clappin' back is our way of declaring
        👏 we 👏 aint
        👏 havin' 👏 it
They go low, we go high
They say no, we defy
They didn't want us to read
Kept us out of libraries they built
Now we are the biggest buyers of books
So, we can read you for filth!!!

Our magic is in our love and tears
Our fears and our flyness
Our sistahoods and insecurities
Our ride or—don't even try it.
We are not the one,
And still we rise,
This is for colored girls who've
    considered gettin' your life and are
RECLAIMING OUR TIME

The Hoe Phase

The Hoe Phase for everyone is different

and in some cases nonexistent

but here are some thangs to keep in mind

while you eat, pray, bump-n-grind!

EVERYBODY ELSE IS DOING IT

Don't feel like you HAVE to have a Hoe Phase. It's not a rite of passage as much as it is a common developmental phase in Western society.

THE DEFINITION *of* HOME BASE IS . . .

Up to you. I hate the concept that if you get physical in any type of way with someone, you're expected to go "all the way." Sex doesn't always have to be the end game to a good time. Especially if you know you are prone to having an emotional attachment triggered by it. Ladies, our bodies are majestic and there are many ways to bring them to climax. No BS, one time, I had a man suck on my neck so efficiently I saw stars. Jussayin, don't feel pressure to have intercourse just because you and a partner have become physically involved.

IT'S YOURS

You are not obligated to tell any partner about your Hoe Phase and who was involved in it. (Unless you're in a committed relationship and it was a friend of theirs or a friend of yours. In which case, you're still not obligated, but I always feel like you're better off letting them know before they find out some other way and insecurities flare!)

HOW DO  WANT IT?

Part of the process of the Hoe Phase is not only learning what you like sexually, but also learning how to ask for what you like. There is no shame in sharing with someone how you like to be kissed, touched, or stroked. Let's throw out the idea that "That will make the situation awkward." The trick is finding a way to do so that keeps your insecurities at bay and doesn't end up disrupting a sultry situation. You gotta set it up like you're putting the person on to a well-kept secret about turning you on.

UPKEEP

If you're gonna be gettin' it in, make sure to keep these basics in mind:

- Use a condom.
- Always urinate after intercourse to avoid urinary tract infections.
- Wash off with water after sex. Your pH balance will thank you for it!

The Hoe Phase does not mean you should be out here being reckless. You know exactly what I mean. Some of y'all are getting periods you don't deserve. You're in a public restroom shouting out, "HALLELUJAH! I'M STILL IN THE GAME!" at the sight of crimson 'cause you know full well you're out here being careless with condoms and the like. Don't play yaself! Have your fun, but don't be dumb! Strap it up!

THE VAGENDA

The Vagenda is a woman's list of real-life individuals who, if presented with the right opportunity, she'd have sex with. Though the Vagenda can be at its height at any time of your life, it's most likely to be carried through while in your good ol' Hoe Phase.

Who's on yours?

1. _____
2. _____
3. _____
4. _____
5. _____
6. _____
7. _____
8. _____
9. _____
10. _____

Mine (you know I'm not listing any real dudes, and gassin' nobody!):
1. Lando Calrissian of *Star Wars*
2. Erik Killmonger of *Black Panther*
3. Luther of *Luther*
4. Julio of *Power*
5. T'Challa of *Black Panther*
6. Tim Riggins of *Friday Night Lights*
7. Thor of *Thor Ragnarok*
8. Khal Drogo of *Game of Thrones*
9. Troy Fairbanks of *Dear White People*
10. Jordan Catalano of *My So-Called Life*

Sex
vs. Intimacy

SOME MIGHT LOOK AT THIS AND SAY, "Sex vs. Intimacy? How is that a versus situation? Sex is intimate." Yes, in the physical sense, sex is intimate—it involves body parts, which make sounds (and sometimes babies), and we can't forget the moisture! (Gross.) It is, in fact, two bodies coming together! However, there is nuance. How many times have you had a friend say, "He started being weird after we slept together"? Happens all the time. In a lot of cases the person who was ghosted is truly at a loss for why and makes a list of reasons, blames themself, etc., which is an exercise in futility because what actually happened is the other person had sex with you but didn't have intimacy with you. You see, sex is the physical act, but in this context, intimacy is the emotion attached to the physical. The common mistake many of us make is thinking that just because you slept with someone, you all have an emotional connection. Then when they don't display the affection and attention attached to that emotional expectation, you find yourself sad, disappointed, and can go as far as to feel like there's been a betrayal of your trust. This is when so many women get bent out of shape, out of character, and end up on an episode of *Snapped*. Let's discuss.

Ahh, Sexy Time. In a nutshell, it really is one of two things, a purposeful act done for the outcome of reproduction or the physical manifestation of lust (and occasionally both at the same time!). Either way, at its root, sex is a physical action that when done right can feel like the first time you see fireworks + the big drop on a roller coaster + getting into the college you wanted + that first five minutes after a full body massage when you're just lying there and that chill spacey music is playing and you feel light as a feather. When ya nail it, your nerves are piqued, your "spot" is triggered, all your senses are on high alert, and you're like, "Elon Musk who? I just went to Mars and back without leaving this backseat!" It's a good time. However, sex and intimacy are not always intertwined, and it is important to know the distinction in order to discern if you're getting what you're actually looking for.

Intimacy is when an emotional exchange takes place between people. It's a connection that resonates deeper than the physical action and delves into consciousness. It's that "thing" that you feel when you're "feelin'" someone and you know they're "feelin'" you back. When intimacy is present it's more than just the pleasure of sex, it's also an energy exchange that can feel supernatural! Remember that Dead Prez record *Mind Sex*? It's that shit that makes folks start trippin' when things switch up. Intimacy is about a closeness in spirit, not just in form, and it is the cornerstone for building trust, vulnerability, and emotional equity. It is the seeds planted in the first state of building a world together.

Some would argue that for women, sex always has an emotional factor attached, and lemme just clarify once and for all that that is not the case. Sometimes the only emotional attachment is, "I wanna see what 'that' would feel like." Just because a woman sleeps with someone, a man in particular, that does not mean she's formed some irreversible bond with him that will have her pining for his presence, sitting in the shower listening to Sade, and looking out the window journaling about when he'll come home from the war. To be honest, it's common for women to have a Vagenda—a mental plan of whom they are interested in sleeping with—whether it's with relationship goals or purely for the pleasure. Unfortunately, many men don't realize that you can fall off the Vagenda quicker than the drop in your credit score if you miss a student loan payment. Say or do the wrong thing and just like that, POOF, replaced. So, to any cis-hetero men smart enough to be reading this book to better understand the women they are approaching, know that we are always listening and all it takes is one dumbass statement like, "Stevie Wonder is overrated" to tumble right on off the Vagenda into "Never, negro" land. On the other hand, there have been times when the sex is SO good, it evokes emotion that you didn't know you had. Some call it "dick whipped," others say you've been "dickmatized"—I've dubbed it a doozy of a phenomenon called, "When the dick touch heart." The doozy lies in the fact that this sensation has *nothing* to do with emotional intimacy and everything to do with physical chemistry, don't get 'em twisted!

Fact is when you're stepping into a sexual space, do yourself a favor and do your best to know what you're getting into before you get into bed. The next time you meet someone that could make it onto the Vagenda, ask yourself, is this someone that's a "Just Sex Sicheeashun," or is this someone you'd like to share real intimacy with. How you proceed from there is your prerogative, but at least if you start out by being real with yourself it makes it that much easier for you to be real with others.

I was a late bloomer. Flat-chested at fifteen and barely a booty by graduation. So when I got to college it was Jasmine and Aladdin out this piece, aka a whole new world. I had never had guys who looked like men actually interested in me. It was empowering and encouraging. By the time I headed out of college and off to the real world, I was in full bloom and ready to mingle. What I mean to say is, I was having all the sex, but I didn't know what I was doing. I also didn't really know why I was doing it.

The Hoe Phase is that era in life that is repeated generation after generation despite having an air of mysticism around it. You're supposed to be "doing you" or "getting it in," and, ideally, it is a process of self-discovery where you use the experience of having sex with different partners to awaken parts of your body (including the mind) that were previously unknown. For me, the Hoe Phase had some glimmers of light, but for the most part, though I remember everybody's names and faces from that time in my life, I don't remember many of our interactions being much to write home about. Sure there were big shlongs, and lil shlongs, and mediocre performances, regardless of size. There were fast pumpers, only from the backers, and robot chickens.* There were perfectly toned bodies and softer frames and manscape specialists and au natural naps and so on and so forth. I was young, ambitious, and, especially in the circle I was a part of, out every night with my friends in the club, drinking shots, and, inevitably, getting it in. Though I was supposed to be on this "sexual walkabout," so to speak, at a certain point I realized I didn't really like sex. I was having it because it somehow felt like that was just what one does.

This rattled me. So, I got still and thought about it. If it wasn't the sex I was enjoying then what was my hoe phase really about? For some people their hoe phase is attached to their first taste of freedom. Maybe they had strict parents, or were very religious, or were in a long-term relationship. For others, maybe they were insecure and had newfound confidence, or perhaps they were like me, still insecure and the attention gave them confidence. It dawned on me that my Hoe Phase was a reaction to finally feeling like I had an acceptance and interest from dudes that I had never had before. I was always the loud, funny, smart chick, but I was never considered fine, fly, or sexy. I came to understand that my Hoe Phase was more about me just responding to being desired physically by someone I desired, than it was about actually wanting the physical interaction. The sex was just a by-product.

Once I cracked that code things changed for me. I no longer felt so obligated to "give it up" when ardently approached by someone of interest. I began to question what I really wanted. I considered the things I was truly attracted to. Sure, bodies and faces are great. I have had some stunnas in my time. Jussayin'! But what I surmised was that, for me, it was always best with the folks I had an actual mental connection with. Even if it wasn't emotional, it was either intellectual or hilarical.† If you could make me laugh, or make me think, it made me moist. Facts. That said, those aspects aren't always evident out the gate. Sometimes it takes time. Once I had this realization, I didn't sleep with the next person I dated for three months. I wanted to build up that foundation of fun, jokes, and mind melding. It was what was best for us. Once the physical came into play it was the first time I had truly, truly enjoyed gettin' the business.

So, in actuality, what I learned was that the Hoe Phase isn't really about sex. It's really about the exploration of self without the limitations of being anchored to one person. It's where you have the freedom to find out, essentially through trial, error, and an orgasm or two, what works for you, not only physically, but mentally and emotionally.

---

* I call dudes who are robotic in their sexy time movements "Robot Chickens" because it's like their heads move separately from their bodies.
† Hilarical is a made-up Harlem word for excessive hilariousness.

CHAPTER 2

Race Realities

Addressing Inequality & STAYING WOKE!

THE REALITY IS THAT ALTHOUGH RACE IS NOT A REAL THING, it has real consequences. It affects our lives in a plethora of ways, ranging from annoying to devastating. For people of color, this can be an everyday, inescapable occurrence if you're even the slightest bit woke. Turn on the TV, and it's still a sea of mayonnaise-flavored sameness. Open your phone, and daily there's a new story of a black person being harassed/arrested/killed just for being black. Go to Coachella and white girls are still rocking Native American headdresses like they're the latest drop from the Appropriation Apparel catalog. It's A LOT. It can be overwhelming and depressing. I'd love to tell you this too shall pass, it's all a phase. But I believe the inconvenient truth that unless aliens ascend from the abyss TODAY, leveling the playing field, and forcing everyone to start over from scratch, race and its trash-ass effects possess the hard-to-live-with-and-even-harder-to-kill traits of the common house roach, i.e., it ain't going nowhere.

Before you label me a defeatist, understand that I would love to have such an unshakable faith in humanity that despite all the evidence before us that shows there are scores of individuals who willfully choose to simply believe that the color of their skin makes them a superior being, I can see a future where their kind is a mere memory. But unless the media and multimedia, which at this point are both consumed in equal or possibly greater portions than parental influence, take bold steps in educating (as opposed to re-educating, which would suggest that the masses were actually taught the truth from the get-go) to project accurate messages of inclusion, non-bias, equality, and tolerance, there will be no true change in the reprogramming of the next generation. That being said, there are levels to this shit, and even if race ain't going nowhere, it doesn't mean *you* can't. It doesn't mean that *you* can't be an impactful part of spitting in its face and refusing to allow it to thrive any more than it has. It doesn't mean that *you* can't be empowered and empower others to live outside of its confines however possible, especially in professional spaces hindered by decades-old practices of nepotism and same-circle referrals. It doesn't mean that *you* can't be fastidious in your undermining of and disassociating with it by popping your own or someone else's white bubble. In actuality, it is because of its steadfastness that we must do all of the above. Yet, that is not the work. The real work is in doing the work and finding the joy in spite of it; finding the funny within it; finding the freedom outside of it. None of which you can do without first educating yourself beyond your experiences, about the histories, practices, and realities of it.

The time to choose sides is now. And by sides I mean will you be on the side of truth and fact, or comfort and cognitive dissonance? Some fancy themselves open-minded by supporting the right for everyone to have an "opinion" without regard for the fact that opinions become laws, which affect people's lives and, literally, the world. So, an unchecked problematic opinion is more than just someone's annoying notion, it is the seed from which grows future problems! When it comes to race, most issues are not a matter of opinion—they are a matter of right and wrong, ethical or unethical, civil or uncivil. The same pens that signed this country into nationhood were dipped in the blood of slaves to sign their lives away. Those pens wrote the book on American race relations, and since it is without merit or value we must burn it and do our best to rewrite it.

Race in the Workplace

Tryna get paid ain't just about skill
You've got to master your job,
and your job's people.
Race in the workplace can be
a bitch to navigate
They don't make it easy to keep
your identity while you integrate.

CULTURE CLASH

The workplace can be a landscape that not only forces various personalities to work together, but one that also creates a place where cultures collide. In America, far too often, the side effects of centuries of white supremacy play out in ways that unfairly demand adjustments be made by individuals who, based on their race/culture, are not the beneficiaries of white supremacy. In other words, folks who benefit from white privilege do things on the regular that folks who don't benefit from white privilege have to adjust to, not because it's more efficient, or practical, but simply because the way this country is set up, white is still "right." When people are distracted they have less time, energy, and attention to pay to being on point, effective, and focused on their *actual* job.

TOKENISM

When you are the only nonwhite person in a room you know it, and it can be uncomfortable when your coworkers always point it out. You become "the other" or "the voice," which are both side effects of being "The Token." The Token is the one person of color who, by simply existing in the setting, meets a quota for diversity.

If you are considered "The Other," you are treated like a different species. It's as if the people you work with don't realize that you're a person, too. They view you with arm's-length curiosity and nervousness. They fear you like an alien they've not yet decided is friend or foe. They keep you in a space of your own that they qualify based on your difference in race/culture/ethnicity.

If you are "The Voice," you are treated like the all-knowing, all-encompassing speaker for your ethnicity/culture regardless of whether that is your area of academic expertise. You are looked to as the ambassador out of the white bubble. It is unfair and uncomfortable. You know when folks say "I have black friends"? They're talking about you.

The flip is that some folks just LOVE being the Token. They like the attention. They feel empowered. They seem irreplaceable. Well, I hate to break it to you, you're none of those things. You're a mascot for your demographic, and the office has you dancing at the game. If you're the only person of color in your office then your office is doing a piss-poor job at recruitment!

ON BEING BLACK FAMOUS

Once we step into certain spaces we are playing a game that never ever included us and actively works to keep us excluded. First, the white supremacy gatekeepers will come at you with the shit you know you did wrong but that never really mattered because you didn't matter. They will utilize it in an attempt to dismantle the crystal stair that you have built to break through their ceiling. Don't allow it. Instead, let them "allow" you to demonstrate your humility. Let them "allow" you to enforce intellectualism. Let them "allow" you to connect with new people, and new ideas, and new ways that you may not have been forced to deal with before. Flip their shit by using your wrongs to right. The wrongs you know you did wrong are the easiest to correct. So save your energy. They're going to come with ones that have been conjured out of wickedness that you can't even imagine and you will have to have magic left over to figure out the way to fight those.

REFERRAL BASED BIAS (RBB)

Which brings us to RBB. I once sat next to an exec who lamented that his marketing department lacked diversity because they hire based on referral, and he said that he did not know any—ANY—people of color in his line of work. His colleagues—SOMEHOW—also did not know any people of color. So, he kept being referred the same types of people with the same backgrounds. I took a sip of my Shirley Temple and gathered my face before asking him the obvious question: "Have you tried looking outside of your circle of WASP colleagues?" He said, "I wouldn't know where to start." This laissez-faire attitude toward diversity is a bunch of bullshit, and it cannot be considered acceptable. Intention is simply not good enough if it is not supported by action. Diversity improves business. Fact. So, it should be a mandate that hiring is based on diversity and inclusion, and this should be carried forth by those with hiring power. These same companies will claim they're diverse for having a gay white guy on staff, or because they have a woman CEO, but let's cut the crap, the truth is not only do they not want to be bothered going out of their immediate circle, they're worried and fearful that if they do, they'll hire a nightmare who is trash at their job, and not be able to fire them for fear of being sued for discrimination OR they'll hire someone awesome, and it will completely undermine the lie they've bought into that says their PWI Ivy education and white skin make them superior.

PASSIVE AGGRESSION AS PROFESSIONALISM

White women have been protected. They were positioned as the companion to white men, and are an essential part of continuing the legacy of white money, thus, they must be protected. For centuries their male counterparts "preserved" them in their homes as nonvoting homemakers, where social expectations forced them to use passive means to achieve their wants, for talking loud and out of turn was no way for a genteel ladylike woman to behave. Eventually, white women broke the seal, and gained the right to their money, their government, and their independence. However, old habits are hard to break, and the passive aggression that was used in the home transferred to the office, and eventually became the standard practice of professionalism for many white women. Tactics like tears, manipulation, and straight-up lying are far too often considered just "a part of doing business." Well, white women, it's time you knew THAT THIS IS ANNOYING AS HELL AND NEEDS TO STOP. Not sure what I'm talking about? Here are a couple common infractions that are driving a person of color or a woman who happens to be white in your office CRAZY as we speak:

1. Going to the supervisor behind folks' backs: If you have a problem, it does not always need to be brought to the supervisor. That is the corporate version of calling the cops.
2. Changing the schedule without conferring first: We're all adults with full lives. If you've already confirmed, do not make decisions about someone else's life without the respect of having a conversation. That is the corporate version of still tryna be "massa."
3. CCing hella folks that don't belong on the email: I KNOW WHAT YOU'RE DOING, AND YOU AIN'T SLICK. But when shit goes down and they ask for an explanation, it's gonna be the corporate version of me, on the day after Christmas, at the customer service desk, WITH RECEIPTS.

BLACKGUISTICS

It is a little-known fact to folks outside of the black community that most of us who work in corporate America or any predominantly white space are a specific kind of bilingual. We have had to learn how to speak on the block and in the boardroom. Aside from the basic concept of what is considered "proper English" versus African American Vernacular English, culturally, black folks deal with things in a more direct fashion than the passive aggression that corporate America has come to call "professionalism." For many of us, it takes actual skill and effort to perfect and navigate the often murky waters of white tears, and it is admittedly exhausting. Some simple translations for those stepping into the work arena:

- "Please advise" really means, "You got us into this bullshit. So, now it's on you to get us out."
- "Per my previous email" really means, "I guess you gon' just ignore the fact that I already said this, huh?"
- "I hope all is well" really means, "I'm trying to be polite before I roast you with a Columbia curse-out*."

WHITE PEOPLE
STOP DOIN' THIS SHIT

- Touching people's hair or asking to touch people's hair.
- Asking, "What are you?"
- Using a "black woman's affect" when speaking, such as, "You go, girl!"
- Referring to your inner black woman when you are not.
- Expecting people to educate you on their culture without having educated yourself.
- Complaining about the smell of someone's ethnic cuisine.
- Assuming everyone had the same upbringing as you.
- Asking, "What did you do this weekend?"[†]
- Asking for a play-by-play of why my hair looks different this week.

BLACK PEOPLE
STOP DOIN' THIS SHIT

- Letting your coworkers make you the representative of your culture.
- Straightening your hair because you think it looks more "professional."
- Selling out your fellow black coworkers to white upper management to curry favor!
- Apologizing for your blackness.

---

* A verbal assault that involves no curse words and takes out the opponent using words and syntax that is so precise and elevated it renders them defenseless.

† A woman once told me she hated this question because when she would answer truthfully with "washed my hair," it required an entire explanation. She eventually resorted to just saying, "Nothing much," and keeping it moving. LOL.

Diversity
vs. What Folks Think Is Diversity

WITH THE RECENT GROWTH OF MOVEMENTS like #timesup, #metoo, and #blacklivesmatter, certain buzzwords have taken hold in the corporate space. Just as quickly as *urban* did in the '90s—btw, *urban* as a synonym for communities of black and brown people is offensive and inaccurate, so if you're a part of the last bastion of people still using it, stop—these words have taken root and in the process they've also lost their value. Oftentimes, the value is lost in the misapplication of not only words but intent. *Diversity* went from a potent word that meant "making sure a staff is not filled up with just white people" to being watered down, literally, by white people. Yes, marginalized groups of white people said, "Wait a minute! We should be a part of diversity, too!" The thing is, there is a different word for making sure that all voices are heard versus making sure that discriminated groups are represented. That word is *inclusion*.

Folks think diversity is about simply making sure that there isn't only one point of view in the room. This may seem like something very easy to achieve, but when *Fortune* reported in February 2014 that just over **4 percent** of Fortune 500 CEOs at that time were minorities, and there were only twenty-four women CEOs in the Fortune 500, it's easy to see how that could require a concerted effort. As we see with movements like #timesup, it's no different in the entertainment space. The bottom-line, go-to voice is still the straight white man's. Since business is so much about who you know, that cycle can keep continuing if there are not mandates, personal interest, or financial or political gain attached to changing it. When I talk about what people think diversity is I am working to widen that space and broaden that POV to include voices that, although they may not be the same as a straight white male, might still have access to some of the privilege he enjoys. Folks is gonna be tight in 3 . . . 2 . . . 1 . . . but being a white woman in a room of white men is not an example of diversity. Folks is gonna be BIG mad in 3 . . . 2 . . . 1 . . . but being a white gay man in a room of white straight men is not an example of diversity. The gag is, so many people are so accustomed to the rigid roles of representation that they've seen for so long that simply meeting the terms of inclusion of any "others" feels like an arduous stretch of comfort that looks like diversity. Keep stretching. Change does not stop at simply including other white people who are not straight white men—that's where change begins.

Ahh . . . "Diversity." You see it all the time: "Diversity Seminar!," "Diversity Showcase!," "Diversity Condoms!" Okay, maybe not the last one, but brothas will absolutely tell you that because of their length/girth they require a special brand 😒. I digress. The word *diversity* has been used so much, so often, that its meaning began to diversify depending on who was using it. Returning it to center, diversity is about giving representation to individuals of marginalized racial and ethnic backgrounds. As unreal as race is (race, like gender, is a completely human social construct that does not have any root in science), it does have real consequences. America continues to uphold and enable systems that provide less resources for, discriminate against, and target individuals simply based on the color of their skin. In addition, the nation that once boasted of borders welcoming the world's poor and its hungry is now riddled with xenophobia that too often throws a side-eye and an accusatory finger at ethnic communities. With affirmative action no longer in place to ensure the balancing of the playing field by law, it is up to companies/schools to consider diversity a priority on their own. Some go as far as hiring an actual person in the position of enforcing diversity as a mandate. Others have scholarships and programs. But the fact is, diversity is often simply a buzzword applied by folks who either don't really know how to or even see real value in diversifying their ranks/halls but more so see the value in looking like they do. Diversity as performance.

The clarification of what diversity is is not petty. It is important. The main reason is that spaces reserved for purposes of increasing and fostering diversity are being diluted with folks who do not require the same level of assistance and inclusivity to break through. White women, LGBTQ white men and women, disabled white men and women all deserve inclusion and to be a part of the conversation. However, their involvement is not an example of diversity. Though they are a part of different societal groups than the majority leadership, their access to white privilege is still very actual and factual in comparison to their racial and ethnically diverse counterparts. Again, this is not to say that women, as well as the LGBTQ community, have not been oppressed, suppressed, and distressed by the powers that be in this country. They absolutely have, and their points of view should be represented and heard resoundingly. However, diversity is about opening a previously unopened door to groups of people who have been disenfranchised and silenced, simply because of their race and/or ethnicity. The argument is made all the time, and it is still valid, that you shouldn't have to, but you can hide your sexuality. Most people of African descent cannot hide their melanin, some ethnic groups can't mask the specificity of their facial features, most polylinguists can't dampen the accent of their first language trickling through like an unclosed tap filling up their identity. Because of that they are facing not only the obstacles caused by lack of inclusion but the impediment of homegrown, still-established, and supported discrimination that requires direct, nondiluted, undisrupted efforts in order to be combatted.

There is a specific conversation to be had about the marginalization of culture and ethnicity versus gender and sexuality. Though intersectionality does exist in the ways the groups are discriminated against, there are UNIQUE nuances to each and the experiences associated with them. That said, the inconvenient truth for some is that diversity is not simply *everyone who isn't a straight white male*. If you are different, you deserve inclusion. But real talk: If you benefit from white privilege, and you're taking space away from those who don't, you are a diversion from the implementation of diversity. When you try to make a safe space for everyone, you end up making a safe space for no one.

When you're not white, and you work in predominantly white spaces, race is consistently top of mind. Perhaps it's because you're the designated "representative" for your particular group, or because you have to be conscious at all times that you're not falling into a negative stereotype, or maybe it's because you work with racist-ass people. I remember when I was just out of college working at Sirius Satellite Radio and I said to someone, "I'm not sure if they have the whip but we can bounce in a minute." A young white woman overheard and chimed in, "Why do you always have to speak 'hip-hop talk'?" It's moments like this that keep race at the top of mind when you're simply just trying to do your job so you can live your best life. When we speak of privilege that is one that we are referring to. The white privilege of not having to wonder if your race or ethnicity is "showing too much."

As a black actress in Hollywood, or a *blacktress*, as I call us, race is so attached to us that we never get a break from it. Aside from the obvious of having to be hyper conscious of how we are being represented on the page, we also have to be aware of how we look when we make it to the screen. This shows up in addressing lighting and making sure that it is properly adjusted to our melanated skin tones. It shows up in our wardrobe and making sure we are wearing clothes that are flattering to our varied and culturally curvy shapes. However, I'm sure many blacktresses would agree that it shows up most in dealing with hair and makeup.

I cannot tell you how many times I have come to a set and had a makeup artist do that white woman with the algebra meme right in front of my face as she attempts to figure out how she's gonna make my light brown skin look right for the camera, with all them peach tones she has on her palette. On the melanin scale, unless I've just recently returned from Grenada, I'm more often than not on the beiger side of pale, compared to my richer-toned sistas. Nonetheless, I find myself in a standoff with someone who knows full well they don't have the tools or the skills to simply do my makeup. You would think, "Well didn't they know that I was coming in?" The answer is probably no. You may ask, "But wouldn't they just have it in their kit anyway?" The answer again is no. Because this industry is still so overwhelmingly white, when there is someone of color it is considered a break from the norm. So unless they've been alerted, they don't bring out their special "brown girl kit." Even if they have the kit, it's not like they get to practice much. So the odds of your foundation matching your hands are slim, honey. Then they be trying to put it on your ears and all down your neck to make it look all one shade. Stop the madness. You'll say,

"I'd like it natural" and they take that to mean, no foundation, just eye shadow, then feel a way when you say, "This is not what I meant." I had a makeup artist tell me, "In my professional opinion, you don't need concealer under your eyes." In that moment, I no longer trusted her professional opinion. EVERYONE ON TV NEEDS CONCEALER. Unless you are *supposed* to look tired or sick or high, or you are the 12 percent who have miraculously flawless under eyes, YOU NEED CONCEALER. Period. There is not enough of a push to make sure that makeup artists are able to do the makeup of a range of skin tones, and artists are not necessarily lauded for their versatility. The true reality is, as a black-tress, if you're not on a show that is considered diverse, or that has regular makeup artists that know your skin and tones, we must always call ahead to make sure that the makeup artist is not only equipped in tools but in skills. Regardless, just to be safe, learn how to do your makeup and always walk with your own kit.

Then there's hair. 😒 I had a producer ask me once, "So what does your hair require?" I replied point blank, "It requires someone who can do black women's hair." Black women's hair is a varied assortment of curls and kinks, sometimes four different types of which are on one head. We have edges, and kitchens, and baby hairs, all of which need to be properly tended to with a skilled hand and a keen eye. Handling our hair is an art. So when you have a natural, and you arrive to a set, and the hairstylist is a white woman with a curling iron in hand, there is always a moment of concern. I don't care if you're offended, I'm going to ask, "Are you versed in doing black hair?" If you're reading this, please just be honest. If you don't do black girl hair, don't claim to, because if you jack my shit up, WE WILL HAVE AN ISSUE. No, I don't want pomade in my hair. No, I don't want you to "bump up my curls with a curling iron." No, this is not a weave. No, I didn't bring my own products, because no, I shouldn't have to. Did any of these white women have to bring their own products? No, they didn't, because you considered them. Is it really too much to ask that a hairstylist keep a baby hair brush, edge control, leave-in conditioner, and heat protectant JUST IN CASE she has a blacktress on set? No, it is not too much to ask. The mark of a professional is displayed when you ask, "Can you do black hair," and the stylist replies, "Yes, heat or no heat?"

Discrimination comes in many forms and indifference is one of them. On behalf of all the black and brown people in all forms of entertainment, we ask you, artisans of the hair and makeup world, please consider us when you are training in your craft. Expand your skill set to reflect *our* world, and it will increase your perspective and your income!

The White Bubble

With perimeters of privilege
It's been built on a lie
Preserved by cowardice
It can only be popped from the inside.

I have been fortunate to know many white allies in my life. A key characteristic to their allyship is the ability to both acknowledge and use their privilege while popping their "white bubble" and not validating the construct of whiteness. When the tragic events of Charlottesville, VA, took place in 2017, Alison Faircloth, a close friend of mine, Dr. Phillips High School classmate, and a woman who happens to be white, wrote this on Facebook. It is valuable for several reasons, one of which is her understanding that as a woman who happens to be white, her voice on this topic is essential to cutting through the noise and reaching the white people who need to hear it. This is how you ally:

A Few Thoughts for Shocked White People Everywhere:

- The event and demonstration in Charlottesville is domestic terrorism
- This terrorism is fueled by racism, anti-Semitism, xenophobia, white supremacy, Nazism, malignant complacency, and run-of-the-mill ignorance
- The protection of terrorism and hate speech under the mantle of "free speech" is another example of institutionalized racism/white privilege
- DJT (though he lacks the intellect, skill, and power of Voldemort, he shares our disdain, therefore we do not say his name) has CONSISTENTLY empowered and emboldened all of the above pre-existing conditions through coded language interpreted as promises by the KKK, David Duke, and anti-Semitic and white supremacist groups
- DJT continues to make veiled appeals to this now unhooded, racist base
- Supporting DJT's presidency IS supporting the amplification of white supremacist terrorism and everyday racism

- Murder and violence is a direct result of the above
- This should not be a surprise, fellow white people
- This is the result of historical, intentional, systemic, institutionalized racism that has been present since the inception of this country
- If you, as a fellow white person, are shocked by these events—I lovingly suggest you are naive at best, complicit, or worse
- For shocked white people who are naive, let these events be a wake-up call to gift yourself a deeper understanding of the shameful legacy of racism and xenophobia in this country
- I challenge you (as I challenge myself) to make it a priority to learn, listen, and identify how you can be an ally to POC and the systemically disenfranchised, and disempower the myth of Whiteness
- If you choose not to do so after the events of today, you remain willfully ignorant and part of the problem
- While I do not support the empowerment of Whiteness as a concept, I acknowledge I benefit from white privilege daily
- White people who feel threatened by equality and protection for POC or simple statements like Black Lives Matter are suffering from highly problematic white fragility at best
- That was a joke—the white people aren't the ones suffering here
- It is the responsibility of white folks to make themselves and those they love distinct from the faces of racism and white supremacist terrorism through BOTH words and actions as they move through the world EVERY DAY, not only on days when it makes the news
- It is NOT the move to ask your POC friends to fill you in. If they volunteer, listen—and be mindful of whitesplaining. If you misstep here, apologize and don't shy away from future conversations.

White People Litmus Test:

Do the phrases "structural racism" and/or "institutionalized racism" bring specific events and policies to mind for you? If not, you need more info.

Quick-Start Action suggestions:

- Watch the documentary *13th* on Netflix
- Make a donation to a relevant organization
- Hope this helps. I have a lot to learn myself and welcome conversation.

That's how you get invited to the BBQ.♥

White Ally
vs. White Savior

I'M GONNA TALK DIRECTLY TO PEOPLE READING THIS who benefit from white privilege. I always say that there are only two types of white
people. People who are white, and people who happen to be white. People
who are white consider their whiteness to be a part of what makes them
great. People who happen to be white know that though they possess white
privilege, whiteness is not based on anything biological or anthropological,
has nothing to do with ethnicity/culture, and is merely a construct created
to oppress others. Before you can even step forward to truly be a part of the
destruction of racial oppression in the world, you must first truly come to
terms with where you fit in the binary. Now, once you've come to terms and
understand and live by the truth that you just "happen to be white," the natural
instinct is to ask, "What do we do now?" . . . to a black person. However, the
reality is, deconstructing the global concept of racism lies squarely on the
shoulders of those benefiting from it stepping forward to actively work against
it. From this notion is born the white ally and the white savior. Now listen, both
folks are coming from a good place, but there are very important distinctions
to be made between the two.

The biggest, most glaring distinction is that white saviors don't know their
place. I can imagine some of you clutching your pearls right now. "My place,
what does that mean?!" Partially because with privilege often comes the entitlement of not ever having to consider that there is a place that you don't have
access to. Your "place," so to speak, is an appropriate position taken when you
enter someone else's space. When you were a teenager and thought you were
grown and came out your whole entire face in the junior's section of some
department store in some mall, your mom had to either give you a few choice
words, or, unfortunately, a quick pop to the mouth to put you back in your
"place." As an adult, the social rules of knowing your place can be a bit hazy,
but in the context of being a change agent against racism they are very basic,

and white saviors miss the mark every time. This is because as a white savior, though you may truly consider yourself to be a person who "happens to be white" you have not checked your privilege. White saviors do not realize that they have lived in a world where their voice, no matter what class they're in, has always been considered more valuable than the voice of a person of color. They fail to grasp that, even when they have had the epiphany that race is a construct and that they are simply a part of a tool used for hatred— that they are, in actuality, late to the party. People of color in the fight against racism been knowed that! You're just showing up. Lastly, they are still coming from a place of distance that views people of color as "an other," versus "another." Because of these obstacles, when a white savior enters a situation where they can be of help by using their white privilege, or simply by just being a good person, they inevitably attempt to dominate the voices of the people of color that are actually in the situation. It sounds something like:

White Savior: Black people of the world, I am Ashley H., and I have come to cure you of all of your woes! I, too, voted for Obama . . . twice! I, too, saw *Selma*, and Ava Duves is amaze! And every first Thursday of the month, I volunteer at an inner-city high school in Chicago for two hours. So, I KNOW YOUR STRUGGLE.
The People: Umm thanks Ashley but actually we had a question about . . .
White Savior: Excuse me, sister, I'm speaking . . . anywhoo . . .

Sit down, Ashley. White saviors show up to the fight thinking they know everything, and they haven't even asked questions. This is not helpful. It is an obstacle. Though it may not be hate-fueled, it is ego-fueled, and white supremacy has spent centuries indoctrinating white people in this way. Making y'all believe the lie that simply because you're white, you're better, and the world is yours. White saviors unwittingly carry this energy into the change space and in doing so mute the very voices that they should be using their privilege to amplify.

White allies, on the other hand, know how to step into a situation and become a part of the landscape that's fixing the problem without consider-ing themselves to be the entire landscape. I'm not saying it's an easy thing to do. Again, FOR CENTURIES, in books, in music, in entertainment, in media, in school, in literally every facet of social existence, much of the world has literally told white people the biggest lie ever told, that your melanin-less skin makes y'all the best. Couldn't be further from the truth. To come to terms with that can be a doozy and requires you to change your way of moving in

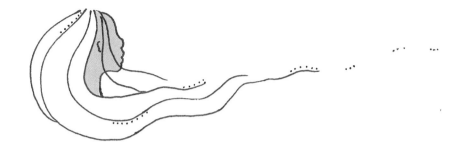

the world and even your language. At the same time, you must balance the understanding that until racism has truly been smote out, regardless of your personal awareness of the fallacy of it, you still, by nature of your snowflakery, benefit from the privilege associated with it. A white ally has successfully done this and therefore knows that when they enter a landscape where they can help underserved people of color, it's really about using their privilege to empower the people that are already there doing the work. The ally carries another, even more important responsibility. I call it the "Get Yo' People Initiative." It is not enough to help give voice, resources, etc. to marginalized people. In addition, the white ally must use their privilege to engage with and challenge the white people who are an impediment to the eradication of racism. The white ally must SPEAK UP when in the presence of racial discrimination. The white ally must ACT when faced with the realities of appropriation of privilege and implementation of supremacy. The white ally must TAKE A VISIBLE STANCE that they are a change agent. I know some might read this and say, well what if they're Schindler's listing and are using their position to do the work on the low. In my opinion the time for that is no longer. When white supremacy was literally the law of the land it was necessary to move in the shadows. However, now, the shadows are the places where the racism continues to live, and they are growing, so allies must be the light of truth that dissolves them.

Let's be real, we could have a festival of "If it wasn't for this white person" films.

- **Dangerous Minds:** Thank goodness this cool white lady showed up in her leather jacket to rap with Coolio about teaching us how to read.
- **Freedom Writers:** Thank goodness this other cool white lady showed up to, once again, teach us how to read.

- **Finding Forrester:** Thank goodness this cool old white man showed up to show me that I already knew how to read.
- **Green Book:** Thank goodness this mediocre racist white man needed money so bad he came along to drive me through the segregated South and watch me be such an exceptional human and teach me, a black man, about soul food and soul music before inviting me to dinner with his racist family.

I could go on! So of course when you're shown constant images of white people being supplanted in a situation and all of a sudden making everything better, you're going to think, "Hey I have the power to do that too!" But guess what, there were a bunch of people there before you showed up wearing your Khaleesi "I shall bring them freedom" cape. A lot of folks don't understand that when you come in and you dominate the situation, you're still a part of the problem—you're not helping the problem. I get a lot of people asking me, "Amanda, I'm a white person and I want to help, what can I do?" The first step to being a white ally and truly being able to help is to understand that it is NOT the responsibility of marginalized people, ESPECIALLY BLACK PEOPLE, to give you an Ikea step-by-step instruction manual on how to dismantle the racism that your ancestors created, that some of your folks continue to uphold, and that all of you benefit from, directly or indirectly, whether you want to admit it or not. White allies create and support platforms and safe spaces for people of color to speak their truths uninterrupted by white privilege, white guilt, and white tears. White allies educate themselves, they research, they listen, they hit the Googles, then they hit the ground however they can be of service. One thing that this movement has that the Civil Rights movement didn't is the internet. Use it, unless you're asking someone about their specific experience as a POC, you have access to the same information we do about the racist past and present. Most importantly, white allies understand that though race is some bullshit, it does have real-life consequences and that it is their position, and their role, to be a part of actively challenging that by speaking truth to action, speaking directly in the face of those who uphold racism, and doing so without speaking over black people who are actively challenging it. You master that and you're beyond someone who happens to be white, you've hit the ultimate goal, "Woke White!" Now, get on out there and figure out how to bring the real to all your problematic family members at the next Thanksgiving dinner!

My mother is from Grenada, and I grew up in a Caribbean household. So, although I had a lot of exposure to all things Black American, from *The Cosby Show* to the *Soul Train* line to what is the precise amount of sugar to add to Kool-Aid, there were certain things that fell through the cracks. One of those was the Negro National Anthem, "Lift Every Voice and Sing." However, my failure to learn the Negro National Anthem was less about my Caribbean mother and more about the white bubble of America, because the fact of the matter is, as a newly anointed American citizen, my mother should have had to learn it along with the "Star-Spangled Banner." The test for citizenship in this country is chock-full of dates and presidents and capitals and all types of rigamarole, but conspicuously leaves out the acknowledgment that black people of American heritage were so marginalized and unique in their American experience that they had to come up with their own damn anthem. Not to mention the national anthem that we are forced to sing at sports events and morning assemblies is actually racist! Yea, second verse. Look it up! In my case, it's no wonder I hadn't learned the NNA. Some of y'all are reading this right now like, "Wait, what?? There's a *Negro* National Anthem???" Yes! Remember when Obama was elected and you were at that party and all the black people started singing along with the CNN feed of a black church congregation singing in unison? You may have looked around with an awkward polite smile as if to say, "I don't know this song that everyone seems to know but it is pretty . . . maybe it's a Baptist hymn???" No! That was the Negro National Anthem, and at a certain point every black person in America learns it and we sing it at black thangs like HBCU events, my comedy shows, and even that one time at Bey-chella. I grew up going to school in regular ol' public schools being taught regular ol' curriculum that paints America, in so many words, as a place that went from Pilgrims to presidents with various random happenings in between, and a "BTW slavery happened, too" kind of approach to US history, so it's no wonder that the fact that there has been a Negro National Anthem since James Weldon Johnson and his brother J. Rosamond Johnson wrote the song in 1900 somehow did not make it to my consciousness until the tenth grade.

I remember the day I learned of its existence. There I was, in the backseat of LaVon's purple Dodge Neon, sitting next to my BFF, Julia, a girl who happened to be white, when Abiya, sitting in the passenger seat, mentioned that we would be attending a scholarship event for LaVon and they would be singing the Negro National Anthem, "Lift

Every Voice and Sing." I was confused. How the hell did I manage to go fifteen years on earth with no knowledge of this song?? Not only was I confused, LaVon and Abiya were appalled! Julia was determined. In the midst of my befuddlement, she found clarity in declaring to all of us in the car that as our friend, she felt it only right that she, a girl who happened to white, learn our anthem. She was right! We sure as hell knew the white girl anthem—"Someday somebody's gonna make ya wanna turn around and say goodbyeeeee . . ." Yea, every black girl born even suburbs-adjacent between the years of 1979 and 1984 knows the words to Wilson Phillips's "Hold On." But I digress. Here's Jules looking like she'd have been down with the abolitionist movement had this convo happened 150 years earlier, and here I was feeling hoodwinked, bamboozled, led astray! Even though I had black American friends, was on *My Brother and Me*, Nickelodeon's first black family show, and was a part of extracurricular organizations like the University of Central Florida's McKnight Achievers and the Urban League, which worked to advance and enrich young black minds, I was kept from knowing this incredibly important and symbolic piece of music due to the white bubble of my education. As this was pre-Google, I had no choice but to rely on LaVon and Abiya to bring my blackness up to speed. Julia, being friends with all the influential black actors/actresses of our prestigious drama program at Dr. Phillips High School ("Never less than the best!") found her own white bubble constantly being poked and pricked, this scenario being another in a successive series.

A week later we attended the event at the Prince Hall Shriners Malta Temple Black in Orlando, Florida, and at its opening, the room was asked to rise for the singing of the Negro National Anthem. Y'all I was READY! You hear me!? I was gon' sing that anthem so Malcolm and Martin could hear me, Fanny Lou and Ida B. would cheer me, W. E. B. and Booker T. would find a common ground, Langston and Zora would make me their muse, Bayard and Baldwin would toast me, Medgar and Huey would rally, Angela and Elaine would call me. I mean, I had the spirit of black excellence alive and well within me that day! I had practiced and practiced the lyrics and the melody over and over again. It was embedded not just in my head, but in my spirit. I felt more connected than ever to the black American side of my experience and my identity. I felt closer to my sisters, LaVon and Abiya, and my brothers, Kenyon, Alano, and Michael, who were also there with us. I felt so proud to be black and in defiance of the oppression in the history of our experience. The chords of the intro rang out and I took a breath, filling my lungs to give support for those first notes. Just as I raised my chin to let all that pride and joy ring out, here go Julia. I don't know where it came from, but she dug deep down into her Winter Park, Florida, soul and found cotton and grits that stuck to her vocal cords, making her voice propel into the room like Simone Biles off the vault. I couldn't even hate. She respected it, so she connected to it. We both threw a staggering blow to our white bubbles that day, and when I went to college and curated my own education, I made it my business to pursue black studies in order to beat it back once and for all. Just like I took that initiative for my own cultural identity, so must we all, to expand our cultural perspective beyond the limited white horizon placed before us.

I have met several men and women throughout my life who in their "happen to be whiteness" have given me hope that there may be an actual end to racial oppression one glorious day. The white bubble seeks to keep perspective skewed, expectation slim, and account-ability nonexistent. It is a vacuum, so that even if you don't consider yourself to be adding to oppression, by continuing to exist within the safety and comfort of its mirrored walls, you uphold it and breathe life into it. Step outside of the comfort zone and wake the fuck up. Be like Jules, and learn the words to another experience. Be like Alison, and "GET YO' FOLKS." Be like Joke, the producer for a pilot I did who, several times, fired back at executives who gave racist-ass notes, and tirelessly defended me using my authentic voice as a black woman. Be like Abigail, a woman I met on a flight, who happens to be white, living just outside of Ferguson at the time of Mike Brown's murder and who realized the level of racism around her, spoke out against it, and continues to raise her children to be activists against oppressive systems. Be like actor Matt McGorry, who stays keeping it all the way 100 on public platforms and defies the rhetoric that if you are outspo-ken against oppression you will taint your "brand." Be like the folks who joined the freedom rides of the '60s, who put their lives on the line knowing that the media would not care about the danger black people were putting themselves in to achieve racial equality and chal-lenge Jim Crow laws, unless their white lives were also at stake. The time is now. Be brave. Be human. Get educated. Get elevated.

PS: All this rah-rah about kneeling for the anthem; fact is we should have been singing "Lift Every Voice and Sing." Damned near every-body on the football field is a negro!

Stereotypes

Is every nigga with dreads for the cause?
Is every nigga with golds for the fall?
Nah, so don't get caught up in appearance.
It's Outkast, Aquemini, another black experience.
—André 3000

CULTURAL NORMS vs. STEREOTYPES

There are shared experiences/practices that bind people of a shared culture. Like black American folks knowing that Frankie Beverly's "Before I Let Go" is the official electric slide song, like southerners knowing iced tea that's not sweet tea ain't really tea at all, like Caribbean homes always being in possession of a cutlass. These things don't become stereotypes until they are used to demean (and for the record, being used to acknowledge uncomfortable truths is not synonymous with demeaning). Furthermore, stereotypes are typically rooted in surface observations that lack context and are presented/critiqued through an outside lens. For instance, when programs present black folks from a low-income neighborhood in a monolithic fashion, replacing the multilayered character development of any human being with the surface traits of an individual observed from a distance, it is also an act of stereotyping. Hence, representation matters!

BLACK
vs.
BLACK
vs.
BLACK

Black folks across the diaspora have a number of unique cultural differences. However, within those differences there have grown stereotypes that are used between each other to insult, demean, and divide. In a world where race, though baseless in biology but real in society, binds us, we have a shared cultural experience in that regardless of our individual culture/ethnicity, as a black person in the world, you are up against oppressive forces and discriminatory practices. Below are some of the more common stereotypes exchanged between black folks across the diaspora, and that hopefully with more education, compassion, and exchange, will be replaced with more unity, tolerance, and perspective.

- **Africa(ns) Is/Are Underdeveloped:** First off, Africa is a continent, not a country. It is made up of 54 countries and more than 3,000 tribes with their own unique cultural practices. Within this myriad of countries are various levels of industry and development that range from the modest villages of Togo's mountains to the sprawling metropolis of South Africa's Johannesburg. Though there are areas of the continent that have had less access to educational/economic resources, it is simply inaccurate to diminish an entire continent, and its people's advancement, based on American or European ideals. Technology may advance commerce, but it is by no means a measure of elevated character.

- **Black Americans Are Lazy:** First off, America was built on the backs of slaves. So let's start with the fact that working hard is literally ingrained in our DNA. The notion that black Americans are lazy is often expressed by immigrants who feel that an unwillingness to do the jobs they have no problem doing is a symptom of being *dotish*, a Caribbean term for lazy. That said, images of black people as lazy slaves and sambos were created by turn-of-the-last-century white folks. It was bullshit then, and it's bullshit now. There is also a judgmental eye placed on black Americans who cite the system of institutionalized racism in this country as a reason for their inability to advance as they may have once hoped. The reality is that being a black American is an incredibly unique experience for the simple reason that we live in the same country where our ancestors toiled and must continually find a way to reconcile the fact that as their descendants this country truly owes us. However, the slave owners' descendants are also still running things, while our own personal successes contribute to the GDP of a nation that has never truly denounced in voice or action the ills of its past and how they continue to affect the present. It is quite the conundrum. Stating that there is absolutely a system in place to prevent the advancement of black folks is not an excuse, it is a fact!

- **Caribbean People Are All Weed Heads:** First off, all Caribbean people are not from Jamaica. We also do not all "speak Jamaican." Caribbean people are also not all rastas, who praise Jah and smoke ganja. Even simpler, we are not all Bob Marley. Granted, Tuff Gong's face is considered to be the most recognizable image in the world, but it goes without saying that not everyone from the countries of the Caribbean lived Marley's Mary Jane lifestyle. For the record, the greenery is ILLEGAL in the Caribbean. If you went down there thinking, "Yaahhh I'm in reggae mode," they will absolutely arrest you and have you in a holding cell listening to soca!

The bottom line is, stop letting them divide conquer us as black people across the globe. We have differences, yes, but they are beautiful and should be appreciated. Whether you are a black American descendent of slaves, a descendent of Caribbean or African countries/tribes, or an immigrant having come to America, we should all be welcoming anyone into our lands that wants to uplift, uphold, and upgrade! Let the differences empower us!

DON'T JUDGE A BOOK BY ITS TWIST OUT

Whether it's a black woman in braids or a brotha in locs, hairstyles are an integral part of black culture. Unfortunately they have also been used to discriminate against black folks. The 1868 ratification of the Fourteenth Amendment to the US Constitution marked the start of government-sanctioned protection under the law for all races, and began the exodus of black folks integrating into white society via schools, neighborhoods, and the workplace. The Civil Rights movement and seminal cases like Brown v. Board of Education—which outlawed racial segregation in public schools—gained steam in their goal to attain voting rights for all and provide black folks with access to open previously closed conduits of education and opportunity. New to those spaces, many opted to utilize the duality superpower and blend in as best as they could, starting with their hair. Natural kinks were pressed and naps were cut low. The '60s, however, saw a reclaiming of African identity and wearing one's hair natural, be it in an afro or locs, which in itself became a statement that represented one embracing their black pride. Not surprisingly, any attempts to wear black hair in a more natural state were met with friction, sometimes disciplinary action, and even expulsion/firing! To this day, kids are still being sent home because their natural hair doesn't meet their school's standards. Regardless of what they tell you, the fact of the matter is, the stereotype associated with natural black hairstyles is simply that they are too outwardly showing of one's ethnic identity, in a country where segregation was law less than seventy-five years before the publishing of this book and still has yet to truly recognize that different does not mean less than.

FACTNOISE

I think of it like this: stereotypes are general characteristics applied to a group of people based on a definition given to them by someone not of them. In contrast, a trend is a specific characteristic applied to a group of people based on repetitive behavior. No matter how truthful a stereotype may seem, when it is presented as fact it is offensive. No matter how hurtful a trend may seem, when it is presented with full facts it should not be considered oppressive. Know the difference, to make a difference.

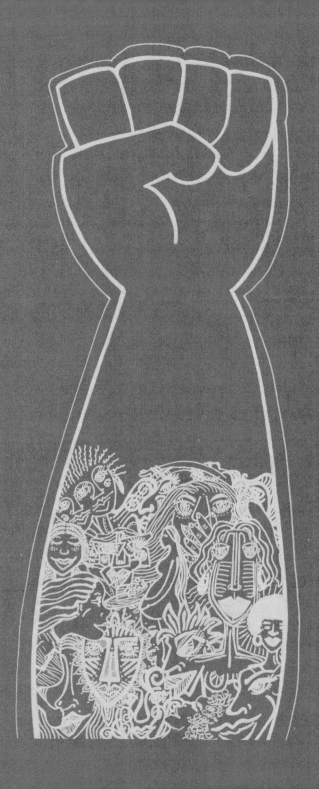

Cultural Appropriation vs. Cultural Reference

OFTEN I GET QUESTIONS IN MY DMS from girls who benefit from white privilege asking, "Can white girls wear braids?" or "Can white girls wear door-knockers??" or "Can white girls do Beyoncé choreography???" I do appreciate the inquiries because I believe they come from a good place. The people who are asking these questions are seeking awareness to avoid being a culture vulture, aka committing cultural appropriation. There are so many cases of cultural appropriation that so often tiptoe into the realm of just full-on, "Oh, you're racist," that even a simple voiced caution in a private forum is a measure that I consider noble. The information age has done more than just make Wikipedia, Pornhub, and IMDB, it's also created awareness for some things that folks in their white bubble never would have even been privy to before. With sports team names like the Indians and the Redskins, and pop stars regularly using culture as a backdrop and ethnicity as a prop, it's no wonder that so many find it confusing when discerning the difference between cultural appropriation and cultural reference.

Culture is of the people. It is born out of shared beliefs/experiences/locations. There is pop culture, which is reflected in media, fashion, and art, and which springs forth and just as quickly dissolves—it is a reflection of the times. There are negatives, like rape culture, which is carried out through systemic means, behaviors, and the upholding of traditions, policies, and court rulings that encourage the objectification and subjugation of women's bodies. There is ethnic culture, which speaks to a collection of people that share in not only culture but common ancestry, language, history, and society. Within ethnic culture, rituals, art, and traditions are essential aspects of connectivity and understanding that have meaning and purpose even if simply to highlight a person who identifies with said culture. Cultural appropriation is the borrowing of aspects of a culture by those who aren't of said culture, who have no valid connectivity to said culture, and who pay no respect to said culture, for the purpose of vanity or commercial gain. This is committed most often by white people who historically have forcefully taken or simply eradicated indigenous cultures in pursuit of dominance. No, a white girl wearing a Cherokee headdress on her Instagram isn't the same as the white people who sought out and committed genocide and thievery against the indigenous people of this continent. However, the wearing of a piece of Cherokee culture and tradition for no other purpose than "because it looks cool" without having any knowledge of its origin or paying any respect to it, is, in fact, cultural appropriation. Fact is, if she had any respect for it she wouldn't have it on her damn head anyway.

People ask me all the time, "Why can't white people say, 'nigga'?!" Now, listen, if you are a black person and you don't want to say nigga that's your prerogative, but you saying or not saying the word has NOTHING to do with why white people shouldn't be saying the word. Along with the fact that its precursor, niggER, was used to demean, oppress, and shame black people, the word "nigga" is a shared tradition of black American culture. Period. Stop shaking your head. Just because you may not like the word does not change the reality of its existence and the trajectory of its etymology from a hateful term used *against* black people to a versatile term used *amongst* black people. It is imperative to acknowledge this, because when white people want to use the word, it is not only an example of the continued entitlement of being included in everything, even when it does not pertain to them, which so many white people feel, but it is also an example of cultural appropriation. If you do not identify as black, put the word back.

Cultural reference is not to be taken lightly or used as a "get out of jail free" card for committing acts of cultural appropriation. Cultural reference is when sufficient homage, acknowledgment, and in some cases, payment, are given for the use of aspects of a culture outside of one's own. If you are a clothing designer and you use prints from an indigenous culture that you are not a member of in your work, at the VERY least, you should be able to specifically reference the source and have researched insight into the meaning/use of that print. Not only for providing proper reference, but also to make sure that you are not bastardizing something sacred by turning it into something trite. In an ideal situation, if you are making any type of profit off of aspects of a culture not your own, a portion of the proceeds should be going back to that community in a nature that either seeks to uplift or preserve it, or both! For centuries, people have left their homes to seek out land and encountered thriving civilizations with deep cultural traditions and roots that originated long before explorers arrived. The internet has continued exploration that, while not violent in the same way as Christopher Columbus and company was, per se, still provides any mildly curious passerby a glimpse, and sometimes entry and insight, into cultures and communities that otherwise would have remained unknown. It is the responsibility of one who seeks to properly provide cultural reference to do their research and due diligence into any culture whose assets they seek to use for any purpose.

Dear Fashion Magazines, stop referring to things as "new trends" that are simply white people finding out about it for the first time. Dear People of the Continent of Africa, stop saying black Americans are culturally appropriating when we wear dashikis. They are worn to pay homage and acknowledgment to our ancestry, which, though varied, is predominantly West African, and to show pride in our roots, which oppressors have systematically attempted to sever. Dear White Girls, stop thinking that just because something is beautiful, unique, cute, vibrant, opulent, has feathers, or simply exists, that it is yours for the taking. It is not. Certain things belong to certain peoples. There are cultural creations and traditions that are sacred and cherished by those who are a part of that ethnic group, and unless you have insight or an invite into that space, KNOW YOUR PLACE, aka show your love and keep it moving, it's not for you. Dear Black Men, stop accusing black women with blond hair of culturally appropriating white women. It is a color, and it is not a part of their culture—furthermore, there are indigenous black people all over the world with blond hair. Dear Americans, stop celebrating Cinco de Mayo like it's an actual holiday when Mexicans don't even regard it as one. You have SantaCon to drink. Also, stop having, "black parties" where you dress up as "black people," it's racist. Furthermore, stop wearing traditional ethnic garb as a Halloween costume. A culture is not a costume. You're not a "sexy Indian," you're a "stupid idiot."

Dear Everyone, stop looking to other cultures for what they have that you can take, and instead look within at what you have. Ideate. Originate. Create. Sure, you can be inspired by others, but there is so much more in creating than simply copying. Check your ego, greed, and laziness when being made aware of other cultures and know that sharing is a gift. Honor the access when it is given and respect when it is not.

Smart Funny & (Less) Black?

THAT ONE TIME

I originally created the show *Smart Funny & Black* because I was fed up with seeing a constant barrage of negative images of black folks in media. The stereotypes of black men as thugs, black women as "angry" and "confrontational" are pervasive and out of control. Furthermore, whereas in the past we had safe spaces like *Def Comedy Jam*, *In Living Color*, and *Chappelle's Show* that comedically spoke to our unique and varied cultural experiences, present day was lacking any such comfort zone. Not one to complain without offering up a solution, I decided to be the solution. When I moved to LA, I decided to take a brand I had already established in NYC as a comedy showcase and reimagine it as a show that celebrated black culture, black history, and the black experience through a comedic game format. I pitched it to NerdMelt, a small comedy venue in the back of a comic book store on Sunset Boulevard in West Hollywood. By the fifth show, it sold out, and I never looked back. The response was incredible. I knew that we, as a people, needed this, but I could never have anticipated how earnestly folks would get behind the show's format and content and the possibility of it being on the TV screen. I was filled with hope and tenacity to follow their encouragement and take *Smart Funny & Black* to the next level by getting it into American households. Surely, this hella funny, incredibly entertaining, super authentic show would be snatched up by a network, "they" said. With the country descending into sociopolitical sewage, any platform would want to be a part of the solution, "they" said. "They" would want to bring other perspectives to the forefront and be mavericks for change, "they" said. "They" would see the basics in the genius of the content and rush to find a space for it to shine, "they" said. "They" would grasp, with both hands, the deep-rooted blackness of it all and unabashedly shine a light on it for all to see! . . . "they" said. I don't know what the hell I was thinking listening to "them," cuz them white folks was not tryna hear it.

Let me just start by saying to all white people and people who happen to be white who are reading this, ALL BLACK PEOPLE ARE NOT THE SAME. I know, I shouldn't *have* to say that, but I do. That is where stereotypes are spawned, and thrive—in the ignorance of thinking of a culture in such one-dimensional terms that you fail to consider that there are different types of black people who watch and make different types of content. For a long time, black comedy was only considered one thing: fast and physical. Even in the black community, if your comedy was on the more cerebral side of thangs, a lot of times, they'd label you as "alt" or a "comic's comic," but you weren't initially embraced by black audiences in the same way as comedians who represented in a more traditional style of what had come to be considered "black comedy." With *Smart Funny & Black*, I wanted to include all the pieces that make traditional black comedy the unique art that it is, but also broaden the scope and acknowledge that different intellect and wit amongst black funny folks about black life is also integral and valuable and representational of the community. That's literally how I came up with the name. A comedy club in NYC was offering me a monthly night to do a show and they coyly asked, "What type of audience are you expecting?" I could hear the tremble of whiteness as the booker tiptoed around Martin Luther King Jr. and Maya Angelou to get it out and to my ears. I told him, "My audience is gonna be smart, funny, and black. In fact, let's just call it that so there's no confusion on what to expect." And that was all she wrote. Needless to say, the title did absolutely the opposite when it came time to sell it.

I was already hosting a show for a network and while in NYC for the week I decided to stop in for a meeting with the exec on the show and the talent person. We had a pleasant meeting and upon my exit they asked if I was working on anything at the present time. I replied that I was launching a new live show called *Smart Funny & Black* the following week. They were shocked and giddy as the executive producer said, "That's crazy because we JUST had a meeting and said we need to acquire intellectual, humorous, African American content, ASAP"! I told them to look no further and sent over the tape of the first show. This launched into a year-long process of twists and turns and nervous execs, and funny style execs, and shook ones execs, and shady backstabbing execs who say sly slick shit and bold ignorant shit, and you feel like you have to exercise more restraint than a black man being excessively manhandled by a police officer, and bite your tongue before you bite yourself in the ass and watch the opportunity dissolve like when Roseanne thought being racist on Twitter would go unnoticed (still laughing btw). I was paired with two execs—a white woman and man—to sherpa the project to the pilot phase. Though I had a fully fleshed-out project that was already on stage every month, they expressed continual reservations on if it was "clear" and whether or not people would "get it." It didn't take long for me to realize that "people" meant "white people" and "clear" meant "safe." However, the most ridiculous and offensive statement said to me in the back-and-forth of development, and which reflects the true feelings behind much of the Hollywood that claims to want diversity, but not if it's going to make anyone "uncomfortable" was: "We just want to make sure we're not making a show just for black people." I'm going to type it for y'all one more time, so you can see, one mo' 'gain, the sentence that was said to me, without a hint of irony, while on a conference call:

"WE JUST WANT TO MAKE SURE WE'RE NOT MAKING A SHOW JUST FOR BLACK PEOPLE."

It was so damn idiotic, offensive, ignorant, and plain ol' white, that before I unleashed the verbal revolution that had sprung on to the tip of my tongue, I felt myself fly out of my body, look down at myself, and say, "Girl, don't even let 'em take you there." When you hear something like that, from your network exec, it's like the first time you're called "nigger." You're almost more shocked than you are offended like, "*Flava Flav voice* WoOooooOOoOooooOoOow, you straight up said that!" It's pity, over anger, that has you looking at the person, like, "What happened? Where did the disconnect take place that has you in this ill-fitting pantsuit thinking that's a suitable thing to say to anyone, let alone a bish like me???" She deserved a smooth read and a quick exit off the phone, but that wasn't possible. You see in these moments you find out what you're really about. Are you going to go rah-rah and give them the "angry black woman" stereotype? Or give her a reason to let the project go? No, because then "they" win. Who's "they" Amanda? All the forces that have been at work for centuries to prevent you from even being in the position to have this call. I'm not saying you don't have every right to rah-rah it up! But there's how things *should* be and how things *are*. That said, *that* moment wasn't the time for my revolution. Instead of reading her for *Hoarders*-level filth, I gathered my calmness and in a very relaxed, consciously nonconfrontational tone, responded with a simple statement: "Well, we only make up approximately 12.5 percent of the population and everything we do is stolen, appropriated, or commodified. So, you have nothing to worry about." Her response: "You don't have to get defensive, Amanda." LOL. So predictable . . . and, actually, YES, I DO. They then attempted to insert token white-guy-who-black-people-like Michael Rapaport into the show to "help bridge the gap with their white audience." Y'all, I need a parade and a stamp with my face on it for the level of grace I exhibited with these fools as they simply couldn't fathom that white people would watch a show about black pop culture as if all their sons, daughters, nephews, and nieces aren't screaming "nigga" at a Kendrick Lamar concert as we speak. As if they themselves don't know the theme song to *Fresh Prince of Bel-Air,* and that Jay-Z is married to Beyoncé, and didn't get their hair braided that one time down in the Bahamas.

Black culture has globally made the world exalt, kept it entertained, ignited it with soul and vibrance and controversy for centuries. White people and people who happen to be white LOVE black culture. The latter take it in because they appreciate it, the former take it in because . . . plot twist . . . they appreciate it, too!!!! And it kills them! So they steal it and attempt to undermine and detach it from its true origin so they can have it for themselves. But like a flower plucked from its stem, it can only blossom for so long before it withers and dies. That is why her concern, and the concern of so many execs who regularly turn projects away, not because they aren't exciting, or well thought out, or innovative, is rooted in a topline narrative that "White people only watch white people, or a certain kind of black people" and is baseless. The question of "Will white people watch this," is not only hackneyed and trite, it's INVALID. White people, black people, Asian people, disabled people, trans people, all people watch the same things, programming that falls into one of these three categories: content that is authentic, content that is an escape, content that is relative to their lives. That's it. To overlook these verticals in favor of race-based fear is to be a part of enabling the institution of racism and the practice of discrimination in this nation.

The truth of the matter is that I, and my show, do not fit what those execs, or any others (with one exception—shout out to Ben Relles) consider to be their stereotypical idea of what black comedy is and the type of black content that black or white people watch. Even though I was literally ON a hit black TV show that defied all of those predetermined concepts, in their timidity they remained static in being able to conceptualize how a show that used comedy and a game show format to explore life through the black American lens would be valuable to their community and to their viewers. Questions I was asked: Are you going to have white guests? Will there be sub-titles for slang words? Why would people in other countries watch this? One exec said, "I don't know what Juneteenth is. Even your guests didn't know what it was, and they're black!" This is exactly why the show is necessary. Dear White People, those of us black folks who went to your predominantly white schools didn't get access to learning about our history, either. We were right next to you as they praised Andrew Jackson like he wasn't a genocidal psychopath who wiped out the indigenous people of this continent. We were right next to you as they praised Christopher Columbus like he wasn't a high-paid thief and rapist who wiped out the Carib and Arawak Indians of the Caribbean. We were right next to you as they praised Thomas Jefferson for writing the Declaration of Independence while he was sleeping with his slaves on Monticello, what is known to be one of the most horrific plantations and is also on the back of the nickel. We heard all the lies and suffered all the omissions. If our parents or an outside resource didn't provide it, a lot of us didn't learn about our own black history and heritage until we went to college and took a class on it. Knowing this, I feel it's important to be a part of preventing that and to do so by continuing to use the number one resource that I have: humor. Though it may not look like what these folks have decided is "black comedy," it is absolutely and innately that. Outside of simply speaking to black folks it's imperative that there be an awakened understanding of the existence and validity of a variance of perspectives. When we shout, "Black Lives Matter," we mean it ain't just about white folks. When we demand "diversity," we mean we want to hear other stories and other points of view. When we sing, "All my niggas in the whole wide world . . . this shit is for US" we mean we are not beholden to making every piece of our black culture, which was born despite oppression, accessible to those who are not a part of it. America and the world needs to not only be made aware of that, but to understand and accept that. Though we may live in a country that does its best to impede that social evolution by always taking measures to divert truth and learning from permeating too deep into the middle/lower income consciousness, I will do my part to continuously challenge and defy that with my voice and my art.

What I learned in the process of attempting to sell *Smart Funny & Black* was that so many people still feel that the only way to elevation and expansion is through the well-worn path of commercial growth and capitalism via big business and corporations. However, it hit me as I was in Grenada, driving 18,000 feet above sea level on my way to the hot springs, that in order for *Smart Funny & Black* to reach the full extent of its potential, it needed to be protected and preserved from the capitalist-driven commerce of the television business. I would need to build it organically, through the people it seeks to service. In order to truly change the narrative on stereotypes that limit black excellence it would require the full extension of its wings so it can affect as many people as possible. The executives who saw it as too black, or not "black enough," or not white-able were less obstacles and more much-needed omens nudging me in the direction of purpose. At the very least, the purpose of *Smart Funny & Black* is to give individuals a point of soulful soul-filled light to revel in and rejuvenate in the seemingly endless fight to freely exist in blackness. At the most it seeks to defy racial barriers and limitations using comedy as our artillery, and to do so while always keeping social justice in our scope.

Staying Woke

Conscious minds who see the truth
While others remain asleep,
We stay awake to the ways of the world
Cuz shit is deep.

WHAT DOES "WOKE" MEAN?

An acute awareness of the racial injustices of black* people.

Wokeness is a constant state of awareness that can undoubtedly be stressful, frustrating, and anger-inducing as one acknowledges the endless stream of racial injustices that continue to plague people of color. In this maelstrom of mayonnaise-based fuckery one must protect not only their bodies and minds, but also their hearts by finding the joy. I am often asked, "Amanda, how do you stay committed to speaking about the cause?" "How do you keep from shutting down and isolating yourself?" "How do you manage all the ignorance being spewed in your direction?" I have my own self-care routines (i.e., watching *Game of Thrones* while playing Candy Crush), but some of them are universal and can help us all as we fight the good fight!

- **Find the Joy:** You owe it to yourself to find even a pocket of joy at least once day. It can be as simple as taking time out to enjoy a scoop of ice cream or laughing/crying at a fave IG account. Whatever it is, whenever possible, pause to locate and possess some joy for your soul.
- **Circle of Dopeness:** When people ask me how I manage all the ignorance coming my way, I tell them it is immensely outweighed by the dopeness of my inner circle. The people closest to you say so much about who you are and also affect the dimensions of your world. Make sure to curate a circle of dopeness made up of people that are pursuing their own excellence and encouraging you to do the same while staying real.
- **Refine the Rage:** You can't be mad at everything, all the time. It's exhausting and leaves you spread too thin for the fights that really matter. Eventually you have to refine your rage to preserve your energy

---

* Over time, "woke" has been somewhat "all lives mattered" into an awareness for all, and somewhat gentrified into an awareness for anything. Initially it referred to black folks who aren't enslaved mentally, understand how injustices function today, and who choose to use their voice to against these injustices.

and at the same time intensify your effect. It doesn't mean you're fake, or you're shady—it's the same concept as choosing your battles. When you sharpen your blade by becoming clear on exactly what your bottom lines are, you in turn articulate your anger and fuel it with information versus just emotion, which is much easier for you to control and wield at your disposal.

EVERYBODY DON'T HAVE THE SAME IDEA FOR SAVING

One of the realities of being woke is that not everybody else is, and you can't wake everyone up. It is incredibly disheartening when this truth hits you in the face like a pair of Chucks falling off a telephone wire, but it's the truth. The sooner you can grasp this, the sooner you can place your focus on assisting those who are woke, and in leading by example, hopefully you cause someone who previously chose ignorance to adjust their thinking.

MULTIPRONGED APPROACH TO REVOLUTION

Everybody doesn't play the same role in revolution. If you look at any uprising in history, whether it be the Civil Rights movement, the anti-apartheid movement in South Africa, or the abolitionist movement, the issues were addressed and attacked via various means. In designing the crest for *Smart Funny & Black*'s logo, I wanted to represent this multi-pronged approach via our "fams."

- **Rebel Fam:** "We Fight." The image of the black panther holding Africa with a black fist donning an RBG wristband represents the physical force needed to challenge oppression. I do not promote violence, but I do promote defense, and when your people are being assaulted and slaughtered, there has to be muscle on your side of the field to defend them.
- **Woke Fam:** "We Read." The Ancient Egyptian holding the stack of books speaks to the importance of education in the fight for liberation. The first thing oppressors do is suppress language and education.

When people can't communicate or read, it limits not only their confidence and intelligence but also their ability to organize an uprising. Black folks, never forget, they didn't want us to read. Simply by consuming literature we are our ancestor's dream and our oppressor's worst nightmare.

- **Cultcha Fam:** "We Vibe." The boom box paired with the pencil, microphone, and paintbrush represent the importance art plays in revolution. Historians may record the facts of the time, but artists record the feelings. We simultaneously create art for educating others and beautiful works that can be a welcome momentary distraction from the hectic state of an injustice-filled world and an idea-filled mind.
- **Fly Fam:** "We Fly." The three faces represent different elements of iconic black style, from Dwayne Wayne's flip glasses and flattop to the young woman's head wrap and septum ring to homie's locs and "Beard Gang" beard. They speak to the history of black innovation, the role style has always played in defining our culture and defying our oppressors, and the need to always be creating new approaches, new strategies, and new inroads to making better lives for those who don't benefit from the privilege afforded others.

HOW THINGS ARE
VS. HOW THEY COULD BE

You can alleviate a lot of unnecessary stress by taking an objective look at the world and acknowledging the fact that YES, it is shitty, but considering and being the change toward the ways it could work.

IGNORANCE AND BLISS

Ignorance is not bliss . . . but ignorance of other people's ignorance is!

Conscious
vs. Trolltep

IN A WORLD THAT HAS MADE CONCERTED EFFORTS to keep black folks ignorant to our greatness, the systems in place to oppress that greatness, and the ability to topple those systems, being aware, empowered, and informed is key to the goal of achieving any semblance of true freedom. Or as the kids say, being "woke." Whether you're about being up on your reading, or being involved in the community, or simply exhibiting black pride in the face of scrutiny, there are many levels of wokeness. Although there are many folks doing work on the ground, this wokeness can most easily be seen super clearly on the interwebs. These innanets and its various platforms have become an open forum for folks who have thoughts, ideas, principles, and ideals that they want to share with the world, or with their twenty-three followers. Amidst this varied array of individuals are everyday people sick and tired of being sick and tired, coons who would sell their own family to the slave ship if the gold was right, self-proclaimed leaders, subversive speakers, actor/athlete activists, educators, and all the rest of us. Though these platforms have provided an incredible resource for information gathering, and sharing, with the intention of empowerment, on occasion they have been the incubator for folks with plentiful information yet limited insight. In an effort to prevent purpose and progress from being derailed, identifying who's 'bout it and who's 'bout the bullshit is imperative.

"Ignorance is bliss" is a crock of crap. Especially if you're a person of color. ESPECIALLY if you are a black person. If you identify as black, and are a member of the black community, blissful ignorance can get you killed, or even worse, labeled a coon! I kid, I kid. Being a coon is absolutely not worse than being killed but as a coon, your support of oppressive ideals and legislation kills not only others, but your access to your black card as well. Thankfully, these days it's become cool to be tapped in. Folks complain about IG THOTs, mumble rappers, excessive video games, and do hella shock value violent music videos that permeate the pop culture space, boldly suggesting that, consumed with the latest dance craze to take over, black Americans have become desensitized to black violence. The same folks then sit back and watch their point proven as the same pop-culture-consuming black folks they are complaining about permeate the pop culture space with the images of the black violence found in the video chiding them for becoming desensitized to images of black violence! But it does nothing to advance the conversation!

Everyone has an opinion. The facts, however, are that many conversations are happening in many settings, from many entry points, about change and solutions as they relate to blackness in America. To be conscious is to be a part of these conversations, even if just as a passive listener and supporter. The dissemination of information is a valuable role in any revolution for change that uplifts the "common" masses and does not require you to be the speaker, but more the seeker of truth and fact; and the sharer of your discoveries with others. True consciousness also requires objectivity and a heightened level of realism. There is how we want things to be, how things were, and how things are. In order to achieve any real change, you have to be able to see things clearly on all of these fronts from your own perspective and consider other perspectives as well.

Hoteps ain't bout that life. *Hotep* is an ancient Egyptian word that means "be at peace." In current black social circles, it is the name given to those who disrupt the "peace" with extreme and evangelical-level concepts of black consciousness. However, they are the unconsciously conscious. The sleepwoke. They are SO woke, they are suffering from sleep deprivation that has them thinking delusionally. A bigger issue, aside from their own disconnect from true positive movements, is that hoteps attack and demean others who don't agree with their problematic insights. Hence my creation of the term *trollteps* aka hoteps who troll. Then again, one could argue that the two aren't mutually exclusive, and by nature, a hotep is trolling the black community. They are unwaveringly homophobic, they attempt to demean women who unabashedly speak their point of view or challenge the toxic masculinity behaviors by black men, and they have a very limited scope in what they consider the true black experience to be and who should be able to speak to it and about it. To trollteps, black women with blond hair are trying to "mimmick massa," even though there are indigenous black people the world over who have naturally blond hair. To trollteps, the voices of gay men, women, and the trans community are of no value because based on Dr. So-and-So's and/or Brother What's-His-Name's teachings they have deemed their sexual orientation an abomination of blackness. To trollteps, ANY woman's challenge to or critiquing of black men for literally any reason whatsoever is an action in partnership with the oppressor. I could go on and on with the BS that these folks drum up and push out. The spotting of a hotep, or a trolltep, or a hotep notep (another term I've created for these fools) can be a doozy. As Joelle learned in season two of *Dear White People*, at first they present as intellectuals who are loving of blackness. Who wouldn't find that endearing? Buuutttt, eventually, they whip out a kufi and some egregious ignorance, and their true selves are revealed as the detriment of their sentiments are made clear. Don't even try to argue. You're speaking rationally into an irrational "The black woman is queen . . . But I am king and should be regarded as such" void. The point is, they're not welcome. Even if their intention is in the empowerment and forward movement of black folks, their rhetoric is grounded in a flawed foundation that upholds patriarchal principles, presents invalid opinion as fact, and is more about ego and dominance than understanding and unity.

The incessant work that has been done for centuries by oppressive forces to brainwash black folks into upholding the supremacist structures that oppress us is on a maniacal level. We, as a community who recognizes this, must work on a constant basis to not only prevent any further brain-washing, but also work to reverse the result of that which has already taken place. It takes mental and emotional stamina and support from each other. It takes gender equality and respecting freedom of sexual choice. It involves intense insight into self and simultaneous ownership of the wellness of your community. The goal is not to merely survive, but to thrive and to encourage each other to do so beyond the confines of what we've been told is possible. We defy them with our excellence and an indifference to their existence. We cannot base how we as a black community operate on the infrastructures of our oppressor. There is no merit to or ethics in their design, which is why I am a big believer that you must call out coons, Uncle Toms, and house negros who push and support agendas that seek to continue the narrative that "white is right." However, trollteps, in effect, and sometimes inadvertently, push that narrative, in presenting their arguments and attacking fellow black folks in the same ways as the oppressors they claim to work toward toppling. In their inability to properly differentiate between coons and black folks who simply do not share their extremism, they widen the chasm within the black commu-nity created by the Colonial and Willie Lynch methods of divide and conquer. In seeking to silence sistas who speak to wellness, accountability, and individ-ual freedom amongst black men and women, they do no more than carry forth a reductive narrative that positions black women as existing solely for the purposes of service, seed bearing, and silence. Nah.

We have borne the mask that grins and lies, and life still ain't no crystal stair, but we stand on the shoulders of giants who have come before us. To be conscious is to understand that we are carrying forth the vision of those who somehow survived slave holds in the shit-filled gut of devil-run ships, those who woke up and put their best ties and kitten heels on to face individuals who threw their worst insults and fists and water hoses at them simply for wanting the right to share the same lunch counter, those who defied the threat of death, simply to learn how to read a language that was denied them, after having their mother tongue beaten out of their consciousness, those who signed their names to petitions that could prevent their families from eating, in the hopes that it would one day allow their family's family to prosper, those who reimagine incarceration as rehabilitation, those who put down their colors to come together in community, didn't take no for an answer, who dared to envision a world where they could see their vision through to fruition, who somehow tapped into the resource within their DNA that extends all the way way way back to when black people of the earth created and thrived in civilizations that are still giving to this world. Hoteps disrupt that legacy when they interrupt with patriarchy, misogyny, homo/transphobia, and more, which does not uplift but instead emboldens fear. As Dap screams at the end of *School Daze*, WAAAKKKKKEEEE UPPPPPP! to knowing, upholding, and no longer denying that we are more powerful as an US.

"I'm not hostile. I'm just passionate." That's what I told Caitlyn Jenner as she sat across from me, in the randomest of settings, her red-nail-polished fingertips clasped in indignation during a YouTube livestreamed dinner hosted by Katy Perry. The gathering, a part of Katy's seventy-two-hour "Big Brother House," done in promotion of her (then) new album, *Witness*, was coordinated to bring a diverse group of minds together, including Van Jones (CNN), Ana Navarro (*The View*), Sally Kohn (CNN), Yung Skeeter (DJ), Caitlyn Jenner (American TV personality), Margaret Cho (comedian), Derek Blasberg (writer, *Vanity Fair*), and myself, Amanda Seales (comedian/HBO's *Insecure*). The mix of guests was meant to encourage the importance of having difficult conversations with people you may respect, but with whom you have diverging and very disparate views. It lived up to expectations. The dinner conversation quickly evolved into discourse, and Caitlyn became bristled by statements I made regarding the current president's proclivity for tyrannical behavior. With urging, she expounded upon her offense at my statements, saying that she "loves this country." When I began to candidly, yet courteously, inform her about how her white privilege creates the lens through which she views America, versus how I, a black woman, view it, shit got real. Everyone could feel it. Everybody knew it. A "moment" was happening.

"Moments" like that, where unfiltered truths are cast against unwavering ignorance like opposing spells from the wands of Dumbledore and Voldemort, have happened at a number of dinner tables since the 2016 election. When they do, they force everyone to play a role in whether the conversation will be an effective one. Our table was no different.

There were Sally Kohn and Katy Perry in the roles of *The Listener*: It's the safest and oftentimes most courteous position to play. Especially if you're a white person and a black person is speaking about their black experience.

You had Van Jones, *The Moderator*: I often found myself side-eyeing him, but that night he was vital in clearing up miscommunications, providing clarity to confusion, and, overall, encouraging all parties to be respectful, even in the midst of horseshit being spewed.

Gotta love Margaret Cho and Yung Skeeter, *The Allies*: May not have said much, but their demeanor and disposition read, "SPEAK YOUR TRUTH!" Margaret's grin as I was breaking it down to CJ was like that of a proud mom watching her kid finally confront their bully. Which is the kind of encouragement you need when you're up against . . .

The Obstructionist: In this case, that was Caitlyn. The person at the table choosing to disengage when the discussion becomes difficult, willfully ignoring facts that are counter to their point, and thus misdirecting conversation from progressive to regressive based on cognitive dissonance, misinformation, and ego, or all of the above.

Lastly, there was me, *The Truth Teller*: The person armed with the information, the honesty, and the tenacity to speak directly to the heart of the issue and educate those involved, while inspiring those in earshot. After the clip of what I now call "The Caitlyn Clinic" went viral, several people asked me, "Do you think she heard you?" My response was, "I don't care." More importantly, who did hear me were hella black folks that felt empowered by the authenticity of our experience being represented.

It may not be livestreaming, but currently, we're all at one big dinner table called America. And though there may not be a right side of the table, as the makers of the media that not only changes minds but can change the world, we must remember there is a right side of history. What role will the work you do play in the conversation to make sure we land on it?

CHAPTER 3

Square Biz

Thriving in Your Career &
Getting That Paper

IN TRYING TO MAKE THE MOST OF OUR TIME HERE on the pale blue dot, some of us are doing a whole lotta BS and tryna make it look like something. Whether it's stuntin' on the 'gram while sleeping on your momma's couch or posting every open bar you attend every night of every week. (Sidenote: You could be an alcoholic. Don't let the social settings fool you!) For the most part, we're simply out here tryna get it how we live it, and though we don't want to be used, we do want to be useful. Many of us define our usefulness by our work. We chart how much we are adding to society by what we do to make money. We solidify our purpose via the level of work we produce and how it affects the world. That said, getting your mind right and then your money right are two of the most basic fundamentals of life. Ideally, you want to do the former first because when you get your money right, you want to be able to enjoy it. As B.I.G. said, "Mo' Money, Mo' Problems," and you'll want a solid mental base that feels connected, from the Coogi down to the socks, to tackle the trials as they come . . . and they will come.

There really is no easy road to the alignment of your professional goals with your heart. With one side rooted in logic and the other rooted in emotion, it takes time and clarity of thought to get the two to work in tandem. That is the process. Within that process there are various stages and developments that seem insurmountable as they're happening, but in hindsight prove to have been requisite elements to your eventual ascent to "shinin' on deez hoes." Speaking for myself as a creative, defining your style, your process, and yourself are paths that will try your whole entire patience at the same time they are shaping you into a creative who is on "a grind" versus just "a hustle."

Now, if you're a multihyphenate, there's also a whole other level of clarity you have to find. Often this clarity is not even for yourself, but for others—for a world that wants to label you—and that can be a confounding space. Bringing your creativity to commerce and corporate America takes some finesse and self-awareness as both operate as their own institutions with their own sets of spoken and unspoken rules. Often, there is no blueprint for either, but there are subtle intricacies and inconspicuous techniques for managing both. As a creative, life can simply feel unmanageable. However, it doesn't have to be. When you do begin to ascend, there are moves to be made to keep the momentum in an upward trajectory. However, if that momentum hits a wall, you gotta find ways to Aaliyah and DMX it and "Dust yaself off and try again . . . try again." In the midst of all that, staying focused on the ways you can support yourself financially and, hopefully, fulfillingly, is probably the toughest part.

Though the path from a dream to a goal to a plan to an accomplishment is tougher than Frodo trying to get rid of that damn ring, it is an inevitable part of the process of gettin' poppin'. Yes, some lessons must be learned by trial and error, but others can be received by learning from the experiences of others and using them as tips and directions to your bigger picture. Think of "the bigger picture" not as a portrait, but as a giant GPS for your life. When you step back, you'll see where you've been and hopefully a path to help get you where you're going.

Being a Creative

Nothing from something is our way
When left with no other options, CREATE.

STAMINA

To choose a creative field takes courage. To advance in a creative field takes talent. To survive in a creative field takes stamina. Pace your energy. Take care of your brain. Protect your heart. You will need all three to handle the rejection, the self-doubt, the deadlines, the critiques, the haters, along with the wins, triumphs, and accolades.

TRUST THE PROCESS

The true struggle of the struggling artist is knowing your greatness long before the people you want to know it do. During that time, somehow, you've gotta find a way to keep going. It's been said before, and I will reiterate it: Trust the process. That doesn't mean sit around and wait for things to happen or that when shit goes left, you shouldn't attempt to make it right. What it means is, there are ups and downs. There are feasts and famine. There are moments when you realize you have outgrown your prior taste and the work you were doing before now seems juvenile in its development. It's all a part of the process. "But Amanda, what exactly *is* 'THE PROCESS.'" The process is the journey to you defining your style.

STYLE

In the case of the creative, your style is your biggest asset. It is what makes your work identifiable and uniquely yours. It's kind of like a figurative barcode. In a sea of creatives gifting their art to the Universe, your style is the constellation by which you spot yours in the night sky. Over time and growth of life experiences and maturity your style will inevitably change. LET IT. When you feel it happening, molt out of your style like an anaconda shedding its skin and breathe into fresher, more fitting, flavas. Be fearless about this. Make sure, however, that it is your inner voice evolving and not the marketplace driving you. The fact is, for every creative, your style, once truly developed, should be an extension of the truest pieces of you. Come up with ten words to define your style. Then knock it down to three. Then see if you can get it to one. Let that be the north star that guides you on your exploration.

DEFINE YOUR ART BEFORE THE INDUSTRY DEFINES IT FOR YOU.

LEARN YOUR CRAFT

Sure, you may have natural talent, but it is still important to learn the fundamentals of whatever craft(s) you're pursuing because they serve as the template upon which you build your own vision.

DETAILS

The dopeness is in the details. The same way mathematicians show their work and can tell you how they got from a formula to a solution is the in-the-weeds level with which you should become familiar with your work. I say this because when you can do this, you are confident in your work and you can call on that knowledge at any time. They say luck is when opportunity meets preparation. When you know your work, what makes it tick, what makes it glow, and what makes it win, you're already prepared for whatever opportunity comes at you.

MOTIVATION

When you're building stamina, trusting the process, and developing your style it can be hard to stay motivated.

- **DON'T FALL OFF.** If you're unable to support yourself with your art and have to work a main job in the interim, it can be difficult to balance. The reality is, it is almost impossible to balance something you need for money with something you hope to *eventually* make money from. That said, it doesn't mean you completely sideline your passion. The key is to keep growing. Even when you are given minimal time, do SOME-THING. So often, we get off track from our creative development because our focus is diverted elsewhere. Challenge yourself to still find a way to fit it in.

- **GET OUT OF YOUR HEAD.** When you find yourself stuck and unsure of what to do next, go watch somebody else do their thang. Whether it's checking out a medium that you work in, or going completely left, put yourself in another's artistic space. When you do this, it takes you out of your creative bubble and, like shaking an Etch-a-Sketch, cleanses your palate so you can see new ideas, make new connections, and expand your imagination.

- **KEEP BELIEVERS AROUND.** The number one piece of advice I can give anyone pursuing a creative career is to always keep people around you who believe in you as much, if not more, than you believe in yourself. You may know in your mind that you're dope, but sometimes believing that in your heart is tougher to do. Make sure there are folks in your world that truly believe in your abilities so that when those times of doubt, slowed motivation, and weakened stamina arise (and they will arise) they are there to put the new battery back in to keep you going!

CREATE YOUR LIFE

Right now some of you are sitting somewhere frustrated that you're not getting the opportunity to spread your creative wings and use your creative gifts and it's killing you inside. But I want to remind you that, as a creative, you have the ability to do something that a lot of people don't. To make something from nothing, including your own path and your own outlets. Take it from someone who has done it time and time again. When you find yourself stunted and feel like you're unable to express yourself creatively, *create your own creative space.* That can mean a number of things, but what it really means is take control of defining your creative outlets for yourself and don't wait for someone to make them available to you. NOW GO MAKE SOME SHIT!

PLATFORM BUILDING

Black women creatives must be the builders of our own platforms. It just is what it is! We must not only make our own art but also our own spaces for that art to live and thrive! Being a creative is not just about artistry. Even if you don't consider yourself an artist, if you're in finance, production, nonprofit work, education, etc., your creativity can be finding ways to amplify black female voices.

 # MONEY TALKS

You take their money, you take their shit. This is the real truth of patronage and working with entities that have input into the work you're creating. Taking notes can be annoying and irritating, especially when they are less about the work and more about someone else's ego or attempt to justify their job. Nonetheless, take it in stride. Rigidity is the creative's downfall. Learn when to adjust (when it's your own ego rejecting a good idea or suggestion), when to find a consensus (when it's BS but you can find a work-around that makes everyone happy), and when to walk away (when what they want you to do is compromising the work).

KNOW YOUR STRENGTHS

You may love to sing. You be killin' it in the shower! That doesn't mean that is your gift. Sometimes we have to be honest with ourselves, that something we love to do may not be what we are meant to do. The creative space is not for the weary, and in order to thrive in it as a career you need to not only be doing your passion but also something that you're talented at. Often, the route we think is our road to success has unexpected turns that lead us into fields and spaces that we didn't foresee. Go with it. Take the twists and turns as they come. In 2006, you couldn't tell me that I wasn't going to be the next soul-singing superstar. But I got real with myself that music wasn't my ministry and made room for other paths to reveal themselves. I never for a second planned on comedy leading me down a road to being a "somewhat" self-help author, and yet, here we are—live and in full effect!

The Hustle
vs. The Grind

FOLKS BE OUT HERE BULLSHITTIN'. Let's keep it 8 more than 92 (100!). There are a lot of people you know who talk all day about what they're going to do and what they want to do but don't make the moves. They're always busy but not really making progress. You ask yourself, "What's really holding them back?" Oftentimes it's themselves and where they're channeling their energy. For some folks, they get caught up in the cycle of the hustle and don't ever commit to the grind. Now, don't get me wrong, the two words have been used interchangeably forever. Especially if you listen to hip-hop, i.e., "I stay on my hustle, I stay on my grind . . ." But I'm gonna apply some more specific definitions to hopefully foster more realistic outcomes! Bottom line, the hustle is what you do to stay afloat. The grind is how you work toward solidifying a career.

There is no blueprint or clear-cut path to going after your dreams. People love to share their stories, and people love to hear other people's stories, but no matter how much advice you get, or how much research you've done, it's a trial-and-error process at best. You gotta figure out yo' shit yo' self. That's what the hustle is—exploring and applying how to sustain and maintain until the momentum is in motion on its own. Keeping busy and keeping funded to keep on moving. The idea of the struggle is very enticing for some, and yes, it is a necessary part of the process, but willfully planting your flag in it is more of an exercise in self-hate than self-motivation. The hustle is not about owning struggle. It's about respecting the process. Within the hustle you get experiences that at the time may seem like more of a nuisance than an applicable lesson. You know what I mean—you have some bullshit go down and you're like, "Why?! WHY is this even necessary!?!? I don't need this right now. I got rent to pay!" (That phone bill is a bitch, too!) It seems completely out of pocket and undeserved. These setbacks seem to you like they're without merit or value. Little do you know, it's all a necessary part of the hustle. Because that irritating instance will eventually be a skeleton key to a new issue. You'll look back like, "OH SHIT! I dealt with something JUST. LIKE. THIS." When you know that the twists and turns and obstacles before you are really just lessons for you to use later, it changes how you manage them and gives you added gumption to continue carrying on. As one of my favorite lines in one of my favorite movies goes, "We have two lives, Roy, the life we learn with and the life we live with after that."* When folks say, "Getcho hustle on" they don't just mean work hard and try hard. They also mean dig your heels in and be a part of the energy moving toward attainment.

Someone once asked me, "How do you get so much work? I've been waiting for a call from my agent for a week." Operative word? WAITING. Do not confuse patience with waiting. Patience is the active decision to allow for something to materialize in a natural and organic way. Waiting is the act of putting the onus on someone or something else to activate you. Bump that. IT'S MOVE TIME. The hustle is you doing what you have to do to discover the goal and plan that extends from your dream. It is the groundwork that determines how you're going to pursue your goal once it's designated. Even if you don't know your purpose. Even if you have yet to identify your passion. The hustle is when you show the Universe how you move. Ask yourself:

Do you electric slide toward things?	or	Do you kick your Timbs up and wait for things to happen?
Do you seek to identify modes of upliftment and point 'em out?	or	Do you let 'em keep passin' you by (like The Pharcyde)?
Do you maximize opportunities?	or	Do you self-sabotage?

I could go on and on because the hustle is really all about finding these things out about yourself and nipping the bullshit in the bud, QUICK! For some, the hustle lasts for decades, for others it may last a couple years. In contrast, the grind is about working smarter, not harder, and refining your tools toward the specific goal(s) at hand. We all have a purpose, and it is not always clear when that will be revealed to us. However, when it is, you want to be in the best possible position to pursue it. And that, my friends, is where the grind comes in.

---

* *The Natural* (1984) starring Robert Redford and Glenn Close.

Like I said, the hustle is the prep for the purpose. The grind is the road to fulfilling it. It can *feel* like the hustle. It may LOOK like the hustle. But it is not the hustle. The grind is driven by a defined end goal. That's why they say the grind never stops. Because purpose begets more purpose. You have an idea that comes to fruition and it bears the fruit of more ideas. Don't get me wrong though, the grind ain't no joke. In some ways it's even harder than the hustle. Remember what I mentioned about waiting and patience. It's really easy to wait, but patience is a whole virtue. The grind is built on knowing what you have within you but having to go through the necessary steps to deliver it. You cannot skip steps. You can speed them up, but you cannot skip them. I taught myself a back handspring instead of learning it the proper way, and it was the bane of my existence throughout my entire gymnastics career. You cannot skip steps. But I repeat, you can speed them up. You speed steps up by simply showing up.

I started doing stand-up, and even though I wasn't afraid of the mic and I knew how to work a stage, I did the open mics. I hung out to try to get spots. I did free shows. Those steps, for many reasons, were necessary to my growth as a comic, and because of them I came to know and respect the fortuitousness of being granted stage time and being paid for it, which in turn taught me to cherish and respect that time rather than take it for granted. The grind is a series of actions and modes designed to move you forward to mastery. When you successfully advance, you're on to the next and must then spread out in that new space and learn it, too, before you can advance to the next level. I always say, the grind grinds you up. Because the grind checks you. It humbles you. It teaches you that although you think you know what you're doing and why you're here, there is so much more that you have yet to consider. It is a beautiful struggle. At its best, it is not a stress but a challenge. It is tiring but exhilarating. At its worst, it is not a burden but a responsibility. It is not a chore but an exercise. When you're feeling empty on your grind, get replenished by talking to or witnessing someone immersed in theirs:

- Go see a live performance.
- Watch a film about a grind that is prosperous in spite of obstacles.
- Check out a museum (painters' grinds be the realest!).

Whatever you do, don't stop. If you made it from the hustle to the grind, you're on your way.

I remember feeling like a hamster on a wheel. I was doing and doing and nothing substantial was really materializing. I was staying afloat, and I would get little offerings of encouragement from the Universe, but for the most part it felt like I was just "doing." I realized I was trapped in the hustle. See that's the doozy. Though the hustle is a necessary part of any process, it has an end. It's so tiring because when you're in it, it feels like there is no end to you giving your all in the hopes of eventually being able to glow up. That's why at some point, you gotta self-check and ask, "What's my hustle really about?" Getting trapped in the hustle is the problem with so many folks who have lowered expectations for what they deserve and are too modest about what they possess. It can be the product of oppression and suppression—an insidious brainwashing that says your only purpose is to survive, not to thrive. Fuck that. Eyes up and stay woke to your purpose so you can get out of hustle mode and into grind mode. The hustle is the cobblestones you hop on so you don't get your stilettos stuck in between the cracks, but eventually you gotta get to the other side of the street and hit the pavement for your grind, baby! The hustle gets you a job. The grind gets you a career. A job gets you a check. A career gets you a lifestyle.

Here and now, I want anyone who is reading this and considers themselves to be a creative to CUT THE CRAP. YOU'RE "WEIRD." Acknowledge it. Own it. Deal with it. This is important, because, and trust me on this, until you do, you will ALWAYS feel misunderstood, underwhelmed, and annoyed by your interactions with the non "weird" world. The world is big and full of people who are, for the most part, not creatives. Especially when it comes to art in commerce. No diss to noncreatives, but y'all think differently. You operate differently. You move differently. Which is fine. Unless you're a creative who has not come to grips with said differences. Your lack of realization of the nature of your artsy idiosyncrasies will have you steady bent outta shape. For instance, being confused as to why the nonweirdos are confused that you didn't turn that piece in on time. You've explained to them that just as you were about to finish it, you stepped back, realized it was trash, and simply couldn't bring yourself to turn it in, but they just don't get it. Your fellow creatives get it! We may not be cool with it, but we understand. However, to someone who is not a creative or is not accustomed to working with creatives, this is some off-beat bullshit. Because business, for the most part, lacks the fluidity of "weird." It works within a grid. It relies on numbers and linear thinking that plans from A to B, often using trends and blueprints. As artists, we innately operate outside of these confines. Again, it is important to know that about yourself, because if you are choosing a creative path as a career you will have to figure out how to work within these specifics without it killing your drive, or even worse, your creative spirit.

Around 2007 I started recording music and eventually found myself performing with The Roots, opening for Lupe Fiasco, touring as a member of Floetry (that's a whole other book, chile), and doing my own solo shows overseas. I released four independent projects, shot videos, did mixtapes, the whole nine! I am a music buff and had spent the early portion of my career as an MTV2 VJ and writer for *The Source*, *XXL*, and more. So, at first, it was incredibly exciting to be able to make my own music and share it with people. Until I realized I was making all this music and I wasn't making no money! That's when I began to consider the business of music more, and it turned out that I hated it. It felt like the music was the least important aspect of the package. Folks were more interested in who managed me, who I worked with, what my story was, what my "look" was, etc. They told me, "You can't sing *and* rap. You have to choose because no one is buying that, and no one is playing that." It was incredibly disconcerting. Essentially, I was being told what so many creatives trying to make a career out of their art are told: "That thing that's coming from your soul is not marketable," aka nobody wants it. So, we can't sell it. What originally had been a passion realized turned into a futile exercise in trying to create art that simultaneously gave me fulfillment and also fit within the invisible lines of the mainstream. Attempting to do something innovative and unique was met with such opposition by non-creative folks before they even heard my music. It was legit odd to them that I would want to forge something from fire, versus pull it off the shelf. I had a music legend once ask me, "Why don't you just make a basic song that people don't have to think about, and buy your mom a house?" My mom would tell me, "I don't think you like money because you're really not trying to make it." LOL. It wasn't that, it was just that as a creative I was moving to the beat of a different MPC2500. Yet, if I was going to stick with this path, I needed to figure out how to sustain myself. That quest led me to eventually dislike music. Unreal! How is that possible!? It happened, honey. I was just OVER. IT. I always say, the measure of when to walk away is when a challenge becomes a stress. A challenge is when something is difficult and outside of your comfort zone, but ultimately rewarding. A stress is when what you're giving to the goal outweighs what you're receiving, and your efforts have moved beyond practical to Pyrrhic. That can be applied to literally anything in your life. In this case, the constant frustration of being unable to reconcile my art with commerce reached a point where I realized it was draining me more than it was teaching me. That was my cue to Neh Neh away from the music biz. It was not the right fit for my artistry.

In hindsight, I didn't fully grasp the totality of what it means to create for commerce. This was a lesson of my hustle. I had to eventually come to grips with the fact that no matter what artistic medium I was pursuing, I'd have to meet the market halfway. The key was to figure out what medium that was. Because you cannot let the "weirdness" be a barrier to your purpose. There's wanting to retain your artistic integrity and there's simply not being willing to use your creativity to deal with the business side of things that feels so restraining. If you know you need to catch a vibe to get the work done, figure out exactly what that takes so you can call on it when needed. If you know that you have a tendency to procrastinate as part of your process, don't accept deadlines that you can't meet, which in turn sends a message of unreliability. If you know that you don't like taking notes from others, sheittt, you may have to just keep your art as a hobby. Nah, forreal though, notes are a part of the patronage. As my mother always says, "You take their money, you take their shit." You just know that the further you go, the more trusted you become, the less notes you have to take. Nevertheless, all these things are considered "weird" attributes by folks who are perfectly fine with getting annual reviews, consider deadlines de facto, and don't have the luxury to procrastinate. I see it so many times, where my fellow creatives let their artsy "weird" shit keep them from advancing. You must find the conduit that instead of creating a clash allows your "weird" art shit to be your method. If he was just a hustla on a Harlem block, Cam'ron would've been looked at crazy for rockin' all that pink and even adding a cape. However, as an MC he carved his own lane, stuck to his brand, never wavered from his "weird" art shit, and now, basically everything Cam does, including getting computers 'putin', is uptown iconic and meme worthy.

It's not to say we artists are illogical, or irrational, but when you are a creative you do just that, you create. To create is to make something from nothing and give it life. In order to do that, to even believe that you can do that, then to have the nerve to think it will be something of worth, requires you to think outside of the grid of limitation, aka you gotta get on some otha shit! For creatives, colors can be alive, objects can be fashioned, music can be made, and characters roused. We walk on a wavelength that is more defined by our hearts than our minds. We consider emotion a tool rather than a hindrance. We can be laser-sharp focused and be disrupted by something seemingly as nebulous as "a vibe." In the spectrum of what is considered normal, artists, simply put, are frickin' weirdos and for centuries have managed to get out of their own way and use that "weirdness" to change the world. So can you.

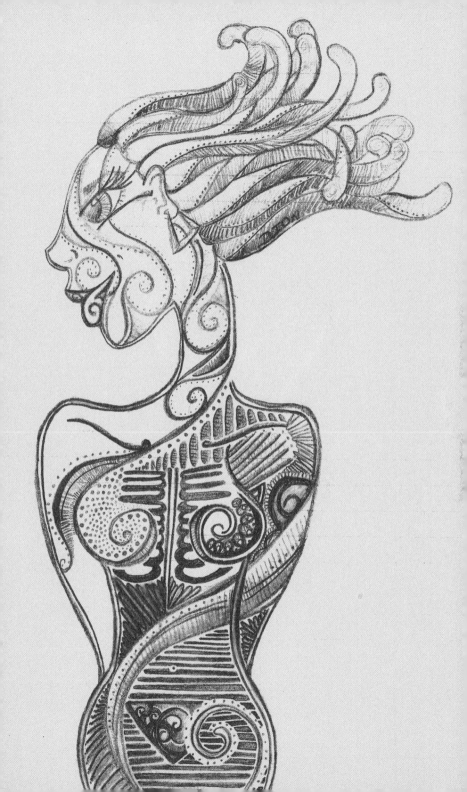

The Come Up

On the rise we move on a mission
And size up competition
But remember,
what's for you is for you;
Actualize your vision.

EGO

On the road to the come up one of your biggest obstacles is yourself. Is your ego bigger than your resume? KEEP IT IN CHECK.

Spend more time listening and asking questions than talking and waxing poetic. Utilize the already formed blueprints of others to create one that's uniquely yours.

DON'T

Don't be a dick. You may think that's easy but especially when someone is being one to you, it can be very difficult not to devolve into their wackness. Do not let their petty moment disrupt your grand vision.

SELF-WORTH AND MARKET VALUE

Don't confuse worth with entitlement. Just because you may know your abilities and what you can bring to the table does not mean you have the credentials to sit at the table—yet. Know your self-worth *and* your market value. When you are clear on the two it allows you to clearly see not only what steps you need to take to pursue your goal and activate a plan, but also if you are truly able to do so.

SECRET *to* SUCCESS

There is no *secret to success*. You're either working hard or you're sleeping with somebody that's working hard. Dassit.

NETWORKING

Some key phrases that I can't stand:
- No one worth your time says, "Let's network." What that reads as is, "Let me get connected to *your* network."
- "We can do business together." If my business is worth more than yours then what you really mean is, "Let me use your money to make my money."
- This one is used by various people, nonetheless, I despise when people ask, "Can I pick your brain?" No! You can't touch my hair and you can't tap into my neural net. Sure, there are questions to ask and things to learn, but the statement reads as, "Can you give me your valued insight and opinion *for free*?"
No dice.

AN EFFECTIVE WAY TO NETWORK

I called Queen Latifah once, and after giving her an earful of why I wanted to connect with her she kept it all the way 100 with me and said that most people with financial resources don't have a lot of time. Therefore, if you're asking them for assistance you need to be able to do so in thirty seconds and cover:

- **What you are doing:** Be able to communicate in a succinct fashion what project you're approaching them about.
- **Why you need help:** Be able to relay in a concise nature why you are in need of assistance to advance the project.
- **How they can help:** Be able to delineate in a clear manner how they specifically can be of aid in the project's advancement.

SLAVE MENTALITY

The slave mentality will have you working harder for other people than you do for yourself. You know that level of detail, attention, and excellence that you would put into doing some work for somebody else? Make sure you apply that when you're doing work for yourself.

ADVICE IN ACTION

People are way more willing to give you advice than assistance, but if you're a self-motivated person, advice really is assistance because you take that advice and put it into action. So often I get questions from people who haven't made a move yet. They haven't lifted a finger, but they want advice on how to do something, and they don't understand why I'm hesitant to give it to them. I'm hesitant because if I'm going to take my time to put you onto something, I want to know that it's going to lead to action. When you are taking real, concrete steps and people see you doing it they are way more inclined to *offer* assistance. Which is better for you! The best way to show someone that you're an action-oriented person is by approaching them after you've already put things in motion. So that if they do take the time to give you advice, they know you've already got something beyond just an idea to apply it to.

STONES

People will give you stones to hop on. Look for the stones to get to your goal and hopefully fulfill a dream. Focus on the next stone, don't get overwhelmed by the ones you don't see yet in the distance.

LOOK BACK AND STEP UP

As you ascend, remember that once upon a time you were looking up for a hand to help you reach the next stepping stone. Be that hand to someone else. ESPECIALLY if you are from a marginalized community. If you are the person reaching out your hand, STEP UP. Too often folks work so hard to get opportunities only to fall short once they're in the position to move up. Charisma gets you in the room, character keeps you there.

GIG PYRAMID

Someone once told me that there are three sides to a job, and it was the best advice I've ever been given.

1. The money
Dolla dolla dolla dolla dolla billz y'all. What are you taking home to the bank?

2. The people
Issa family affair. Who will you be alongside for this ride?

3. The content
What it is, hoe? Wassup? What are the goods you'll be working with?

The key is that in order to take/keep the gig, at least two of these have to line up. If not, you're more than likely going to feel like you wasted your time, and don't **nobody** got time for that!

PEOPLE-PLEASING

If you're the kind of creative I am, you're a bit awkward when dealing with people, especially as it relates to business, *especially* in the corporate space. It's a bitch, and to be honest, they say artists are sensitive, but corporate folks have one-ply skin. Below are some tips on managing the folks who are managing you that I've learned the hard way:

- Start emails with a salutation. "I hope all is well," "Happy Monday," "Good Morning," etc. People like it.
- In a general meeting, find a common interest and make the meeting about that. Business is boring. Bring entertainment to their day. Talk about anything but business and make the meeting feel like recess. They'll not only thank you, they'll remember you.
- Keep relationships. You don't have to be a creep, but check in and invite folks out to your events. If you had a genuine connection with someone, they will not think it's odd that you want to follow up down the road with a dinner or lunch to check in.
- It's not just about who you know. It's also about who knows your skills. Sure, you can be the life of the party, but if no one knows what you actually do they won't keep you in mind. I'm not saying walk around announcing your name and profession like, "Hi, I'm Amanda, comedian slash common sense specialist!" But I am saying in any field a smidge of narcissism is necessary, and finding a chill way to make folks aware of what you're doing and what you want to do ain't never hurt nobody.
- Sometimes the revolution just ain't for that day. Get the job. Then, sit by the door. Get in the door, and fight from within. Other times leave that job right there. It's gonna kill ya or get you incarcerated!
- Thank people. Always. Thank everyone! I don't care how big you become, thank folks, say excuse me, and let people know you appreciate them.
- People are going to say whatever they want to say about you, so give them very little to go on other than the integrity of your work.
- You aren't going to like every person you work for. You aren't going to like how every person works. It's not forever and it doesn't mean a bridge has to be burned. This road is long and twisting. You never know where it will lead you and who will be there when you get to where you're going. So, if you're unhappy with a work situation, always look for a way to move on that allows you to still hollaback!

IT MAY TAKE ME LONGER TO GET TO THE TOP

BECAUSE I'M CARRYING MY INTEGRITY WITH ME.

OWN YOUR MUSIC.

Fame
vs. Prestige

SOME PEOPLE JUST WANT TO BE KNOWN. For whatever reason, they have placed value on random people knowing who they are. Maybe they're from a small town where they felt stifled and unnoticed. Maybe they're an extrovert and really just like hugs, shaking hands, and kissing babies. Maybe they were a nerd and think being famous means you've gone from Steve Urkel to Stephan Urkél and now that you're accepted, Laura will finally love you. Thanks (or nah) to social media, we live in a world where everyone has the opportunity to be known. People crave likes and followers so badly they will pay money for them. Kids are committing suicide based on the pain of going viral for the wrong thing. I've had a dude holler at me, go to find me on Instagram, and then have his whole demeanor change once he saw my follower count. Folks are making hundreds of thousands of dollars not as traditional celebrities known for their work in the arts but as celebrities in the digital space where they can be known for any number of reasons. That said, being known has become a currency in a very quantifiable way and folks want in. But as always, there are levels to this shit. Being known is not just about people knowing you, it's about why they know you, which leads to: Do you just want fame or do you also aspire to prestige?

Fame is fleeting because it's often not really rooted in anything. It is the most basic level of being known. There are varying degrees of it, but it simply means people know who you are, for whatever reason. You're out in the world and they're like, "Hey, you're so and so" or "Hey, you're *that* guy!" or "Hey, did you go to Piedmont? No, wait, aren't you on that one show?!" It can be a by-product of hard work, but these days it's very often a by-product of just being "out here." Think about it: At this point it doesn't even take much to be famous. Fifteen minutes are being stretched to months and even years by folks with a mediocre booty that's constantly in Lululemon pants, or just being kind of crazy and willing to do some stunts involving cinnamon or sitting in a bathtub of milk and cereal, or simply just being stupid or racist, in which case they're more infamous than famous. Popularity is nothing new. High school was a doozy! For a lot of us, how many people liked you determined how much you liked yourself. Which is actually WILD and should absolutely not be the case. So, at a certain point, many of us grew up and had to check that. I mean, my IG profile literally says, "I'm not 4 everyone." Nonetheless, I feel like we're checking it even less these days because fame and popularity have become an actual goal for people in their daily lives. *How many likes did you get? Did you use the hashtag? You should have used the hashtag.* When you step back and look at the big picture, fame is hella empty and may get you some free 'fits and a couple of dollaz but if you want more you have to do more.

Prestige, in contrast, is about not just being known, but being revered for what you're known for. It is not just about *you* being known, but *your work* being well regarded. For some this may not matter. You just want people to know your name. With fame you're simply riding on the surface of acknowledgment, and that doesn't really last. Like a ten-second twerk vid on Snapchat, it's potent but ethereal. Again, anybody can be famous. Anybody can do something to get people's attention, but can you *keep* people's attention? Can you affect them? Can you influence them? That is how you gain prestige. Excellence and quality are the cornerstones of attaining this status, and too often they have become irrelevant or striving toward them is misconstrued as elitist. The fact is we need folks to be shooting for that goal. Especially in the America that's swirling around me as I write this book. We are in an age of misinformation and alternative facts that seek to keep the masses numb and the real ones mum. In this kind of environment, the encouragement to think bigger, work harder, and go beyond gets trampled beneath a quest for mediocrity. The outliers and overachievers cannot let that happen. They cannot let ignorance and complacency win. They continue to create with a trajectory toward prestigious achievement because they know that it is a signifier of being outside the box and pushing the world forward. We're all here together so we should all be trying to add something of tangible respectability that aims at making this a better place.

I feel like when people are just reaching for fame, what they're doing is creating a void. They're adding an element of nothingness to a world that needs much more realness in it. And eventually if we don't pay attention, the people with the highest influence are going to be the people with the least substance. You might have prestige without fame but you still have something of great value, because with prestige comes legacy. Then you have something that is actually tangible.

Hey man, get it how you can get it but if you can get it with greatness why not give it a shot? Prestige is what I aspire to because I don't want to add to nothingness. I want you to know my name because of what I bring into this world. I don't want to continue to create the void. I want to fill the void. I want you to know why I'm this kind of person, why I'm contributing things, and what I'm contributing, not just that I'm here. Don't get me wrong, we're all here and everybody deserves to be acknowledged for their existence on this planet. Both fame and prestige can trick people into thinking that because more people know that you exist, you're better, or you're of more value. Guess what? We're all valuable. We all belong here. No matter how many likes or followers you have, it doesn't make you any more valuable. You may have more influence, which gives you more responsibility and means that your message needs to be clearer. But it doesn't by any means make you more important. I encourage young people to strive for prestige, not fame, because I want them to consider a greater output and a longer path. I want them to think in terms of how they will be known, understood, and remembered. With the "just add water" fame of today, people seem to forget that there is a whole life to live and the stronger the foundation upon which you build your dreams the more solid that platform will be to help you reach for them. When you build from a place of wanting respect vs. just wanting attention, your goal may take longer to realize but your outcome is more likely to have a lasting effect.

I know I wrote a whole essay on the difference between fame and prestige, but Black Famous is a whole other kind of famous and a whole other level of prestige. You see, Black Famous is when you reach a level in your career where you permeate all realms of Blackness. From the hood to the HBCUs, the church to the group chats, the club to Capitol Hill, the ratchets to the righteous, the niggas to the negros, and everywhere in between, folks know who you are and are down to show love. It's a seminal moment in any notable black person's career when they realize they've attained this seemingly impossible prize. It's like you're Avatar Ang and you can bend all the elements!

I remember the night I realized I was Black Famous. I was in DC speaking at the Brave Summit at Georgetown University, a day of lectures and panels by women of all different backgrounds providing empowerment and information. I was the keynote speaker, and I had an incredible time sharing stories about my experiences coming up as an artist and coming into my own. Jeanise, one of my oldest homegirls, had come to town to hang with me for the weekend. After the event we were headed to Anacostia to go see my boy, DC-native-to-the-bone-bristle Tabi Bonney, perform at the Black Love Experience, an annual gathering of vendors, music, art, and just beautiful black errythang in Southeast DC. On the way there, we linked up with two of my day 1.5 homies, Thomas and Lameen, and went through squaded up. Rolling in to the event with Tabi, who was rockin' a gratuitous poncho and giving pounds out, the vibe was conscious but not hotep, classy but not stuffy. I was immediately struck by how many folks went from dapping Tabs "the mayor" up, to saying familiar hellos and what's ups to me! So many smiles and such genuine reverence. For years I had gotten "Ain't you from that one show?" or "You look mad familiar," but here people not only knew my name, they knew my work, and knew my point of view! They commented on specific IG posts I'd made, bigged me up for my performance as Tiffany on *Insecure*, and showed love for my "Black Girl Magic" poem on the BET Social Awards that year. It was surreal. We stayed at the event for a few hours, we danced, we laughed, and I took more pics with folks than I ever had outside of an actual booked appearance.

Three hours later, after closing down the spot, we hopped in the whip, bumped Migos's "Stir Fry," and made our way back into the city to The W hotel. We stepped into the rooftop bar and immediately recognized that it was a totally different flava. Folks here were fancy, sipping champagne while dancing to classic '90s hip-hop and R&B

while overlooking the Washington Monument. We got our two-step on like no one was looking, only to eventually realize HELLA people were looking. When a young woman approached me and asked timidly if I was Amanda Seales I said yes, and when she gave her table of girls a confirming conspicuously covert eye nod they erupted with glee! I couldn't believe that just my being there had brought them a moment of joy. She told me the crew loved me and she loved my IG stories and she said, "Keep going! We're listening!" I was about to sit down when the manager of the club began to approach. My authority-bucking ass got my mouth all ready to respond to whatever BS he was gonna say about my friends when he leaned down and said, "If I would have known you were coming we would have taken care of you and your friends." SAY WHAT!? He went on to say, "This is our security guard, and you're his Woman Crush Wednesday." Hilaaaaaarious. I took a picture with him, me and the homies had a couple more laughs, reenacted the choreography from the New Edition "If It Isn't Love" video, and then it was on to the next joint.

We pulled up to a spot called Park. From the curb you could already peep that it was pure ratchetry at its finest. I hadn't been to a joint like this since niggas was rockin' throwback jerseys in the club. We rolled up and money at the door was giving us the business saying that we had to drop $20 even though the club was closing in an hour. The homies were flummoxed. They tried to reason with him, saying, "My mans, this makes no sense tho!" Mid-negotiation that was going nowhere, a young woman steps out of the club giving you a full stiletto, with a head of laid edges to inches, dawning a black, skin-tight, long sleeve, sheer onesie, adorned in pearls of various sizes. I was enraptured by the look when she exclaimed, "IS THAT AMANDA MUTHA FUCKIN SEALES?! IT'S MY MUTHA FUCKIN BIRFDAY! AND I WANT A MUTHAFUCKIN PICTURE!" Everyone craned their necks my way and I sheepishly obliged. Who did she give the camera to, to take the photo? Money who was giving us the business at the door! After that, the homies gave him the, "Now what!?" look and we were in. Once inside, folks was getting it in and we were sliding our way through the people like a plumber using a snake to clear the shower drain of a woman with a natural. This room was a totally different flow than our first stop with the afrocentric turn up, and our second stop with the R&B grown and sexies. With O.T. Genasis urging us to "Push It" and Future mumbling something indiscernible, we joined in waving our hands in the air like we just didn't care! Even in this ShadeRoom—esque environment, without skipping a beat, the love continued with folks crossing the room to snap a pic, even stepping away from the dub they were diligently providing to come say wassup. It was surreal.

I've had a life of people telling me, "People don't like you," "You're too much," "You're extra," and at a certain point I began to believe them and not like myself. Then I went to therapy and worked through that and it made my truth clearer, which made my voice stronger, which made my style sharper, which made my work tighter, and the next thing I know my energy is on flow and the fake ones is coming and going and the real ones is recognizing real and I'm moving and grooving to the beat of my own drum but instead of folks screwing up their face, sayin', "What's she doing???" more and more they're rocking with the rhythm I'm bringing and joining in step with my movement. That night I saw it live and in full effect in the Chocolate City. Everyone from the brothas and sistas up in Southeast in ankh necklaces and naturals, rocking everyday Wakanda wear and kickin' underground raps, to the squad in the rooftop spot sippin' my drink of St. Germain and prosecco, with their Chanel and Gucci bags, hard bottoms, and fedoras singing out Jodeci and Mary, as well as the fam in the turnt-up hot box, in snorkels and Timbs, tube tops and miniskirts, fresh wraps still smellin' like the flat iron and door knockers from the beauty supply, not only gave greetings, but showed genuine heartfelt love and appreciation for my work, my wisdom, and my spirit, and it felt INCREDIBLE. I pride myself on being a person who speaks fearlessly on behalf of justice for everyone but from a place of pride as a black woman. That night I felt the connection I had made to the present in order to hopefully change the future. I felt the highest honor of prestige one can garner: to be lauded by your community.

At one point in the epic evening, as the music played and bodies waved and whined around us, Thomas, who'd seen the full extent of my journey from Purchase College spoken word poet to now, turned to me, and in a moment straight out of a feel-good black movie about struggle and triumph, where the protagonist finally makes the team, or gets out of jail, or scores a date with the flyest chick in the school, he said, "You did it, kid. You did it." It's been a long time comin', but we here and it feels good.

The Fall Off

It ain't over 'til it's over
Know when to walk away
Then get back to the middle
There's another dragon to slay.

NO.

Someone else's "no" does not have to shut down your yes. Let it motivate you to find a better option.

MORPHING MISTAKES

When you attempt and fail it can be jarring. You question yourself, your instincts, your ideas, and it can stop you in your tracks. Give yourself the same consideration you'd want someone else to give you. Go over the steps that were taken and examine where the mistakes were made. Commit them to memory and morph them into lessons learned.

KNOW YOUR LIMITS

In the quest to succeed we can be our biggest obstacle when we take on not only more than we can handle, but more than we can handle well. You don't have to be good at everything. You have to be good at knowing who is good at what you're not good at. Let others be experts at their specialty, and it will give you the space to execute your own.

THE FAIL FUNK

When you take an L, it knocks the wind out of you. It's real. Thing is, what you gonna do? Stay down? Nah, we don't stay down. We've got work to do. Allow yourself twenty-four hours to cry, panic, beat yourself up, whatever you gotta do to get the emotion out. ONLY twenty-four hours. Then you get up the next day, get focused, and start working on the new plan.

BROKE BUT NOT BROKEN

Living below the poverty line is a financial state that is incredibly difficult to ascend from due to capitalism, class structure, inflation, taxes, racism, etc. The cards are stacked against the poor in a deliberate way that forces a "lower class," in order to be able to define an "upper class." In the context of this chapter, "the fall off" speaks specifically to those who are not poor but have seen financial success only to lose it.

Here, being "broke" means there has been a break in money momentum. At the time it's hell. It's uncomfortable. It's stressful. Anyone who said, "money can't buy happiness" has never not had money. The wackness of life is way easier to deal with when you have money to throw at it. That said, if you're reading this right now, and you're broke, remind yourself, "This is just a phase." It does not have to be your destiny. You may have to put your pride aside for the moment, and do what you gotta do, but as cliché as it sounds, it is all a part of the journey!

If you're poor and you're reading this, I hope you are the exception. I hope you are the sword that finds a way to cut down the limbs shading your path to financial security. I would say I hope that policy makers make the necessary changes to break the cycle of poverty that exists in this country, but I know better than to rely on politicians for principles.

Selling Out
vs. Buying In

SUCCESS IS VERY TEMPTING. You've put in work. You've seen struggle. You've painted the bottom of your shoes red to look like Louboutins. It's understandable to consider taking an easier trek to triumph than the one you're on. From presidents to pointless "personalities," there are many examples of people who have taken a shortcut to the top. What's the big deal, right? Everyone else is doing it. Why should you be the only one bustin' ya ass and working hard? You know why? Because you have some damn ethics and you're not easily bought. Especially if you are a black person in this country, letting a price be put on your identity and integrity is an irony I simply can't stomach. For the most part, I remain objective in this book, but when it comes to this topic there is only one right side. We ain't 'bout sellouts.

But *Why, Amanda?!*, you might ask.

1. Because it's weak. It demonstrates brittle backbone and callow character. If you're not strong enough to fight for your integrity you can't be relied on to withstand being tested to protect anything else.
2. Because it's shady. It exemplifies a lack of moral compass. You know what they say, "If you don't stand for something, you'll fall for anything."
3. Because it screws up the curve! It is hard enough to win without folks being willing to stoop beneath a standard of basic hard work and dedication to get a leg up. It makes it harder for everyone else and drives the quality value down.

Sellouts come in all shapes, sizes, genders, races, ages, you name it! A sellout is someone who trades in their integrity for personal gain, often getting the gift of advancement from someone who doesn't have their best interests at heart, but instead sees a way to benefit off them. In contrast, when you buy in, you retain your integrity to create further opportunities despite those not having your best interests at heart.

You can be considered a sellout for a number of reasons. Perhaps you've flipped the script and are going against former principles you steady stood by and hashtagged all day in exchange for money, power, or status. Perhaps you have turned your back on your squad or individuals you share commonalities with in exchange for money, power, or status. Or perhaps you've given your interests to a person/company/system that is known to be www.shadyboots.com and problematic for positivity in exchange for money, power, or status.

When it comes down to it, being a sellout may get you some paper, some pull, or some likes, but it also earns you a legacy of wackness. In addition, you inadvertently, and sometimes advertently, empower the oppressor. You may tell yourself that boldface lie of "it's just business!" However, your actions trickle down to hurt others and continue, and sometimes embolden, problematic behaviors. For example, if a company notoriously lacking in diversity finally hires a person of color as an executive and that person then carries on the same tradition of not increasing the diversity in hiring, and still has the conference room looking like that season of *Friends* when Aisha Tyler was dating Ross, they are, in fact, a sellout. Another example is if you create a TV show that brings you fame and fortune yet at the same damn time it knowingly perpetuates a stereotype that continues to negatively permeate the social landscape and cause real consequences, you are absofrickinlutely a sellout.

The term "sellout" is a signifier for selling your soul and/or, as I was once told, "selling your folks down river," a euphemism born out of the act of trading slaves on the Mississippi River. It was known that the farther south you went, the worse the conditions of slavery were. It's not to say that selling out is solely related to black people. By no means. People regularly consider music artists who change their sound when they get a record deal or visual artists who change their style in order to gain popular acclaim to be sellouts to capitalism. I consider women who support the shaming of other women for their sexual confidence to be sellouts to the patriarchy. The bottom line of a sellout is that their actions advance the foulness of others, more often than not for the preservation of one's own personal gain. Is that something you want on your conscience? Is that the shade you want cast on your karma?

Buying in is when you double down on the fact that you know not only your product, but also your path. You understand that if the terms of selling your product prevent you from your path then you must seek out other options. In the interim, you have to have the resolution to stand your ground, like Okoye next to that rhinoceros in Wakanda, and know that even though folks may not recognize your path right now, by sticking to your guns you're going to create opportunities for them to recognize it, and eventually they will bow to you, like her husband, W'Kabi, did to her. When you buy in, it's you knowing not only the market's landscape but also your worth. It's you declaring, "I am not going to involve myself in this unless I'm being offered something of equal or greater value than what I'm bringing to the table and which allows me to use my earned money, power, and status to influence actions in a positive direction." You are investing in you. You are investing in a message, and you're investing in having a seat at the table for change. You are creating stock. When you're at that table, integrity intact, people cannot buy you out. They know that you are not the one. They know that they have to approach with a DJ Khaled–personality-size level of deference because the best way to demand respect is to demonstrate having respect for yourself. Don't nobody respect anybody they can put a dollar amount on.

TRIED AND TRUE SELLOUTS:
- **Stacey Dash:** Went from Dionne in *Clueless* to getting a check for being clueless on Fox News.
- **Omarosa:** Up in the White House talking 'bout she had a list of black people that are enemies to the Trump administration, then wanna be up in the *Big Brother* house talking 'bout she had such a terrible time there.
- **Ben Carson:** Former genius surgeon turned Trump administration member who said, and I quote, "Slaves were immigrants." Look it up y'all, he said that on a microphone in front of people, and it was not *Def Comedy Jam*.
- **O. J. Simpson:** "I'm not black. I'm O. J." Mmmhm 'til they locked yo' black ass up!
- **Jonathan Capehart:** Pushing the narrative that the "Hands up don't shoot" slogan was built on a lie, because he asserts that the late Mike Brown did not have his hands up when he was murdered by officer Darren Wilson that fateful day in Ferguson, Missouri. This cat found his way from the *Washington Post* to TV in the midst of the ongoing travesty of the case and felt this was a valuable concept worthy of discussion in spaces where Mike Brown was being vilified and was part of undermining the very necessary movement against police brutality of unarmed black people born out of his death. Before @CapehartJ blocked me on the Twitters for telling him his actions were coon-worthy, I tweeted him, and I quote, "You have no idea who I am. But u will & you will feel very uncomfortable that ur matched intellect is checkin' your BS."

BETTED ON BUYING IN:
- **Oprah:** You already know.
- **Ava DuVernay:** Pivoted from PR to director/producer, beginning a track record of seminal work from *Selma* to *13th* and using her influence to create

Array, a grassroots distribution, arts, and advocacy collective focused on films by people of color and women.

- **Magic Johnson:** Retired from the NBA and uses his fortune to bring franchises to underserved neighborhoods, providing jobs and bringing a higher quality of life experiences to these communities.
- **Charles D. King:** Elevated through the ranks of William Morris with a practice of hard work and reliability before leaving to create MACRO and using his access to open doors for black creative entrepreneurs to flourish via their craft.
- **Issa Rae:** Created her own show on YouTube, took the brand all the way to big business without compromising her own creative vision, and used the inroads she made to give other creatives space to do the same without compromise.

Listen, I get it. In times of hardship, selling out can feel like the only option. In the process of progress you need funds, you need support, and you need creativity. We are in a capitalist country. Everybody is trying to get on, and everybody is trying to make ends meet. You've got kids and a family to support. You have dreams that you want to achieve. You're tempted to say, "Damn, if I just take this lil bit over here, I could probably do this whole thing over here." Sometimes that's true, but it's only true if this lil bit over here doesn't also take the bottom out from what you're trying to do over there. Remain conscious of that. Snakes will come for you all up and through the grass. I urge you to use the creativity within you to try and take different modes to get those needs met without forsaking your integrity. If you can wait it out, when you buy in you have the autonomy to determine your product's value versus bundling it with your integrity, which is priceless. When you sell out, you're letting someone make you believe that what they have to give you is worth more than your integrity. It's not. Don't let anyone sell you that lie. For years, I was surrounded by so many examples of selling out and it got tougher and tougher to encourage young women, and my peers, to stick to their integrity when they could see so many folks that seemed to be shining and winning for doing the opposite. Nonetheless, I knew that if I could eventually get here without doing that, I could be yet another example of buying in. I am so thankful and honored to say that I have never had to compromise my principles and sell out in the process of getting here. Surround yourself with the right people and fill yourself full of resolve so you, too, can come up without coming out your worth.

I'm a little fuzzy on when exactly folks started calling me "Diva." I was in a crew called "Da Divas" while at Dr. Phillips High School in Orlando, Florida, and I used to tag it EVERYWHERE. Literally. So, I'm pretty sure it was born out of that. Once I moved to New York and started school at SUNY Purchase, it continued as a nickname and in some cases was shortened to simply "Deev." It is astonishing to me how many people didn't even bat an eye at my desire to be referred to as "Diva," which is a testament to not only how free-thinking NYC can be but also to how full of artsy weirdos my college campus was. That said, I still had a lil insecurity about it, and when I went to the Sugar Shack, a restaurant in Harlem proper, and signed up for their weekly spoken word open mic, I wrote "Diva" on the sign-up sheet and added (Amanda) in parentheses, to let them know I wasn't buggin' by asking to be called "Diva." When the host introduced me she saw the two names pushed up against each other like trying to parallel park on St. Nicholas Ave. in the middle of winter, and said soothingly into the mic, melodic and warm, with a melted-See's-caramel-candy-in-hot-chocolate timbre, "Amanda Diva." From that day forward, that was me.

The name Amanda Diva had its ups and downs, but for a new name with an old connotation, I wore it well. As a poet, it set me apart as more hip-hop than neo-soul and simultaneously sent a message that though I was young, I was to be respected. Some folks made it very clear with their stank faces and shaded hellos that they weren't feelin' that message, but it was clear nonetheless! Once I transitioned into hip-hop as a career, serving as a radio personality at Sirius Satellite Radio (pre-XM merger) and writing for AllHipHop.com, *XXL*, and the like, the name became as much a part of my brand as the array of Kangols I insisted on wearing. Sidenote: Y'all, there were so . . . many . . . Kangols. Line up pics of me from '03–'08 and my head looked like a bag of skittles. But I digress. In a game of pseudonyms meant to aggrandize and define what matters to you before anyone knows you, Amanda Diva worked. What mattered to me was that you knew I was larger than life, I was not for the nonsense, and I was a true talent. For me, that is what "Diva" was about. The opera sopranos of their time, like Maria Callas, who played no games, and demanded her needs be met because she was going to go on stage every time and give the audience everything, now she was a DIVA! However, in the age of my donning the moniker it had begun to lose its luster. Sure, *VH1 Divas* did its best by bringing the divas of our age together to belt their wigs off in full sequined numbers, but simultaneously the term was being used as a descriptor for a woman with all of the needs and demands of a world-renowned theatrical force of nature and none of the talent. The moniker was tossed around like video chicks creepin' on a come up. If, at a shoot, you made any request, no matter how minimal, you were called a "diva." If you had a point of view differing from the group think, like, "Nah, I'm actually not really feeling folks wearing Chinese slippers in the club" you'd get a, "OHHH, OKAY DEEEEVVVUUUHHHHHH!" It was really annoying. Nonetheless, I had planted my flag.

I remember going into a meeting at Hot 97 that the homie DJ Envy had secured for me. I was already doing radio at Sirius but to be on Hot was a dream. It was a New York staple at the time, the home of Angie Martinez, and a mecca of hip-hop greatness. It was Hot 97 that Jay-Z raced to to tell his side of the story when R. Kelly was maced backstage at their Best of Both Worlds Madison Square Garden concert. It was Hot 97 that first delivered to me the horrifying news that we had lost Aaliyah to the ocean from above. It was the mixtape era, and every Saturday a different DJ would do a set for *Takin It to the Streets.* It was DJ Green Lantern that had me end a date early and run up to my dorm room so I could hear the first post-"Ether" record off of Nas's *Stillmatic.* My roommate and I sat on our extra-long twin beds in awe as "You're da Man" reverberated throughout our suite in the Outback (or as I called it, The Wack Back) at SUNY Purchase.

So, to be going there for an interview to possibly join this illustrious cavalcade of icons riding the backs of hip-hop greatness was momentous. I sat down across from the man in charge, Ebro, and after a brief exchange about what I was doing and wanted to do, he got to my name. "It's corny," he said. It was like a swift jab to my proverbial sternum. "Corny?" I asked. "Yeah, nobody wants to listen to somebody with 'Diva' in their name. It's played out," he said, with his bearded fine nigga arrogance spilling all over the desk like a garbage bag bursting before you make it to the curb. Envy, the homie who had been the mouthpiece so I could get this sit down, chimed in here as well saying, "She's been doing great for listeners over at Sirius with her show, *Breakfast at Diva's.*" Ebro wasn't tryna hear it. "Meh, it's tired. If you're trying to come over here you'd have to lose the name." Now, y'all, I was young, but this was just stupid. At this point I was a VJ on MTV2 and had a global radio show on Sirius under the name Amanda Diva. I was twenty-two and thriving! People were recognizing me in the street and I was getting press and bylines under the name Amanda Diva. It simply made no sense to leave my name, which was gaining traction with the masses, behind at a point when I was ascending in the same field. Yet, here I was being told that in order to pursue the dream of being a part of this formidable family I would have to toss it to the wind like a loose weave track now languishing on a sidewalk. I am not a stubborn person. I am a best-idea-wins person. At that juncture, it was not the best idea. I left feeling deflated, but defiant. After all, I was Amanda DIVA, and no real Diva let a nigga diminish her shine simply because he didn't recognize it.

I would go on to work at Sirius for three more years, four years in total, while writing and doing spoken word, then transitioning into pursuing a career as a recording artist myself. Independently releasing four projects and a mixtape, touring as a member of Floetry, appearing on a number of albums including Slim Thug's *Already Platinum*, Pitbull's *El Mariel*, Curren$y's *This Ain't No Mixtape*, and Q-Tip's album *The Renaissance*, along with opening for The Roots, who, from day one, welcomed me into their illafifth dynamite family with open arms and always willingly gave me a stage to spread my musically inclined wings. At the same time, I was producing my own web series, *DivaSpeak TV*, on this new website YouTube, and another called *Diva Diva Ya'll* on streetwear-savvy Karmaloop.com. The point is, Diva was ingrained in my presence, whether I was singing, rapping, writing, or hosting. I felt married to the name. All that said, I was a no-nonsense person in a FULL-nonsense industry. Lemme tell y'all something, hip-hop was (I can't speak for the climate now) not made for type-A personalities, ESPECIALLY if you're a woman. I am a very direct, very smart, very free thinking, very on point, very detail-oriented, very particular person. The hip-hop music business is exactly the opposite of all of this. It's a lot of folks passive-aggressively or over-aggressively posturing their limited scope of knowledge and views while far too often being wildly inefficient and unreliable. If you're reading this and getting mad, I'm talking about you. On top of that, it's a cockfest, and as a woman, you're the party favor. As this was the climate, over time I became conditioned to having to exert said "Divaness," which gained me a reputation for being "difficult," "stank," and "extra." In actuality, I just possessed a keen eye for fuckery and lacked the alacrity to address it with finesse—a skill I'm honestly still working to commit to muscle memory. Before I knew it, Diva went from the fun flamboyant addendum to my government name to an albatross around my career's neck. It was even brought to my attention that I was losing out on opportunities because of the name. Before I'd even have a chance to speak for myself or let my work do the talking, my name would repel interested parties who were disinterested in dealing with a woman who carried a pseudonym that, by then, had become synonymous with reality TV stars known for throwing "diva-like tantrums" without cause or skill to support them. It got really real when I was cast in a pilot for a new hip-hop show and the executive producer called me the night before our first day. Along with words of encouragement and regular prep, she offered me the advice, "Your job is to go in there and prove you're not a diva." Remember that proverbial sternum? Yea, mollywhopped once again. Cuz yo, that absolutely was not my job! My job was to go in there and be the funny, witty, opinionated, hip-hop knowledge cannon that I am! So to consider that this name had so much weight that it overpowered my actual skill set was horrifying for me! If I were on my full *Sunset Boulevard* Norma Desmond diva-level shit I would have gazed into a mirror watching my soul vanish as I smeared my lipstick. Instead I got off the phone and spent the next couple hours reassessing my life.

I had turned thirty a few months earlier, and it was like I had walked through a door to another dimension. Nothing looked the same. Maybe it was the Saturn Return* or simply entering a new decade, but I IMMEDIATELY felt a shift in my consciousness. Though Ebro was the first to tell me my name was lacking in luster, he wasn't the last. The biggest champion for the eradication of Deev turned out to be DJ Green Lantern, the same DJ who ten years earlier had me cutting a kiss short in order to hear Nasir's premier. Over the years, he, along with DJ Self, Q-Tip, late manager of The Roots Rich Nichols, Nelson Taboda, Swizz Beatz, Ron Stewart, Erik Pettie, Dwight Willacy, and Lenny S, had become a glowing standard of purely platonic brotherhood in a sea of sharks who made sexual harassment a daily affair in a fraternal field that had little to no sororal safe spaces. On a regular basis DJ Green Lantern would chide and cajole me to "Drop the diva." "You don't need it," he'd say. "It's limiting," he'd urge, and I'd admonish him about how it's a part of my brand and it's how people know me and all the logical reasons I had given Ebro in that office

---

* In a nutshell, the Saturn Return is an astrological rite of passage that takes place every time Saturn completes a full orbit from your time of birth. This is about every thirty years, and is considered to be a time of reassessment, discovery, self-evaluation, and upheaval on your road to a new phase of life.

at Hot 97 so many years before. However, after walking through the door into the Narnia of my thirties, they admittedly began to feel more like excuses than explanations. Hip-hop suddenly wasn't speaking to me the way it once had, and I could feel something greater pulling at my purpose. I didn't know yet that it would be comedy, but I knew, intrinsically, that a shift was coming. Change. Something so dreaded yet inevitable. I began to toy with the notion of reinvention. What did that look like? What did it entail? I'd seen major celebrities do it before—Gaga when she toned down, Badu when she turned up, Janelle when she broke from the monochrome, Prince when he became the symbol, etc. But I didn't have the sturdy following they had. Would people even notice if I switched up?

It came to a head in the spring of 2011 when I was doing a show called *The Spark*, which I hosted and created for AOL Black Voices. The first shapeshifting moment was when Nick Cannon came on the show. It was a comedy-based current events show where two guests and I discussed topics relating to the black community through the lens of humor. After his guest appearance, me and my old homie chopped it up and he told me, "It's time for you to come back to TV. You have a voice and people need to hear it." I was taken aback but I knew he was right. I just didn't know how that was going to happen. After talking to him about it, it weighed on me. Doing *The Spark*, I had begun to find my comedic tone and learn how to channel my passion through its lens. I knew that I needed to pivot, and I felt that the universe had sent me someone I trusted to give me a sign about where to pivot to. Shortly thereafter, I was simultaneously haranguing Wiz Khalifa's "people" for an interview while the legendary Quincy Jones's people were reaching out to us for one. It was surreal. I was talking to Green about it and he laid it plain: "Wiz is super dope and would be a great look and interview, but Quincy is an icon and his people are coming *to* you. That's who you need to be aligned with and in order to be taken seriously in those circles you'll need to drop the 'Diva.'" For the first time, I heard him. Because for the first time, I could see even a glimpse of truly realizing my dream of being a voice of value for and of the black community. Something about the juxtaposition of where I was at the moment versus someone like Quincy Jones, a living legend of stature and merit whose work I have loved my whole life, awoke in me a clarity that I had yet to experience previously. Reinvention was not only near, but inevitable. About a week later, I was walking up to an event and when the woman holding the list asked my name, I told her, "Amanda Diva" and she exclaimed,

"OKAY GURRRLLLL!!!!! OK MISS DIVA! I SEE YOU!!!!" Yeah, at the point I knew it was time. "Diva" had to go.

The next day I changed all my social media handles and that was that. Amanda Seales was back. Some folks said it was a bad idea, that "Diva" was an integral part of my brand. Once upon a time, they would have been right, but I had simply grown out of that brand. Though I didn't know exactly what direction I was going in, I knew innately, in my gut, that in order to find my purpose I would need to relieve myself of the past to make room for a rebirth. I guess it was my own type of Baptism, except instead of being saved by Jesus I was being saved from myself. My brand wasn't based on my name, it was based on my work. In trusting the transition to my new truth, changing my name, and reinventing myself, I began a new path and trajectory that allowed for my voice to find its purpose without a name drowning it out. The reality was reinvention. Though a daunting, seemingly impossible concept for some, the change, drastic in nature, was an essential step in the right direction to unlocking my purpose and stepping into my full self as the funny, world-changing, spirit-empowering, no-nonsense diva I was truly meant to be.

Being a Multi-hyphenate

So much we do,
but there's so little time
Folks may not understand our hustles,
but they can't hate on our grind.

SYNERGIZE

As a multihyphenate, the goal is to be able to utilize all of the gifts at your disposal. This requires synergy. Synergy is achieved when you unearth the skeleton key that unlocks access to all of your skills and instead of operating as energy moving in different directions, they feed each other. If the skeleton key makes the skills available, synergy is the thread that strings them together. It's like looking at the hem of a pair of pants and seeing the thread keeping things in place—those stiches look like hyphens. When you start to look at your various trajectories under the same scope, you begin to see how they connect, and the synergy emerges.

KEEP TIME, STAY SHARP

If you can't make the juggle work, then you need to change how you're juggling. Part of being a multihyphenate is finding the actualized way to implement all that you desire to do. Key parts of that are time management and discipline. Sure, you're a free spirit and you move outside the confines of normalcy and blueprints. That's all the more reason why you have to have some sort of method for managing what others consider to be your madness. When I was writing this book I had to literally add hours to my day by getting up at 5 every morning in order to make sure I would have time to write on top of continuing to juggle everything else poppin' off in my multihyphenate universe. Make to-do lists. Keep your calendar up to speed. Assess and reassess your priorities as they come. Hold yourself accountable. All of these can be helpful tools. That said, it is not juggling if you're always dropping the ball. Know your limits.

NO BLUEPRINT

I find the biggest frustration for most when it comes to being a multihyphenate is the fact that there is no blueprint. This is not only frustrating for the multihyphenate themself but for the folks who care about the multihyphenate. Even though there has been no shortage of folks who are multihyphenates, it hasn't worked its way into the mainstream as a common career choice. So it is no wonder that it can feel like you're that feather at the end of *Forrest Gump* while trying to nail down your path. Change your perspective and up your courage. The world was expanded (and, in many cases, destroyed) by folks who had the backing and the courage to venture out beyond what had already been charted. If you're a multihyphenate you, too, gotta gain the gumption to chart your own course and know that there will be wrong turns along the way (and if that wrong turn lands you in someone else's space don't just claim it for yourself. Learn from them and then keep going). If you're in the lane of the folks who care about the multihyphenate, support them. Sure, it may cause you worry. It may be unorthodox. You may be West Indian, or from the Continent and culturally it feels almost physically impossible to support someone in a career choice with no conclusive direction. However, do it. We must support those willing to explore new lanes of expression and establish new boundaries of human ability. Without them, we are stagnant.

WHAT IS PASSION?

Passion keeps you moving when you're exhausted.
Passion knows no bounds and always pulls you further along your path.
Passion excites you.
Passion inspires you.
Passion makes you feel full when you take part in it.
Passion feels right even when you're wrong.
Passion feels like winning even when you fail.
People spend their entire lives looking for their one passion. You may have more than one. Or your passion may be the work of doing multiple things. Whatever it is, it may take time, and it will definitely take self-exploration, but if you're trying to discover your passion, ask yourself if what you think it is/they are line(s) up with most or hopefully all of the above.

"YOU HAVE TO PICK ONE."

People will tell you this lie all day long. YOU DO NOT HAVE TO PICK ONE THING TO MASTER. It helps, however, to find one thing that allows you to do everything.

Phrases like the above are common comments when you're a multi-hyphenate, and sometimes you find yourself stuck on how to reply. No worries, here's some clap backs to give 'em back! You're welcome!

- It's like you do so much you do nothing.
  That's a common sentiment from those who find it unfathomable that one can be multitalented, because they are not.
- So what *do* you do?
  I utilize my many gifts, to the best of my abilities, across a number of commercial fields.
- You have to choose one thing.
  It would be irresponsible of me to limit my gifts to one box. Instead, I think outside of it, where there's plenty of room for me to be all of me.
- How do you make money?
  As long as I'm not asking you for any, it's none of ya damn bidness!

Multi-hyphenate
vs. Dabbler

SOME MIGHT SAY WE LIVE IN AN ADD WORLD. So many things are constantly pulling at our attention. If I'm not on Instagram, I'm on Twitter. If I'm not on Twitter, I'm texting. If I'm not texting, I'm FaceTiming. If I'm not FaceTiming, I'm daydreaming about a boy I currently like and wondering if he's daydreaming about me. If I'm not daydreaming, I'm bingeing a show. If I'm not bingeing a show, I'm shooting a show. It's sensory overload! I believe this has been a gift and a curse for a lot of folks. It's like having a lot of clothes. Super fun and makes you feel like Barbie, but also, a bit overwhelming when you're hella tired and hella hungry and all these colors are coming at you and for some reason everything you put on either looks foolish or hoeish and you. Just. Need. To find. Something. ANYTHING. To wear. With the advancement of game changers like the interwebs, gender equality, and an increase in black college graduates, ceilings are being broken, doors kicked in, and thus there is more access than ever for individuals to explore various career interests. Fields like coding, finance, sports, etc. are no longer considered "just for men." Areas like marine biology, psychology, and fashion are seeing a more diverse pool of interest in terms of culture/ethnicity. That said, with endless possibilities can come a lack of direction. We've all heard the adage, "Jack of all trades, master of none." In determining your direction you must first determine whether you are a true multihyphenate or a dabbler.

A true multihyphenate is someone who has dedicated significant time to mastering a number of skills that work together synergistically. That's not just to say you're good at a number of things. It's that you are professionally adept at a number of things. For instance, I am rather athletic and can knock down threes from the top of the key, have a mean backhand on the tennis court, and at the time of writing this, can still do a backflip. However, I would never claim to be a basketball player or a tennis player because I have never given dedicated focus to mastering either and consider them both hobbies. Gymnastics, on the other hand, was my life for five years, with daily practices and competitions, and had a lifelong effect on the person I would become. Therefore, when asked about my athletic interests I simply say, "I *play* tennis. I *play* basketball. But once a gymnast, always a gymnast!"

In order to become a multihyphenate, the first thing you must master is time management. The second is knowledge of self. These two things are integral because once they are synergized you must be able to effectively juggle the different strains of your trajectory or, just like a plant whose roots aren't thoroughly watered, they will dry up. Knowledge of self comes into play because you need to be truly honest with yourself about the frame and inner workings of each of your hyphens to know how much and what type of attention needs to be paid to them respectively. For instance, working on the illustrations involved in this book has forced me to up my focus on my visual art. That's a skill set that has been a tad neglected due to the time I've put into my writing and performing as of late. You must nurture each of your hyphens like they are your children. Though they are a part of a cohesive picture formed from you, they each have their own identities and uses and require unique attentiveness that you can only determine from being conscious of them. I will speak more to the concept of synergizing your hyphens in a bit, but for now, just know that as a multihyphenate, even though folks may not understand the multiple layers of your professional profile, the work is to refine your varied skill set into tributaries that all serve the mainstream of your cashflow.

A dabbler is not a bad thing, it's just not a multihyphenate. A dabbler is someone who has a number of interests that exist as hobbies. They may be good at them. They may even be great at them, but they have never committed time and effort to any of their interests enough to have mastered them. When people pursue different avenues of interest but cannot claim them professionally or on a mastery level, they are a dabbler. They enjoy partaking in the practice of play versus profession and are driven more by the variety of things life has to offer, versus having a multitude of serious passions in various areas. Dabblers are often people who have dedicated a significant amount of their life to one specific thing and have hobbies that serve as a useful tool of balance. However, the hobbies that they have interest in, no matter how dedicated they may be to them, do not have a bearing on their professional trajectory. Again, to call someone "a dabbler" is not a diss, but it feels like a diss when it is mistakenly thrust at someone who truly finds life's purpose in a myriad of things, versus just one. Furthermore, you may enjoy partaking in many types of art, but if you have never attempted to sell or display your art, be it as an actor, writer, director, painter, sculptor, graphic artist, poet, musician, DJ, songwriter, etc., I consider it a diss to those who have. Be thoughtful in claiming titles. For example, though by linguistic standards if you paint, you are a painter, by artistic standards there is far more nuance involved. It takes incredible nerve, courage, and discipline to lay before this unrelenting world a creation that has come from turning passion into purpose. Sure, dabblers can attempt to sell their work, but when you are coming from a place of simply using the craft as a tool to pass the time versus as a conduit of channeled focus, it is a pastime, not a priority. To dabble is to try, to be a multihyphenate is to commit.

As a multihyphenate myself, this topic is very near and dear to me. For so many years, I was told that my being able to do many things well was a detriment. I was told it was a sign of lack of focus. What I learned, however, was that it wasn't that I lacked focus—in fact, it was that my blur of interests, passions, and endeavors made it difficult for the world to know *how* to focus on me. I'm speaking from the point of view of an entertainer, but this applies to any multihyphenate looking to make money. Unless you're independently wealthy or Wakanda's Prince T'Challa with vibranium on swole, you're going to have to present yourself to outside parties to gain access to economic growth. In which case you have to look at yourself as a brand being sold to the marketplace. Basic marketing will tell you that if a product's identity and purpose is not clear, consumers will not purchase it. Now, I know some of you are reading this and are talking to the page, saying, "But Amanda! I am not a product! I am not a brand! I am a person!" Sounds good, and yes, in real life that may be true. You, boo, are a whole human being with a life and a past and a present, but if you want a future—in ANY field—you have to understand that you are a part of a business model that looks at you not as a person, but as a resource. The question isn't to be or not to be, it is what type of resource will you be? That is where your autonomy comes in. Though it can feel very sobering to know you're not in control of said marketplace and its diminishing of individuals down to dollaz, what you are in control of is how you enter that marketplace and how you want to be defined versus sitting back and letting it define you. As a multihyphenate this can be the absolute most difficult, frustrating, overwhelming task. Yes, you are passionate and skilled in a number of areas, but what is your passion, what's your "thing"!? People will ask you this all day because your passion is how they label you. No, most people don't like to be labeled, but the world as we know it craves assigning labels to people. That's why there is a genus species name created for every animal, insect, and plant. The human race likes to know how to identify things so that it knows what to do with them, how they work, and how they can be utilized. Unfortunately, plants and animals don't have agency in deciding that, but you do. People will also tell you that you have to choose one thing. Oh, they say this shit all the time. "You have to focus on one thing. Put all your energy to that then let it open the doors to allow you to do other things." There is a level of truth to that but not in the context they imply. They say that with an underlying notion that not only is it not a good idea to pursue varied interests but that it's not truly possible. A lot of people are only good at one thing. Which is phenomenal, but it is limiting when they place their constraints upon you. My experience, in contrast, is that the "one thing" is not necessarily one skill or interest but one overarching concept that brings all that you do together in a cohesive fashion that clearly defines your brand and its purpose. I call it "The Skeleton Key" because it is able to unlock all the doors of your interests and let them thrive together under one roof. In order to find that key I suggest not looking at the breadth of your skills but instead considering the outcome you seek. Once you've identified that outcome, look for the different pathways that lead there, consider others who have successfully achieved the outcome that attracts you, and research the path they took to get there. What parts of their path align with yours? Where do they diverge? The answers to drawing up your own blueprint are there.

Being a multihyphenate can feel overwhelming and empty at the same damn time. On one hand, you have seemingly endless energy that you must channel through various means that can often feel like you're being pulled in opposing directions. On the other hand, because of all these opposing directions, you can feel like you're going in no direction at all and are simply turning in circles or building at an interminably slow pace. You're not. Your process is just different. It requires hella patience, stamina, and discipline. It also requires freedom, flow, and fun. If this world were comprised more of people doing what they truly love than what they have to do, it would be a better place. Give yourself a shot at the former, by being real with yourself about what you really are. As for the dabblers, let your myriad of interests continue to color your life and punctuate your landscape with oases of fun and fascination that bring you joy.

Comedy Key

THAT
ONE TIME

In October 2013 I got an email from a young woman asking if I'd like to be a part of the all-black women stand-up showcase she and a friend were putting together. It changed my life. *Saturday Night Live* was in search of a negress to add to their cast, as they'd been conspicuously lacking one for quite some time. One of their cast members even went so far as to say the reason for the lack of black women was because none had stepped up to the plate. Imma just leave that there, because it's so preposterous a notion it is undeserving of rebuttal. Instead, the rebuttal was a slew of black women comedian showcases popping up all over town with lineups of funny sistas tryna get their shot. I had never done stand-up before but there I was, in my apartment looking down at my phone, wondering, "Do I do it?"

"What do you do?" had become a treacherous question that I dodged and ducked when hurled my way. It is seemingly innocuous but to a multihyphenate without a clear direction it was like a Hattori Hanzō sword in my eye every time. The inquiry was an immediate reminder of what I deemed my own personal failure. Sure, I'd been an artist all my life and had committed hours upon hours to mastering the various skills in my tool belt. Yet I floated above the surface from one gig to the next, wearing more hats than you'd see at a Sunday Church service in Atlanta. I wanted to be grounded. I wanted to be able to clearly tell people what I do in a concise fashion. Even better, I wanted them to know what I am without some long, convoluted explanation that twisted and turned like a map of the Underground Railroad. But as of late that seemed like a notion out of reach. I mean, even I didn't know how to describe myself in the creative space. I was LEGIT a DJ, a comedic actress, a host, a writer, a singer, a rapper, and a painter. I had more than dabbled in each and attained a level of professional prowess that, though impressive, made my business card look like I had multiple personalities. Speaking of personalities, the word *personality*, too vague and disconnected to encompass the true breadth of my depth, was the latest summation I had come up with for my branding after trying and discarding everything from "humorist" to "content creator" to "renaissance woman."

I remember once going to a meeting at an agency that a friend had referred me to. (By the way, having someone who is already making them money let them know that you, too, could make them money is the best way to get on an agent's radar.) I walked into their NYC offices, somewhere in the low twenties, off Broadway, and sat down with a large, white, red-faced man behind a cluttered desk who proceeded to tell me that if I only "had a twin sister and owned a cup-cake shop," he could do *something* with me. My head fell to the side, perplexed. He went on to say, "Looking at your resume and materials, you're just a smart, funny, black girl who knows a lot about hip-hop and there's **nothing** I can do with that." I took it in. He was dead seri-ous, and I couldn't even counter. I rose, told him it was only 9:12 a.m., and therefore too early in the day to stomach that kind of rejection, thanked him for his time, and headed out. It was the latest frustration in a constant stream of "no"s, "not interested"s, and "We just don't know what you do"s. I had spent my twenties diving head-first into a bevy of artistic realms that had given me a tool belt of skills that was matched by few, but also an overwhelming sense that I would never find my niche. That feeling of no direction is the number one night-mare of being a multihyphenate. All at once you feel full of promise, and yet devoid of purpose. You envy those who have a singular clear directive and wish that you too could have a bottom line to come back to. I was no different. My talents felt in the way.

I began to tackle the unsolved mystery from a more logical angle by looking over the landscape of my work for a through line that could help shape it. What I found was comedy. Regardless of the medium, I always sought to infuse humor into my work, and after a couple seasons of *Best Week Ever*, two YouTube series, and a humor-based show on AOL called *The Spark*, it had become clear that I was funny. Once I peeped this, I began to obsess over Carol Burnett. Her sketches and ability to be consistently funny across TV, stage, and movie screens was incredible to me. It was dope to see someone who was a true multihyphenate shine. Watching Carol drove me to look at other entertainers who had managed to do the same. Names like Wayne Brady, Chelsea Handler, Maya Rudolph, Ellen DeGeneres, Queen Latifah, and Chris Rock came to mind. They were all multi-hyphenates who had managed to successfully crossover into differ-ent lines of entertainment work. I pride myself on my logic and skills of deduction, and they came to use when I looked at the differences between these great talents. Side by side they all share similarities in their pursuits, but in fully dissecting their blueprints I figured out the main thing that some had and some didn't: their own voice. Sure, Queen, Wayne, and Maya are super dope and woke and steeped in goodness, but their work was not rooted in their point of view in the same way Ellen's, Chelsea's, and Chris's was. They all had their own points of view but unlike the former three, the latter had built their entire brands on not just their performance style in the comedy space but on their identities as comedic personalities. As outspoken as I was, this was a doozy of a realization. I was looking at three of the most poppington entertainers of our time and comparing their path to mine and realizing that just like them, I could host. I could write. I could act. I had a strong point of view. I had a big personality. As far as repertoire went there was only one thing they shared that was missing from mine: stand-up comedy.

Stand-up is not something to be taken lightly. People swear they're funny cuz their homeboys be knee slappin' at their lil jokes, or they caught a chuckle or two at a dinner party, but to have to be funny, on cue, with written material, on a stage, by yourself, is a whole other ballgame. I remember telling a homegirl and fellow comic that I wanted to get into stand-up and she said, "You can't shortcut this." I didn't know why she presumed I would. Now that I am a stand-up I can see why that was her natural response, as I've had MANY a person tell me that they're "thinking of doing stand-up" when they have never in their life been funny, focused, or, did I mention, funny? My case was different because as a performer I don't take any stage work lightly, and as a lifelong fan of stand-up I held it in such high reverence that I knew if I was going to step into doing it I not only had to be good, but I needed to be GREAT. I put it out into the Universe that stand-up was next for me, but I will admit, I was tenuous.

Though I had been a poet, a host, and a musical artist, to go on stage and tell jokes was an entirely different level of performance and required a whole other level of courage that I had yet to muster. One night my boyfriend at the time and I were watching a stand-up special that had us merely chuckling and he paused it, turned to me and said, "Tell a joke." I was like, "Uhhh, what do you mean?" He said, "Take the next five minutes and write a joke then stand-up and tell it to me." (This ex, in particular, was trash on many levels but every so often he had a shining moment like this, which kept me around. But I digress . . .) Surprisingly I had one swimming around my head and jotted it down. Then he had me stand in the middle of the room, with the remote as the mic, and tell the joke. He laughed. Like a forreal laugh. Then said, "Now see, you definitely funnier than this dude. You should do it, yo." Then he went back to watching the show, and I went back to picturing myself as a stand-up comedian. It felt a little clearer. A few months later I had written my third one-woman show, "It's Complicated: Hilarical Answers to Serious Questions on Love" and was looking for a place to perform it. I sent out a tweet about my anxiety being high that day. Out of the blue, a comedy club in NYC tweeted back and said I should come by and ease my anxiousness with some comedy. I DMed and said, "It's funny you're reaching out like that because I am looking for a place to perform my new one-woman show and your venue would be perfect."

Performing the show in a comedy club was a genius idea if I do say so myself. I had done my previous one-woman shows in theaters, but I wanted to do this one in a comedy club because I felt that, to a lot of folks, a comedy club feels more accessible as a venue than a theater does. He replied back, "Let's do it." That was all she wrote. Three months later, I did five shows over five weeks, selling out the last three. In that time, I got to spread my wings onstage for an hour and half being funny, in my own voice. Even though it wasn't stand-up in the traditional sense, I was in a comedy club, I was onstage, and I was telling jokes. I knew from that point on that I had it in me. A month later is when I looked down at my phone and saw that email about the SNL stand-up showcase.

I did the showcase and killed. You can watch it on YouTube. I don't know if I would have kept going had I not, but I did. From that point forward, I was all stand-up, all the time. I hit up open mics. I hung out. I emailed and begged and traded for stage time. It was the middle of the polar vortex and I was troopin' up and through them city streets to do five- and ten-minute sets for free. You know why? BECAUSE THAT'S WHAT YOU DO. You dig in! You commit! You grind! You learn the ropes and then you double Dutch with them thangs.

Immediately I felt a change in me. Not just because I had a new focus but because it felt like the right focus. Sure, there were haters (there's always gonna be haters) who thought I was just another TV personality dabbling in stand-up as another means of exposure or another stream of income, but for me it was different. I found in stand-up what I had originally found in hip-hop, that I could be my WHOLE ENTIRE SELF. Though I did dopeness in the other artforms I had pursued, I thrived in stand-up. The things about me that people had told me were flaws—I'm opinionated, I'm intense, I'm detail-obsessive, I'm a know it all—were essentials to my ascent in stand-up! Though I had looked at the blueprints of people doing what I wanted to do and saw that stand-up was the missing link, the true teller of its role as my skeleton key was that it was a challenge that invigorated me. Even in the awkwardness of being at the comic's table with a bunch of folks I didn't know and feeling like the new girl in seventh grade, or the loneliness of taking the train home from Williamsburg at 1:30 a.m.

after bombing to a room full of "I don't see color" hipsters, or the frustration of being asked, "What kind of crowd will you be looking to market to" and replying, "They'll be black. Smart, funny, and black," I never at any point felt like quitting. I was home. I had found my tribe.

I refused to consider myself a comedian until I was consistently being paid to do it and even still, to this day, I pinch myself that I get to be a part of this exclusive society of X-Men given the superpower of bringing people laughter. I was right. For my career, stand-up was the skeleton key. Once I had "comedian" as my "label," everything else came together. Execs in general meetings took me seriously, agents became interested, and most importantly I homed in on the springboard from which everything I did would be launched. As a multihyphenate, I have been blessed with many gifts, none of which I take for granted. However, it took comedy to unlock not only the *what* but the *why* in my purpose. When Rich Bova, a professor at SUNY Purchase, stopped me on campus one day and told me, "You need to get your master's because you are going to change the world and you will need it to do it," he knew I would need the knowledge to speak to folks but I had to discover I'd needed the jokes for them to hear me.

CHAPTER 4

Bae Watch

Navigating the Dating Pool & #Relationshipgoals

A FRIEND OF MINE ONCE TOLD ME, "There should be no strategy in relationships." Sounds great, but I think we can all agree, no matter your sexual preference or gender, if you're looking for love, it can be very difficult to get out of dealing with "games" and figure out how to navigate the playing field. Who should be the one to approach? How should you approach? When should you call? Is a first date too early to sleep together? What even is a first date? If he sends a panda emoji does that mean he's a freak?? And so on and so on. . . . With movies like *Two Can Play That Game* and *How to Be a Player*, books with titles like *How to Be a Lady to a Man Who Knows the Lady a Man Wants*, written by ***insert thrice divorced man right here***, and the daily public displays of computer love on social media, we've been groomed, taught, and conditioned to exercise strategy throughout every phase of courtship. The question becomes: What goal is your strategy tuned to obtain?

Some just want sex. Hey, do you! But are you being honest with yourself and the other person in that pursuit? For far too many, simply having a relationship is enough. Whether it's for financial purposes, for the kids, or just to be able to say, "I have a man," they'll forsake their own happiness, trying to function through dysfunction and remaining blind to their inalienable truths. Others want companionship without obligation and familiarity without family. There are fuckbois, and THOTs, situationships, and cuddle buddies, cuffin', talking, ghosting, and more. Plus, technology has added all types of new help and hurdles to the quest, simultaneously bringing folks together and, in more ways than one, widening the chasm. Then, of course, there is the bigger picture of the evolution of gender, the change in social norms associated with gender, and the call for economic equality, which have all been incredible steps that have delivered a heavy blow to the toxic masculinity far too many find comfort in. With all the above swirling around, these days it can seem like relationships are harder to get into and even harder to stay in.

Be that as it may, I am a realist. So, though the path to love may be peppered with potholes, one must keep driving toward the paved road. In this section, we'll dig into "data" on Dating in a Digital World, tackle the Hoe Phase, get Booed Up, and juggle those Breakups to Makeups. I don't believe in the term "relationship expert," and as I type this right now I, myself, am going through the growth needed to make me a partner to someone in the way I want them to be one to me, but at the root of all of this dating madness is the question, "What are your core principles and fundamentals?" Throughout these "side effects of . . ." you'll find out those answers, and next thing you know, you'll still be a cat lady, but perhaps you'll be one step closer to finding your person.

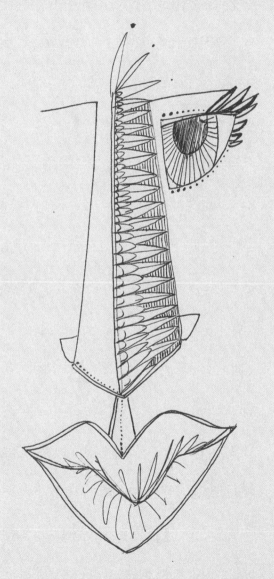

Dating in a Digital World

Analog is person to person.
Digital is computerized.
Technology now works
to bring us closer
but don't let it get in the way
of keeping love alive.

TEXTIQUETTE

"I'm not good at texting" is no longer a valid excuse for simply being inconsiderate. Basic rule of thumb: If you wouldn't be cool doing it in real life, it probably isn't cool via text either. Here are some basic rules to NOT texting like an asshole:

Phantom Texter: Don't be the person who just disconnects, like POOF, without warning from a back-and-forth convo. Sure, we're all busy, but we can't let being busy cancel out being decent. If that person were standing in front of you, you wouldn't just walk away. Unless, of course, you are an inconsiderate asshole who has to return some tapes.

The Tittie-or-Two Hours: Everyone knows that late night "U up?" text nine times out of ten is not about discussing your hopes and dreams. It is reserved for sexy time. Which is why only certain folks should garner a response. "But Amanda, why is it called, 'The Tittie-or-Two Hours?'" Because, the only person that should be contacting you after 11 p.m. should have already touched a tittie or two of yours.

Dot Dot Dotters: When you're seeing someone and the ellipses bubble comes up on the phone, the anticipation goes through the roof. "What are they gonna say?!" And then, just like that, it's gone. And if five minutes or more goes by, it's like that thought didn't even happen.

Read 'Em and Sleepers: If you're gonna have read receipts on you gotta respond once you read! Unless you're trying to send a message that you're ignoring someone, know that it's simply distasteful and low-key savage to read a message, have it marked as read, and not reply within a reasonable amount of time.

FACETIME FAUX PAS

There are rules to this shit.

FaceTime is not for everywhere. Stop with the FaceTiming in crowded public spaces. Walking down the street or in a place where you're generally alone is all good. But otherwise, you're loud! YOU ARE HELLA LOUD! I was on a tour of a plantation in Louisiana and a dude was having a full FaceTime convo, in German, while we were being shown the slave quarters. Y'all! NO ONE wants to hear your convo, let alone see it happening as you weirdly hold your phone in front of you to talk eye-level to someone you can only see neck-up. Stop the madness.

Unless you have an established relationship you can't just be FaceTiming folks all willy-nilly. You gotta give a heads-up. It's only right. Can I at least have time to put some lip gloss on? These phones are HD! Some folks even need you to make an appointment. I don't blame them. Folks gotta earn being "scarf worthy."

FaceTime is not a substitute for actually seeing someone. In some situations, it's the next best thing! Of course, if your person is across the nation, getting to see their face (and maybe even a lil more) is a cherished technological advancement. But I've seen it get out of hand. I once dated someone that lived literally in my apartment building (don't ever do that) and he would be tryna FaceTime face-to-face level convos that it would take him a ten-step walk to have. NO DICE.

THE RISE OF THE FUCKBOIS

The digital age has played a critical role in going from the dawn to the rise of the fuckbois. A *fuckboi* can be loosely defined as a man who wants to indulge in the perks of having a relationship without accepting the responsibilities that come with it. The invention of dating apps has been their Godsend. Why "put up with" this woman who has growing expectations, when you can simply swipe to find a brand-new broad and you can start fresh with none?! Add in texting and it makes noncommittal communication a breeze! A fuckboi once told me that all good women want the same thing, time and consistency, two things he claimed he had none of. I asked, "So why do you keep hollering at those types of women?" He said, "Even if you can't afford nice things you still want them." He was deadass serious. Thing is you don't keep trying people on without being expected to actually commit to them. The digital age, when wielded by a fuckboi, can have you thinking someone is truly into you if you don't know how to properly read their behavior. Beware of them and their technologically advanced narcissistic ways!

BRB/TTYL/WYD/TBY

BRB: Be right back
TTYL: Talk to you later

WYD: What are you doing
TBY: Thinking 'bout you

Use of all of these at the right time and for the right purpose can save your entire relationship and make you look wayyyy more considerate than you truly are in real life. They're not a substitute for action, but a helpful bridge to it when you're working to keep your priorities feeling prioritized!

TECHNOCURITY

With all the different ways that folks can be shady due to these technologies, there's a specific type of security of self that you must have, technocurity. That's right, a special brand of self-knowing that is technology-proof! Between, phones, DMs, catfishing, and more, it's no wonder people lose their damn minds wondering what someone could be doing to deceive them. The only way to stay sane is to keep your eyes up and your integrity strong. The same confidence we talk about in Side Effects of Insecurity has to carry over to how you navigate this new romantic space that travels via fiber optic wires.

SHOW SOME
ANALOG LOVE DIGITALLY

When it comes to finding analog love in a digital world, I feel the key is to consider the digital aspect as an enhancement but not a replacement of the organic ways of making and nurturing a human connection. Yes, technology adds convenience and ease, but it should not replace effort and action because at the end of the day no Wi-Fi connection is stronger than an actual human connection!

Attention
vs. Affection

IT MAY SEEM LIKE THEY'VE BEEN HERE FOREVER, but the idea of having a phone on your body, at your reach, all day, is fairly new. In high school, one person in my friend group had a cell phone and it was to be used only for emergency purposes like to call and tell my mom to tell my dad, who decided to come visit and play father for a week, that I would not be going along with his, "I'm here. So, I'm runnin' shit now" act, and instead would be going to Denny's with my fellow drama geeks to celebrate the close of our show. Anything less than that could either wait or required all hands on deck to find a quarter for the pay phone. Now, however, it's an actual oddity, and in some cases, simply irresponsible for someone not to have a mobile communication device. Which is why the expectations of communication and connection have inevitably changed, and we're still learning how to maneuver being so reachable and so able to reach out. Add to that texting, which is now a concrete form of exchange that can truly make or break a relationship if not utilized properly. Whether it's via a dating app or following through on someone's number you got at a party, the phone is now, more than ever, a key conduit in making a love connection, but it can often be difficult to tell, via the digital device, if there are analog feelings. One way to be transparent with your intentions is to make a clear distinction between if you are showing/receiving attention or affection. Paying attention is doing a transaction, showing affection is making a connection.

I came up with this concept because I feel like a lot of times I'll have homegirls who be like:

Homegirl: "He likes me!"

Manda: "Well how do you know that he likes you?"

Homegirl: "Because he texts me on the regular and you know I get my good morning text every morning and, you know, he just shows me attention."

Manda: And I'm like, "Okay but does he show you affection?"

Homegirl: *mad silencio* "Whatchumean?"

A lot of us feel like just because someone is acknowledging our presence, that means that they like us or even love us. I, however, think there's more to it. Especially when it's in the form of a text. Ya see, technology has made paying attention easy. It takes close to nothing to pay attention within the context of today's technological standards. You can be fixing a car while breastfeeding while getting a pedicure while paying your BFF attention as she texts away about how annoying the dude at her job is who keeps telling his boss he's scared of her because she's a black woman who is unafraid to correct him. All you have to do is respond intermittently with a, "Oh, hell nah," "Shut up!," or "You go to HR on his ass yet?" and you've paid ample attention. You can text a guy a Ntozake Shange choreopoem-length piece on your feelings, and even if he's on the other end of the phone at a strip club puttin' dollaz in a thong strap, as long as he responds in a timely fashion (for most that's five to ten minutes, for others that's five to ten seconds or five to ten days) with some form of acknowledgement, i.e., "word," "cool," or "I feel you 😶 " you feel paid attention to! Not saying it's wrong, but it's surface. It takes nothing to send you (and ten other people) a good morning text every morning. It creates expectation and consistency, but it lacks content and true connection.

It's literally the difference between watering your plants and talking to your plants. When you water your plants, you're giving them the basic necessities they need to keep growing. However, when you talk to your plants you're nurturing them and giving them personal attention that actually taps into their consciousness and allows them to flourish in a whole other way. This is scientifically proven, y'all! I'm not just talking out my ass. Affection is shown in many different forms, but most of all it's curated and direct. It lacks generalities and is filled with nuance. In the case of our technology-based world, it's about taking time (and data) to show someone you care. Instead of just texting Happy Birthday, it's making a bday playlist just for that person. Instead of sending another text that says "TBY" (thinking 'bout you), send a voice memo of what part of them you're thinking about that's making you smile. Instead of sending a pic, make a lil slideshow set to a song you know they like, or will like, or simply call someone, or, even better, schedule a (or if y'all are at a certain level, pop up on the) Skype/FaceTime. In this fast-paced day and age, affection can seem as dead as chivalry, but all it takes is a little bit of applied consciousness.

It is also valuable to examine the distinction between affection and attention and how they are applied beyond the context of technology. It is important because it really is the difference between you settling for some shit or nah. When we think that someone just paying us attention is enough, it can send the message that we don't need to make an emotional connection with them. I'm sure folks read this and had an epiphany about what they're receiving, and in some cases, what they're giving, because some people don't even know that *they're* just paying attention. They're in a relationship right now like, "I show my girl love. We watch TV together. I send her GM texts." That ain't affection. That's attention, which, contrary to the popularity of being "busy" these days, is the easy part 'cause affection requires you to be present emotionally, spiritually, mentally. Which for hella people can be very scary. And that's the shit that be making people be like, "Nah Imma just stick to them GM texts." Because once you open up in those ways, then you start to have a real connection with somebody. You know what can happen when you have a real connection with somebody? They can break your heart, they can tear you down, they can shatter your world! You might say, "It ain't worth it! I can't come back from that!" So you let fear get in the way. You know what else happens when you make a real connection with somebody? They can open your world up. They can inspire your spirit. They can bring a frequency to your space that helps you heal your wounds. You gotta get over that fear because when you show affection and you make connections with people, you're making a connection with yourself. When you find a connection with yourself, it makes it possible for you to connect in other ways, beyond your current levels, to your purpose, to what you're here for, and to where you want to ascend to. So when it comes to attention versus affection, find you somebody that ain't just gonna water you, but someone that's also gonna nurture you.

The 'gram and these innanets have been a gift and a curse to dating. We've discussed some of the curse of it all, from texting, to faux connections, unsolicited dick pics, and more. However, there are positives. Some would say it's a gift because it brought them together. A slide into the DMs or a swipe right and "You're a match" on Tinder has led to people actually having children together or in some cases full-on marriage. Creating spaces for like-minded folks has given hope to those who had given up on finding "the one." For the long distancers, Skype and FaceTime and being able to talk over Wi-Fi has been a Godsend. When it comes to missed connections, it was these interwebs that have been able to reunite two ships passing in the night. However, there is another gift that the digital age has provided many of us with, and that is the gift of the dodged bullet! It's almost enough to make you think, You know what, maybe the machines do want us to win. I cannot tell you how many times the internet has prevented me from wasting my time. I'll give you some of the highlights!

OMA-NO-SIR

One time I met a dude at a friend's birthday party. He was all the basics: tall, handsome, witty. I was smitten. Then I got home, and settled into an IG deep dive to learn a little more about my potential future beau. FOUR PICS INTO HIS IG he was hanging out, all chummed up, with Ms. No Ma'am herself, Omarosa. Not only was he in pics with her, he was referring to her has a friend and as a black queen. No sir. I forgot his name as I quickly clicked through to look at a cat profile to cleanse my palate of the bullet dodged!

THE LYING LAWYER

One New York night, I was post-breakup at an event my homeboy was throwing, and on my way out of the door feeling hella "Stella had her groove hacked," when the DJ threw on So So Def Bass All-Stars's "My Boo." My. Jam. I had to stay. So, I did an about-face and headed back to the dance floor to get my solo groove on. Then, out the corner of my eye, I realized (dun Dun DUNNN), I was not alone. A tall, quite dapper, mahogany-toned gentleman was doing his best Bankhead bounce to my left, and once he caught my eye, he started closing the gap between us. I obliged as, one, it was THE JAM, and two, he was fine in a "in college I would have a crush on you if you were my professor, but now we're both adults and I can act on it without fear of consequence" kind of way. So, there we were, jammin' on the one, and when the song was done, he sidled up to me and we did the obligatory name ask, ***insert joke* *insert laugh*** exchange. We headed to the bar and the convo was great. We had shared interests, he was a lawyer, he had played football at a noteworthy university, he loved all cuisine aside from Thai, he lived in Jersey, he knew all the words to "Shawty Swing My Way." After one dance the man was giving me a total download of the important elements of his existence, and considering his gorgeous smile and the meticulous tailoring of his suit, I was there for it! Shortly thereafter the event began shutting down and folks were exiting, but before we were out the door my dance partner asked for my digits. I happily shared and spotted a homeboy who lived in my neighborhood to share a cab uptown with. While grabbing a slice before heading up the West Side, I got a message from Sir Suit saying he was so happy to have met and that he'd love to take me out. I WAS BEAMING. I'm surprised my smile didn't derail oncoming traffic. Aside from the fact that I really enjoyed our convo, this meant that "I still got it!" Even after being dumped, mama could pull 'em on or off the dance floor! I was floating. And a lawyer, no less! This was Jackpot City, USA! I got home and, excited at this new prospect, texted my homegirl the good news. I was expecting a response like, "That's wassup!" or "Okay, girl!" But no. She replied, "Did you Google him?" I hadn't even considered it. She told me that before she gets even REMOTELY hype about ANY man, she gets to the Googles and does a background check. It made sense. Employers always do a Google search to check if anything glaring comes up regarding their new employees before hiring, why wouldn't we do same thing regarding a new prospect for baeness?

I took her advice and entered his name into the search engine. Y'all, I DIDN'T HAVE TO GO TO THE SECOND PAGE BEFORE THE FUCKERY WAS REVEALED. I begin to read a recent interview with his alma mater, skimming and scanning for a red flag, and four questions in, there it was. Surprise, this man was married! With a whole wife, a whole child, and an ENTIRE newborn baby at home in their beds while he was out cutting a rug and asking newly single sistas like me on dates and inquiring about our fave cuisine! The nerve! Somewhere between, "I played football" and "I'm not a fan of Thai food" he managed to skip over the part where he had a full family! I was livid. Not one to let someone get away with thinking they pulled the du-rag over my eyes, I replied to his message with a link to the article. He wrote back saying that he was going to tell me eventually that he was married. I told him I hope his wife (whom I'd already found on Facebook, btw) eventually realized her man is trifling and left his ass. Bullet dodged. Thanks, innanets!

INSTAGRAM FORENSIC SPECIALIST

I consider myself an Instagram Forensic Specialist. Honestly, so many of us are! Using critical thinking, comparative analysis, and the powers of deduction and research, I am able to get a pretty good rendering of a person simply from what they post on IG. It's a very useful skill and has come in handy more than a few times in the bullet-dodgery category. One particular evening comes to mind when I found myself on a date with a dude who I'd met on the train. Since we had no mutuals, my IG forensic skills were in need more than ever. I skimmed and scoured, went down rabbit holes and up through comment threads until I felt like I had enough info to feel like this was not a complete waste of time. So, when he asked me out for a hang, I obliged. While sitting in high-ass chairs at a high-ass table in a restaurant on the lower west side of Harlem, his IG meandered its way into our conversation. I mentioned that it was rather revealing, and he was taken aback. Hesitantly, he asked how. When I divulged that I was a certified IGFS he grew relieved and laughed. Surely, I was joking. There's no such thing. What could I possibly know about him from his Instagram that wasn't conspicuous? I asked if he'd like me to share. He hesitated, like you would before a psychic asks, "Do you want to know if he's the one?" and then said, "Yeah, sure, why not" and took the plunge. I began by first asking him how he's liking his new job.

> **Him:** Okay okay, how'd you know I had a new job?
> **Me:** You had a bunch of pics at a job. Then no more pics there and weeks of pics of you doing absolutely nothing during the day, then a pic of you with new coworkers in a whole other setting. Clearly, you got a new job.
> **Him:** Alright, that's impressive. What else?
> **Me:** I dunno, it's a bit dark. Not sure if you wanna go there.
> **Him:** *(Pausing for the psychic again)* Nah, I do. Spit it.
> **Me:** *(measured)* Well, how are you dealing with your brother's passing?

He cocked his head at me like a dog hearing a new command and wasn't sure what to do with the accuracy of the information. He hadn't outright said his brother had passed anywhere on his IG. This is true. He did, however, have pics of him and his brother and then alluvasudden posted a #tbt with them and the caption "I can't believe this is real." One of the comments said, "I just heard about your brother on the news. So sorry." I Googled, and voila there it was, the news story about his brother. He didn't inquire how I knew. It didn't matter.

> **Him:** It's been hard but I'm doing okay.
> **Me:** Good.
> **Him:** Okay something else. We can't end on that note.
> **Me:** You sure?
> **Him:** Yea, you really are good at this. I'm impressed.
> **Me:** Okay. One more . . .

I go to his IG and scan the pics 'til I locate the one in particular that had given me pause. I show it to him

> **Me:** Who's that?

The pic is of him and a pretty brown-skinned gal at a chic NYC brunch event. They're dressed to the nines and are posing together in a familiar, non-suggestive way. The caption, on the other hand, is telling to the knowing eye and reads: Him and Her.

> **Him:** *(looking at the pic)* Oh, it's complicated.

When he said, "It's complicated," it confirmed the inconvenient truth I had deduced from the pic, that he clearly had feelings for this unnamed styletastic woman in a real way. In which case, what am I even doing here? I'm not a space filler nor of a mind to win one's heart away from another.

> **Me:** And just like that, this has gone from a date to an outing.

Bullet dodged. Preshate ya, innanets!

HAUNTING HASHTAG

I had just broken up with my boyfriend of almost two years for what I was committed to making the last time. We had a habit of breakups to makeups that typically came when my loneliness would swoop in like Santa with an unwanted gift, and I would fold and welcome him back into my home, my bed, my body. It was a terrible cycle that had to end, but what would it take? It seemed like nothing could get this breakup to stick! It had been a week, and he was leaving my favorites, Sweet Chili Doritos and Red Plum Nantucket Nectars, on my doorstep every day. He was also leaving carnations. Now, listen, I love and respect all flowers, but carnations are not a strong choice of apology flower. They basically say, "this was the most convenient option and so I got it cuz women like flowers?" Don't do carnations. Nonetheless, the other snacks were moving me because everyone wants something nice to be done for them and, real talk, everyone wants to be liked and cared about. I took these tokens as an example of his love and remorse for being an unpredictable, mean ol' prick. I was becoming fragile, the chinks in my armor began to show, and I decided to look at his page to see if maybe viewing his IG would either fill up the empty space that was missing and tide me over 'til tomorrow or reveal some wack shit that would set me straight. I devoured his page a pic at a time hoping it would suffice, but I still craved his companionship. Then I had a brain-wave to look at the hashtag he had created for himself. There it was. Him, in a club, with a girl straddling him, a week ago. So basically, this took place, and then the same hands he had on her thighs in the pic were the ones he used to pick a yellow carnation out of a PVC bucket to leave on my doorstep!? I was mortified. I called him and demanded to know who this woman was. Without hesitation he said her name and that he'd slept with her that night. I couldn't believe it. Here I was still pining over this fool, and he was out in his proverbial black dress taking pics and banging chicks. I asked him, "Why? Why would you do this when you've been coming here every morning trying to get me back?" He replied, "Because I'm weak." He was weak?! **He was weak.** I think he thought that saying that would be an impressive self-aware response. In a way, it was, because he had shown that he was weak in so many ways, so many times, but this time, I finally heard him. Then I heard myself. I heard my inner voice reminding me that I am strong. Strong women cannot thrive with weak men. A revolutionary woman's love will not be won passively. I told him all of the above, and it was the first real step I took in not going back to stand in front of the target where he'd fire his next bullet. Nope, not this time. Bullet dodged. Merci, innanets.

So, you see, the interwebs have come to my aid more than a few times, making sure that I am not wasting my time, and that I am clear on who I'm giving my time to. I know some will consider this cynical and taking the natural process away from learning someone. There is some truth to that, but at the end of the day, like most technological advance-ments, the innanets are a gift and a curse, and if it can help you avoid someone who is a curse, then it's the gift that keeps on giving!

The Curve

Nobody likes it
But it's something that we
all have to manage
How to give it and how to take it
Without your ego getting damaged.

THE TROUBLE WITH THE CURVE

Let's start off by saying it is okay to curve. You do not have to be interested in everybody, and everybody is not going to be interested in you. There's this misconception that says you have to give everyone a chance or you're mean, or picky, or difficult, and that's not true! If I am not interested in your dick, we are just friends. That's it! And it's not a diss. It's just a curve. And you can do that in a way that's respectful and doesn't shade or demean anyone.

The friend zone is not a diss.
The friend zone is not a diss.
The friend zone is not a diss.

HANDLING THE CURVE

Taking a curve to the chin can be a harrowing experience. You gotta pick up your whole face off the ground and get on with your life, which, in the moment, can seem like an impossible feat. The most important thing is not to let the curve take away your confidence or leave you bitter. Let it steer you in a better direction. As Michelle, a hairstylist on the set of *Insecure*, once told me, "Man's rejection is God's protection."

ENTERING THE FRIEND ZONE

"The Friend Zone" gets a bad rap, but let's clear some things up. First: Yes, it's a curve, but it's not a diss. If someone isn't interested in you romantically, but they still enjoy your connection, that's fair! What's not cool is when the "friend zone" is used as a tactic to keep you romantically accessible without the commitment of a romantic relationship. In the beginning of seeing someone, it's like Mufasa introducing Simba to the Pride Lands: "Everything the lights touches is yours." The possibilities are endless: We could be just dating, we could be just friends, we could fall in love! It's open season. But as you get to know each other more, you might just feel like, "You know what? We're more suited for the friend space." However, once you've breached the physical intimacy barrier, the boundaries have to get clear. The person you thought you were moving into bae life with can slide you right into the friend zone with benefits, i.e., a situationship. So, be careful with the wielding of the "friend zone." If you truly only like the person as a friend, all good. If you like more than a friend but don't want to have to do more than a friend, that's wack. Bonus: If you're actually "friend zone-ing" because you know you're a piece of shit and you don't want to get any deeper with the person and "ruin the friendship" when they find out, you should stop dating and work on YOU.

AFTER THE CURVE

Can we be friends?: The good news is, yes, perhaps you can be friends, but if you're the curver it's really not on you to determine that. All you can do is be present. A lot of folks don't grasp this and think that the curve can just be brushed off. But you always have to take into account that feelings are real, and some—ok, *most*—people need space to get back to the middle after they been curved to the left!

No curve then kiss: You cannot curve then kiss. YOU CANNOT! You can't one minute say, "No, this wouldn't be a good idea," and the next minute try to go in for the kiss. It sends a mixed message! The curve is confusing in and of itself without then having to figure out why this person is still coming after you physically when they just said no dice. Curve your lips that way!

On to the next . . . friend: If you curve me, you can't just try to holla at my friend next. Sorry, unless there was already a previous vested attraction it's just shitty to curve somebody and then direct your interest to the person next to them. That's not even a curve. That's a swerve, which means you are outta control!

KIND OF CURVE

Then there's the curve that's not a no, but a possibly. It could be for a number of reasons—timing, location, being broke as a joke. Regardless of the reason, it's not the ideal outcome and thus, a curve. Then what? How do you curve but still keep things cool so that if the cause of the curve shifts there's no baggage to step over to get to the good stuff? The balance comes in walking the line of practicing restraint without coldness.

GHOST RIDE THE CURVE

The worst curve is the ghost. It's basically a very strong action that says, "I don't want to deal with you" for a bevy of reasons. Maybe the person is afraid of a tough convo, maybe they're unsure of how to handle their Dru Hill '90s R&B-level romantic feelings, maybe they're just not that into you. Whatever the case, the ghost is a method of curve that I DO NOT support. Communication is so important to advancement and elevation, and I always feel it is important to at least speak your piece before saying peace.

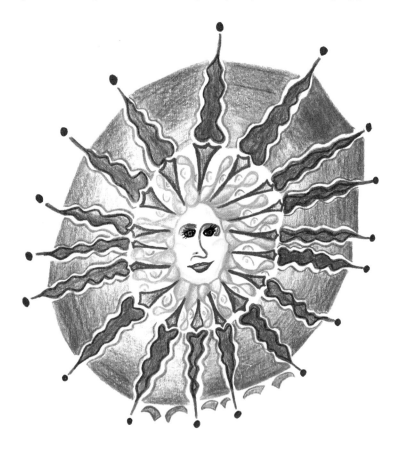

GHOST STYLES

Ghosting has become so commonplace that, like Inuit tribes possessing fifty words for snow, there are now words for specific ghosting techniques!

- **Bread Crumbing:** When somebody drops little words in here and there like, *Hey!/Sup/You good?* just to keep you on the trail to their affection but never actually follow through with action.
- **Stashing:** When they just keep you in the stash. You don't meet their friends or family. You don't have consistent convos. They give you intermittent rewards that keep you on ice until the next time they want to see you.
- **Submarining:** When they dip out mid-convo and then resurface days, weeks, months later like, "Hey, wassup? You good?" only to dip out and resurface again with the same lingo.

That's three different kinds of ghosts. Again, some folks ghost because they're in fuckboi/trife gal mode, some do it out of insecurity, some do it to avoid confrontation. Regardless, no one likes to be curved, but the ghost curve is def the worst because it has no explanation! I'm not sure when it happened, but this narrative that says "don't tell people what issue you have with their behavior, just bounce" is no bueno. I get it—the disappearing act protects you from confrontation, but it also protects the person from having to face the facts of their wackness if, in fact, they're acting wack. So, what ends up happening is they carry on thinking that their behavior is okay, and they bring it to the next person. I'm not saying there has to be a discussion. I'm not saying there has to be confrontation. All I'm saying is keep it 100. Tell somebody what's up, *then* bend that curve like a body wave!

Small Doses

Curve
vs. Diss

EVERYBODY DEALS WITH REJECTION DIFFERENTLY. The mollywhop to your ego is real and can truly have you feeling some type of way. Some folks cry. Others go ham in their kickboxing class. Others down a fifth of Hennessey. Everyone has their own method to deal with the wackness of being on the receiving end of a NO. However, it doesn't always have to be that way. Step back, get out your feelings, get out your ego, get some perspective, and you can possibly save yourself some heartache. For a lot of folks, even if they were simply rejected, they take it personally and as an affront! They think just because they got curved, they got dissed. They attach the rejection to disrespect, but often that's your ego on overtime and has nothing to do with the situation. There are definitely disrespectful modes of curvery, but a lot of times it's just the basics of someone not being on your same plane, and that's ok. The key is learning the distinction between the curve and the diss and how not to let either disrupt your magic.

The curve is simply, "I'm not interested." News flash, you don't have to be interested in everybody. As I've already explained, there's this false rhetoric that says everyone deserves a shot, and guess what, they don't! If you're not interested, you're not interested. You don't owe anyone a chance just because they were nice to you. You don't owe anyone a chance just because they like you. You don't owe anyone a chance just because they showed up. Context matters. Timing matters. Preference matters. You are entitled to all. Your bottom lines may even be trash inspired, but you're entitled to them nonetheless. And because you're entitled to them, you reserve the right to curve. The nuance is in how you deliver the curve. There are ways of curving that can come very close to disrespect. For the sake of your karma and your car not getting keyed, it behooves everyone to try their best to deliver the most direct curve possible. It's like playing that game Operation. For all the folks reading this born after 1987, Operation was a game with a weird-looking white man on a board and all over his body were little openings that had different bones and organs in them. The challenge of the game was using little tweezers to pull out the bones and organs without touching the magnetic rimmed walls of the openings and making a buzz sound. That's what delivering a curve is, except you're essentially trying to put someone's heart back without touching the sides and making a buzz sound that translates to a series of deep quote memes and an overdose of depressing R&B. A lot of folks say honesty is the best policy, but when it comes to the curve, I would swap honesty for tact. That's not to say you don't have to keep it real, but sometimes—actually most times in a curve scenario—it's just not necessary to say everything. Especially if everything borders on being straight-up mean. DON'T GET ME WRONG, sometimes a mean curve is ABSOLUTELY earned! However, if the curve is simply based on lack of interest and not on earned disinterest, you simply need to say enough to make it clear why you're curving, and keep it moving.

Things take a turn when the curve has a bite to it. That's when we step into diss territory. *Diss* is short for *disrespect*, and rejection is bad enough without that extra bit of bitter added to it. However, I repeat, just because you got curved doesn't mean you were disrespected. The disrespect is really about the reason you were curved and how the curve went down. Any time someone feels it necessary to attach something demeaning to the curve, you've entered disrespect territory. For example:

Curve: I just don't feel like there's chemistry here but thank you for taking me out.
Diss: You're hella corny and it doesn't turn me on at all but thank you for taking me out.

Curve: I realize that I still have feelings for my ex, so before this goes any further, I think it's best to just be friends. ***You know you're not really gonna be friends, but it's a nice gesture.***
Diss: ***They don't hear from you, then see you out with your ex.***

Now, in the first example, the diss came when you unnecessarily felt the need to call out the corn. Unless you're pressed for some very specific indicator of why this person doesn't make you wanna put your phone down, so to speak, you can be clear without being OD and you can be tactful without being vague. That said, some folks don't abide by this and really be going for folks' necks. I'll be the first to tell you, I've doled out a murdergram or two in my time, but those disses were in response to being disrespected, so they had it coming!

The key to all of this, though, is that when you are rejected you have to ask yourself, Was I dissed or was I curved? Either way, you must take a look at the lesson that can be learned, your own behaviors, and wish that person love and light as you continue on your journey. Be that as it may, we're all human and you'll inevitably feel a snuff to the ego when someone you're feeling just ain't feeling you. The thing is, we all do feel a bit better about a situation when, even if it didn't go our way, we can still regard that person as a good person. The curve gives you that. Let it give you peace of mind. It may not have been a match but at least you have good people around you. When you get hit with the disrespect, the natural inclination is anger. "Who do they think they are!?" "He gon' see!" "Oh HELL NAH!!!" All are valid responses, but you can't let their diss take you down. At our most evolved we're able to look at someone giving us an unwarranted diss and say, "That's unfortunate" and send them, too, on their way, with love and light!

If you're dating, you're gonna deal with curves and maybe even some disses, but the most important thing is realizing that you have to find what's good for you and so does that other person. If they curve you and feel you aren't good for them, that's on them. You don't need to convince them, or pitch them, or campaign to them. You simply have to walk in the confidence of what's good for you and whether someone's winding up a curve or crafting up a diss, they're not it. Someone will be!

I remember it like it was yesterday. There we were, in the midst of what I thought was great sex, when out the blue the brother currently inside of me said, "You ain't gonna cum anyway," pulled out, and strolled out of the room to go play video games. At first I wasn't offended. It was like when you're dancing with someone at a party and they walk away: You figure they went to the bar; they'll be back. He must have been joking, I thought! Nope. He was deadass serious. My box was not producing enough bass for his liking, and he exited the club. To him I was a waste of sexy time because I didn't easily arrive at the Ozone, a climax, the big O. I was shocked, for obvious reasons, but also because I really was having a good time. I didn't really need to orgasm. The rest of the elements were on point! Needless to say, that was the end of that. I gathered my things and did a walk of shame, not because I'd slept at someone else's spot instead of mine, but because I'd been curved mid-stroke for something that at the time I couldn't even control! Eventually, I chalked it up to his ego, and the fact that the curve had devolved into a diss was beneath my accepted level of treatment anyway. Good riddance! But then it happened again. A few years later a different partner told me mid-thrust, "I don't know why you're not letting it happen; you're making this tough for me." It hadn't occurred to him that perhaps *he* was not making it happen! Nevertheless, in so many words, these two told me they thought my vagina was broken.

I always say, men have the Tonka truck of reproductive organs. It goes up. It goes down. Voilà. For women, the engineering is like assembling a LEGO Millennium Falcon. One piece in the wrong place and EVERYTHING goes into disarray. The pussy is very pesky! Women spend our whole lives tryna get a handle on this thing. It's got all kinds of modes and mechanisms. It's like Instagram and switches up its algorithm without *any* notice. Perhaps to an OBGYN there is some order in the cooch court, but as an owner of one for more than three and half decades, I have found that the "magic middle" has no blueprint, rhyme, or reason. Everyone's is built different, with different instructions, which are less helpful than an IKEA booklet. Each vajayjay requires a different set of skills, which can take a while to perfect, in order to get taken to "the promised land," so to speak. You watch Samantha on *Sex and the City* and it's like she can orgasm just by thinking about it. However, for most, that couldn't be farther from the truth, and for some women it's simply not even in the cards. This is not kept on the hush-hush. It's known that an orgasm is like finding the gem at the end of the obstacle course on *Legends of the Hidden Temple*. So why do some men shame women for something that's notoriously hard to reach? I'll tell you why: Our climaxes are attached to that fragile construct of hypermasculinity.

For the first time, women are in a position, at least in the US, where, even with the duplicitousness of pay inequality, taxed feminine products, and rampant sexism, it's possible to make a completely independent life for ourselves. As recent as 1975, women needed a husband's signature to get a bank account. If you've seen *Mad Men*, you know that husbands were even given access to your conversations with a therapist. It's no wonder that for so long the goal of so many mothers was to make sure their daughters were married. Until fairly recently, we were still living in a Jane Austen–novel-esque society where things were set up to force our reliance on men as providers. However, times, they are a changin'. As women become more and more independent, thriving in our single lives, working in careers previously unavailable to us, holding abusers accountable, having children on our own terms, marrying for love not for necessity, reclaiming our time and our sexuality, some men feel compelled to assert their dying roles as providers in a heterosexual relationship by taking ownership of our pleasure. Don't get me wrong, some men simply enjoy pleasing their partner sexually and want to see them happy, so they go for gusto. Others, however, root their desire for their partner's sexual pleasure in a reflection of their own prowess, value, and masculinity. On some "Sure, women may have made inroads, but in the bedroom, man still reigns!" type shit. So, when we don't orgasm, they see it as an emasculation. Like we're intentionally disarming them of their penis purpose. No wonder so many women have learned to fake it to preserve their partner's manhood. Well, I never got that memo, so I never faked, and I'm here to tell you YOUR VAGINA IS NOT BROKEN.

Along with the fact that the O is simply not a button that is pressed, not all dudes are able to, interested in, or good at getting you there! Just because you have a dick doesn't mean you know what to do with it. It takes both people having not only self-awareness but awareness of the other person as more than just a hole, or a pole, in order to make this thang pop off! I eventually found my orgasm thanks to a now ex who—due either to love or the fact that he didn't have a job—dedicated himself to locating it like Waldo in what I consider to be a sea of internal chaos. For some women, getting to yours may take sexual maturity, a certain position you have yet to discover, a patient partner, or some dedicated self-exploration. Not everyone will be able to climax via the johnson or want to, either. And that's cool. Regardless, let's all agree: There's no room in your vagina for a penis *and* an ego.

Booed Up

The road to coupledom
is full of twists and turns,
you live, you love, you like,

Keep baggage light,
enjoy the ride,
and in tune with this insight.

FROM HOLLA
TO HASHTAG BAE

The steps to sealing the deal between you and boo are def not as clear as they once were. A guide:

- **Hollering:** When interest is being shown but action hasn't been taken to advance the desire.
- **Talking:** When both of y'all have shown interest but have yet to verbalize real romantic feelings.
- **Dating:** When both of y'all are going out in the world to get to know each other better.
- **Smashing:** When y'all are going out and getting it in.
- **Cuffing:** When you're sleeping with only each other but not committed emotionally/mentally.
- **Rockin':** When y'all on your Ashford & Simpson, together, and solid as a rock.

WHAT EVEN IS A DATE?

As society shifts and changes, so do some people's concept of what a date is and why it's important in the development of a relationship. On the surface, it's simply an outing between two people with romantic interest in each other. On a deeper level, though, it persists in the midst of technological advances and social shifts as one of the strongest continued traditions humans use to meet other humans and eventually reproduce more humans. The date is where folks get to know each other, and for that reason the first date can't be overlooked. It sets the tone for whether or not there'll even be a second date! Just in case you need a refresher, here are some basic bottom lines for date numero uno:

♥ **A first date is NOT at someone's residence.**
Boundaries, folks. I don't know you like that to be all up in my apt meeting my cat or to be all up in your apt with you trying to get "the cat."
♥ **A first date is planned in advance.**
There are exceptions, of course, but typically, spontaneity is earned. Planning shows that you're not only respectful of my time, but that you actually give enough of a damn to think this through.
♥ **A first date is not about sex.**
Now listen, if by the end of this encounter you've been so swooned by their smile, impeccable manners, and vast knowledge of '90s cartoon theme songs (*Darkwing Duck* was a classic!) that lust is a must, DO YOU! But, setting out on the auspice of objectifying/being objectified isn't the best jump-off point for connection.

Dating is about doing. It ain't just nice words and emojis. It's about demonstrating, through action, that you are interested in learning the contents of someone's character . . . and doing some dope shit in the process.

THE SIXTH MAN

Don't approach anyone with the full court press if you aren't really trying to get to the goal. Because there's gonna be defense, there's gonna be screens, man-to-man or zones, who knows?! But if you ain't really trying to drive to the basket, please just stay on the bench.

PEOPLE ARE PLANETS

Ok, let's get geek life about this. There are various social generalities to dealing with people, but especially when you're dealing with a person on a one-on-one basis in a romantic space, I consider everyone to be an individual. To that end, I look at people as planets. (Told you: SCIENCE!) Ya see, each planet has its own climate, core, and history, just like people. In understanding that, you realize how much of a feat it is for two people to truly come together. Regardless of the gravitational pull of two people, their "planets" must have compatible climates/cores/histories to be able to find and retain a stable orbit.

- **The Climate:** Someone's patterns and ways of dealing with life. Are they prone to storms? Are they cold? Are they temperate? Are they dry?
- **The Core:** Someone's value system and foundation. Are they solid like granite? Are they flaky like limestone? Are they nurturing and giving like minerals?
- **The History:** The way someone's experiences have shaped them into who they are. Are they eroded after years of bumping into other planets that were not compatible? Are they soft sand beneath hardened volcanic rock that formed in order to protect? Are they fields of green that rejuvenate when watered by their own atmosphere system?

No matter how someone's planet is designed, just like with our home, Earth, you study the climate and you can predict how it will function. You look into its core and you can see what properties it's made of. Lastly, when you dig deep enough you can see all the phases we've gone through in history to get to where we are now. If you're lucky enough, someone will trust you to explore their planet and will want to do the same with yours. However, unlike we have done with the Earth, make sure that they only take what they can replace. Be clear that your orbit can end any time they attempt to keep you from getting the light your planet needs to thrive.

AND ON THE SEVENTH DAY...

When you meet someone and you start seeing them and you start feeling them and they're feeling you and it's fun and laughs and jokes and quality time, you may not realize it, but you're building a world made for you and them. A space given life by what you both breathe into it. A wavelength for you to ride while you discover each other's energy. Ride it. Swim in it. Revel in it. Don't be afraid to live in that pocket of joy and stop worrying about whether or not it is forever. Just know that no matter what happens you will always have had that feeling and it is true.

UNDERAPPRECIATED PERKS
of BAE LIFE

Good sex, emotional support, companionship are all great elements of a good relationship. However, there are some added perks that make having a boonopolis the wave!

- **The Airport Pickup:** I'm not saying we gotta run up and do the *Dirty Dancing* lift at baggage claim, but it sure as hell is a great feeling to land safely after being squished in a flying metal box and see someone you like ready to take you somewhere you really like: HOME.
- **Zippers and Buttons:** Have you ever been by yourself and damned near had a panic attack because you couldn't get something zipped up or unbuttoned? It ain't pleasant.
- **Holiday Bae:** The annoying and, for some, anxiety-ridden thought of, "am I going to spend _____ alone" is now eradicated!
- **Blame Bae:** If you've been together long enough they can be a get-out-of-that-shit-you-said-you-were-gonna-go-to-but-don't-really-wanna-go-to-free card. It's not your fault they made plans for y'all to see their parents that weekend and didn't tell you! Dratz!
- **Cooking for Two:** You know how hard it is to cook for one? It's really tough! You buy all these ingredients then after you cook it all up you have all these leftovers. You plate your creation and there's no one else to appreciate the masterpiece beyond the folks on your IG who double tap when they see the pic scroll by. When there's a second person there, though, you have brand-new inspiration! All of a sudden you're Martha Stewart in this piece and Miss Patti with the pies. It's great to have another person there to cosign with, "WOW, the cilantro really gives it a kick!"

RESCUE DOGS

Some folks may not like this comparison, but I think it's very helpful for explaining the dynamics of new relationships formed in the midst of old wounds, because whether it's a puppy or a person, it's the same cause and effect that leads to mistreatment in a domestic setting by someone who is supposed to take care of you. Rescue animals are often in the position of needing adoption because they have been harmed or neglected. Therefore, they seem to always have a certain level of distrust and jumpiness with their new owners due to their conditioning. As an owner, you possess a heightened level of compassion, patience, and duty because you know the source of their reactions. Often these habits are eventually reversed or greatly diminished simply by the animal experiencing the new norm of consistent love, kindness, and support. Now, I'm not by any means saying people are dogs. But what I am saying is that a lot of us react the way we do to new partners (defensive, skeptical, side-eye strained, etc.) because we are accustomed to being treated a certain way. However, we are not some poor pup in a kennel who doesn't have a say in its next home and has to cross its paws that a kind soul will come along to begin our rewiring. We can change that ourselves. We determine our rewiring by who we allow ourselves to intertwine with and how. It feels very natural to state your past negative experiences up top, to let the other person know what you've been through and what not to do, but it can send the wrong message. You are so much more than the bad experiences. When you lead with the positives, you let someone get to know you in light, without having to step over the baggage you've placed at the door of your temple. That said, if you see moves that look like they match the set of baggage you already have, be very deliberate in not negotiating asshole mannerisms. By refusing to accept abusive behavior that undermines our joy. By, at the first instance of fuckery, tactfully and compassionately expressing displeasure at how you're being treated and respectfully disconnecting if the response is dismissal or deflection. YOU cannot control anyone else, but you CAN control what you take in. When you allow yourself to be treated better and given the kindness that you deserve and that you put forth, you rewire yourself to trust, to receive goodness, and be centered in peace versus paranoia. There is goodness in this world. In other words, if he's coming with the shade, ***O.T. Genasis voice*** YOU NEED TO CUT IT!

THE FULL SET

Whether it's a carry-on or a five-piece set, everybody has baggage. Everyone. The question is who is unpacking theirs.

CAPTAIN SAVE A NO

In an effort to be nurturing, supportive, and there for our partners it can be tempting to take on the role of therapist. However, even if you are a licensed therapist, you are not your partner's therapist! A therapist is an objective party who is trained to treat people for their mental wellness. As a significant other, objectivity is out the door.

In that same breath, be careful of when your support becomes enabling. When you love someone, you want them to prosper and you don't want to be in the way of that happening. However, too often in our not wanting to get in the way, we are inadvertently encouraging someone to stay in their own way. You can inspire and you can influence, but you cannot do the work for someone—that they have to do for themselves. Remember, everyone has a candle within them, but only they can light it.

UNCONDITIONAL LUHHH

Love is often spoken of as this singular all-encompassing entity to strive for. However, it is far more complicated than that. At the very least, it is important to consider that there's the love you have for a person and the love you show to a person. You can possess love for someone in a real way, but that doesn't mean that they are in a place to receive/return the actions associated with the emotion. It's a distinction that many of us are forced to make before we make the choice on our own. The feeling of love may be unconditional, but the action absolutely has conditions and it's up to you to define what those are for you.

ARGUMENTS AND DEBATES

Debates are fact-based discussions on opposing sides of a topic. Arguments are debates with emotions involved. Truth is, debates are way easier to navigate, but arguments are way easier to have. Tryna to figure out if something is worth having either about? Don't just choose your battle, choose your weapon. Not every issue requires a Hattori Hanzō sword, and yet some require far more than a NERF gun.

NO CEREBRO, BRO

Truth is, no one is telepathic. I would love be out here Jean Grey-ing everyone on some X-Men shit, but it just isn't in the cards. That said, often people simply don't know they're on some BS unless you tell them. The work is figuring out how to tell them in a way that doesn't demean you and doesn't put them on defense. That's when you gotta come from love. Your partner is going to truly piss you off. They're going to inevitably disappoint you. They're absolutely going to make you question their IQ. When this happens, when someone you like does something you don't like, the toughest part is not going at them from an angry or judgmental place of what you didn't like, but instead digging down and anchoring your argument in the love you have for them. Approach critique from a place of compassion rather than correction, and you see less of an argument and more of a debate. It's not about being phony but finding a more effective way of being sincere. I know, issabitch, but if the person really rocks with you, they get it and respond in kind. If they don't, get to steppin'!

SOLID AS A ROCK

Take some advice that I was given. Don't try to build something sturdy on shaky ground. If someone isn't solid in who they are and what they want, they will more than likely not be solid with what they want with you. Until there's clarity on where/how/why you fit in each other's lives, consider your interaction with them a pocket of joy on the journey.

Relationship
vs. Situationship

A DANCIN' ASS R&B SINGER ONCE SAID, "Situations, will arise in our lives, but you gotta be smart about it . . ." No truer words could be spoken when it comes to the dating game. Even if something may present itself in a certain way, there's what we want something to be, and what it actually is. The two don't always align. For instance, you may be showing up for someone in a real way, but that doesn't mean they have requited love for you. So, in order not to be misled, have your time wasted, or your heart broken, you have to be smart about it, which takes being real with yourself about what you're actually involved in. Is it a relationship or a situationship?

At its best, a relationship is a shared commitment between two folks, on terms both agree on, that fulfills both parties in a positive way (I know there are polyamorous scenarios but for the sake of most readers we'll just keep it a bae + boo equation!). In the best of times there is physical, mental, and emotional equity, and in the worst of times there's understanding, compassion, and consideration for legitimate reasons why any of those first three tenets are lacking. There is no one way to do a relationship, other than the overarching bottom line that it's gotta be mutually consensual for it to be a real thing. It doesn't simply mean both of you have posted one another on your IG pages. Though I can't front, once upon a time the Facebook claim was a **very** definitive move. A relationship is clear. It's defined. It is what it is. In some form or fashion you've each said something to the effect of, "Hey, I like you. Let's let the important people in our lives know that this is a thing." With that declaration, there's a concerted effort made to consider the best for the other person and to be self-aware about how you're affecting their life. It's an "us" scenario. Don't get me wrong, there's a spectrum to the "us" of it all, but on the most basic of terms, when you're in a relationship it's a paperless contract that says you are consciously aware of the fact that there is another person along for the ride and you're not tryin' to drive 'em off the road.

A situationship, however, can feel similar but looks a lot different. A situationship has many of the ingredients of a relationship without the bowl to mix them in. Sure, you may both genuinely like each other, and yea you may both have each other's best interests at heart, but typically in a situationship, one side of the equation, for whatever reason, does not want to commit to being on the ride with another person. The reasons vary in quantity and content. Sometimes it's because they're focused solely on their own direction and feel they'll be distracted by the need for concern for another's direction. Other times it's because they like being available to hop on and off any ride they please (or have anyone ride them as they please), so they want to remain untethered to a specific direction. There's also just the fact that some truly just aren't that into you, and thus don't see the value in your presence on their path beyond a certain point. That said, what makes it a situationship is that even with any or all of those limitations you are tethering yourself to vagueness. If your friends ask you, "So wassup with so-and-so?" and you reply, "I don't really know what we are," you're in a situationship. When you stay Netflix and chillin', and laughing, and talking but you've never met anyone of note in their life, you're in a situationship. If you always have time for them, but they only have convenience for you, you're in a situationship. To be clear, the situationship should not be confused with a "fuck buddy" or "friend with benefits." Those scenarios are straight-to-the-point understandings. The situationship, on the other hand, is less of seeing eye to eye and more of an acquiescence to something that you talk yourself into, thinking that with patience and an unwavering demonstration of compromise, it will eventually switch up into a relationship. It rarely does.

You've seen it or done it before: You and someone are hanging out a lot, you broach the topic of hanging out with each other exclusively, and they say, "Well, I'm not really ready for that. I like things to just happen naturally." Even though you know that you have reached an emotional place in the union that they have yet to reach, instead of reconfiguring the boundaries, you proceed as you've been doing, your emotional attachment continuing to grow, often at the same time as your physical and mental availability. Then a moment happens when you expect them to react or show up or behave a certain way based on your attachment and they don't. You challenge them on it, and they say, "I ain't your man/girl." They aren't. You knew that. However, your expectations were mismanaged because you allowed yourself to get emotionally attached to someone who has made it clear either through actions, words, or both that they are not on the same ride as you.

Do yourself a favor, if you realize you're in a situationship, have a conversation. Find out where their head is at. From there, assess your own value and desires. If they cannot/choose not to provide what you need, send them off with love and a peace sign. If you're in a relationship, communicate. Though all this technology has helped bring folks together to find love, there still is not an app for mind reading . . . yet!

When it's my turn
It will be beautiful
It will be smooth and sunny and sweet
It will be saccharine on my tongue
Snowflakes on my lips
Honey in my tea
Hands on my hips
Kisses for whatevers
Dancing in aisles
No buttons pushed or pulled levers
Smiles, laughs, and smiles.

Bad days and stormy moments
Nestled 'tween comfort and warmth
Weird ways and funny style
Replaced with good form
Bare feet on sand
Bared souls
Held hands
Fearless friendship
Two who understand

"It's my turn," I'll say
With an exhale of acknowledgment
The sky will be blue
I will see clearly now.

When It's My Turn

THAT
ONE TIME

Breakups to Make Ups

I don't believe in fairytales
But I DID believe in you.

Breaking up is hard to do, and even harder to stick with. Listen to your heart, and even more closely to your instincts.

THESE ARE THE BREAKS

Don't bring up breaking up unless you really mean it.
Don't get back together unless you've truly forgiven.
Don't stay together unless you're both in it.

"NICE GUYS"

Some men are nice guys. Some do nice things. Learn to spot the difference.

FIGHT FOR LOVE

Fighting for your relationship is noble. It's honorable and, hopefully, worth it. Far too often though, folks don't start to fight until the relationship has already been dealt the final blow. Some confuse fighting for a relationship with fighting for forgivenes. Which they're screwing up, by choice, and then asking for forgiveness. No, that's not fighting for a relationship. That's a cycle of toxicity.

THE GRAND GESTURE

We've all read the fairytales where a prince kills a dragon, or shows up with a glass shoe. We've seen the rom-coms, where the rich guy scales the fire escape, or the guy in the trench coat stands outside the window with the boom box. The grand gesture is a common trope used to demonstrate love. However, in real life, it must be used thoughtfully.

An unthoughtful use of the grand gesture is in the "take me back" context, which can often end up toxic when performed by the person who's created the negativity in the situation, trying to control the situation. They're trying to control the narrative, but when they had the power to control it they chose to be hurtful. They no longer have a right to the direction of the narrative.

Many of us think the grand gesutre is a demonstration of vulnerability, but often what it really is is an emotional manipluation used to pressure the other into going along with their estranged partner's desired outcome. It's an example of, "I'm gonna do what I want to do to get you back, versus doing what you wanted me to do to keep you." If you're the one that did the F'd up action your only recourse is to apologize, let the other person know that you are aware of your missteps and their repurcussions, and that *when they are ready* you are available to be given the opportunity to correct. Once you do that, SIT DOWN. While you're sitting down, work on yourself, FOR YOU, not for a pat on the back or because someone is watching, or to win your lost love over. Work on yourself so that whether the person takes you back or nah, you're not taking the issues that caused you to fail in this relationship into a next one. Truth is, too often folks are fighting to get their relationship back, versus regaining the trust of the individual they betrayed. What they really feel like they lost is a posession, not the love and respect of a person.

CH-CH-CH-CH-CHANGES

People don't change. Life changes people. Meaning, no one just changes, like, "Voila! I'm this whole other person now!" They have to be moved to change and usually it is "an act of God," i.e., a literal or figurative death or a birth or a fail of epic proportions that does it. That said, if you think you are going to change someone, you're wrong. Did you get that? You. Are. Wrong. They have to have the desire to change. Sure, you can inspire that. Yes, you can influence that, but no, you cannot make them do anything they don't genuinely want to do themselves. Folks think a label, whether it's boyfriend, girlfriend, husband, wife, dad, or mom, is going to make someone alter their behavior or even their personality. Know this, IT WILL NOT. So if you're sticking around with your fingers crossed that someone is going to spontaneously become who you want them to be and in the interim you're hurting while waiting it out, lemme save you some time and pain. Unless they inwardly make the definitive decision to do so, people, like a leopard's spots, will not change. Keep it movin' to the K.I.M.

CHEESE EGGS *and* SELF-IMPROVEMENT

The person you're seeing can recognize how dope you are, how hard you work, how good your cheese eggs are, how smart you are, how good you are with money, how well-behaved your kids are, how good your pussy is, but it doesn't matter. If they're not trying to be the best version of themselves, they don't deserve the best version of you.

INTENTIONS

Intention and action are not the same thing. Even if someone has the best of intentions, if they're unable to see that through in action it turns from intention to disappointment, which becomes resentment. If you recognize in yourself or in someone else that they may have the best of intentions but they continuously fall short of that because of their inability to act, then the best thing to do is just cut it before it gets dirty and nasty.

A KEEPER

Get you somebody who's not always fighting to get you back but who thrives on seeing you stay.

BREAKUP ⧢ MANAGEMENT

Ok, so you broke up. It's terrible. You're all effed up. Here are some basic ways to manage the aftermath:

- **Listen to Up-Tempo Music:** I know you're tempted to go full Jhené Aiko playlist, but don't do it. Make a playlist of joints that always get you turnt and wake up with it every morning ('cause I don't know about you, but for me, mornings are the toughest after a breakup). I've gone a step further and went on a full salsa music diet where every song is up-tempo, but because I don't understand the words, there's no way for any of them to be a trigger!

- **Stay Busy:** Seems obvious but no, really. This is what friends are for. Get you a full calendar of distractions from thinking about someone who more than likely is not thinking about you. The mall, the museum, the crab spot, the movies, the game, whenever, wherever, whatever— keep your mind occupied.

- **Program Affirmations:** All this technology has got to be good for something, right? After you block them from all social media so that you don't have the possibility of stumbling upon them unwittingly, put your phone to further use. Program affirmations into your calendar that will pop up through the day and remind you, "Everything happens for a reason," "You're the catch!" "SHINE ON!," etc. You'd be surprised how uplifting a nice note to self can be!

MAKE IT WORK

In this day and age of instant gratification and relationship options literally at your fingertips, it can feel like people are disposable when things don't line up out of the gate. Truth is, none of us show up to each other perfect. There's always some level of shifting that has to happen to truly fit into each other's grooves. If you're meeting each other in the middle, I say ride the wave. Sometimes it's not that y'all don't work, you may just need to put in a little work.

I WILL ALWAYS LOVE YOU ...
KINDA

I think sometimes when we say, "I'll always love _____," we're mistaking always loving the memory of somebody, or the memory of that love we had, with continuing to love them. Until you get that perspective you can't get out from under it. You'll always have remembrance for the love you had for them but once people show you another side, you can't keep that going. You absolutely have to be careful with giving love to people who aren't giving it back. We get caught up in "I will always love _____," but no, you'll just have love for that love that you had.

BE FAIR

Once the breakup happens, it's fallback time. It's a wrap. Let the dust settle. Let the other person collect themselves. Don't:
- Keep liking all their pics on IG.
- Expect them to be your friend right away.
- Continue trying to be cool with their friends/family.

It's not fair.

WWMBFFD?

(WHAT WOULD MY BEST FRIEND FOREVER DO?)

I once had someone tell me that you need to hold the people you're dating to the same standard that you would hold your homegirls. At first, I didn't really know what that truly meant. But when I thought about it, I would let dudes get away with all types of behaviors that I would never let my homegirls get away with. My homegirls flake on me, and I'm asking, "What the hell?" My homegirls don't call me back or don't reply to my text and I'm asking, "What's going on?!" Dudes do that and I'd be afraid to say something, because I'm afraid to sound naggy or I don't want to bring it up because I don't want to sound too pressed or too thirsty. FUCK THAT. We're all busy. Be considerate in your communication. However, if someone of supposed importance in your life is consistently too busy, too detached, or too "I'm not a phone person," it's time for a recompartmentalization 'til further notice! You ain't gotta be a dick about it, but nobody in your life, whether they're your friend or they wanna be more than friends, should get away with being inconsiderate. If you call them, they should call you back. If you text them, they should text you back, and if not, then you need to step back.

GHOSTING

Ghosting is the *Phantom of the Opera*–type behavior of vanishing off the face of the phone earth. It's happening right now. As you read this someone is deciding that they will no longer reply to texts or calls or emails and is not giving a lick of an explanation of why. As covered in Side Effects of the Curve (page 172), people ghost for all types of reasons, most of which involve being petty or scared. Listen, unless it's a matter of safety, there really is no valid reason to simply disappear from interacting with someone you've been having a credible exchange with without giving some type of explanation. Don't misunderstand me, I'm not saying it's gotta be a three thumb-swipe essay or even a discussion, but trust and believe that unless you're escaping abuse (or fleeing a cop) when you ghost, it's an act of avoidance and cowardice, and that never puts positivity out into the world.

BEWARE OF FUCKBOIS

A fuckboi is somebody who is basically unleashing an onslaught of fuckery and expecting only the consequences of a boy. (See Side Effects of Dating in the Digital World [page 158]). Fuckbois and narcissists share many of the same traits. The difference is that narcissism is a personality disorder with no cure, and fuckboism is a phase that can end. These are individuals who are solely out for their own enjoyment and gain, and fail to have or express any concern about others. They are not anchored to anything or anyone. The awareness comes in how to avoid getting ensnared in their web and how to avoid being someone who slings such webs!

HOW TO SPOT A FUCKBOI:
- Inconsiderate of your time
- Lack of accountability
- Takes without giving in equity
- Intermittent rewards that keep you hooked

THOT-LESSNESS

Though THOT technically stands for "that hoe over there," I consider it to be a euphemism for a woman who isn't necessarily loose with her body (because, whatever, it's your body. Be responsible and you're good) but more so loose with her principles. You're basically a female fuckboi. I'm not going to bother breaking it down. See the above and apply it to a woman. If that's you, you're being THOTty, or my other term for this classification, a "trife gal." Stop that shit. ASAPtuously.

END OF THE WORLD

When you build a world with somebody and you have your inside jokes and the experiences you've shared in private and out in the world, you carry that with you. It's like a whole other realm that you've built with somebody on a wavelength that's all your own. So when they cut it, it feels like they've eradicated that world and you're basically standing there looking at the ashes by yourself. Whether you were seeing somebody for three months or three years, it feels like a death because it's not only the loss of a person, but the loss of this place that you came to love. That's why when you're building that world you have to build it on solid ground. So that even if it gets smote out you still have fertile soil. That's what it is to know who you are and what you're bringing to a relationship. Thus, when you suffer the loss you still have not only the soil, but the tools within you to build again. The silver lining is, you get to have these different places that were beautiful that you can visit every so often. You can walk in the door, just don't set your bags down. You gotta remember the good things but know there's a reason why you're remembering the good things, as opposed to continuing the good things with that person, in that world. That's how you continue moving forward. You can't stay in an old space. There's no air left in there for you to breathe. They sucked the air out. Never forget that.

HOW 'BOUT NOW

Never let someone's wackness devolve your decency. It's easier said than done, but when it's all a wrap and the dust clears, and the subtweets and IG posts are gone off the timeline, you'll feel better if you didn't descend into being mean or nasty.

CHANGE COURSE

You can't control people, but you can control who is in your circle. If you keep allowing folks in your space to bring you negative experiences, you will continue to condition yourself to expect that behavior. Over time you either become desensitized to it or you become hypersensitive to it. STOP IT. TODAY. Make the decision to stop allowing yourself to be mistreated/abused/manipulated. Learn to spot it quickly, identify it, address it, and if it does not change immediately, discard it. Period. Set a code of ethics, become the bouncer at your own club and announce, "I ain't lettin' NO-BODY in that ain't coming through correct!"

YOU DESERVE LOVE. LOVE DOES NOT DEMEAN YOU.

Differences
vs. Dysfunction

YOU ALWAYS HEAR THE ADAGE, "RELATIONSHIPS TAKE WORK."
Sure they do! You need to put in effort to stay present and attentive. You need to consciously put aside time to spend quality time. You need to keep up your side of the partnership. That's the work. Yet, a lot of folks are in relationships and they're working really hard and they don't even know why they're working that hard. People are in a relationship and they say, "You know, we keep clashing. We *keep* clashing because we're so different. We're *so* different." I'm no expert, but it just seems to me that the work in a relationship should not be about making the relationship work. At a certain point you have to ask the question, are y'all different or are you just incompatible?

Everyone has idiosyncrasies and unique points of view, i.e., you may like to sleep naked. Your partner might like to keep their socks on. You might be a Trekkie. Your partner is a Jedi. "Hey, I'm a vegetarian, but I don't mind if you eat meat" or "I like cats, but dogs are fine too." Those are differences. They are inevitable. As humans, we may share basic similarities but overall we are very different and that is a beautiful thing, especially when it aligns. Two different people coming together in a match creates a whole new world for each person to have access to. Some fear differences because they see them as a signifier of the unknown. They find it uncomfortable to experience something other than what they know as a part of their inner circle. Personally, I find differences to be intriguing and growth-building. It can be so exciting dating someone very different from yourself, because when those differences align it forces you to open your mind and often allows you to face things that you may have been actively avoiding but that could elevate you. It can be challenging having to adjust and shift in the presence of someone who is not innately like you or who operates outside of the norm of what you're accustomed to. That said, a challenge is a good type of work. It's like when you go to the club and they play "Knuck If You Buck," followed by "Shorty Swing My Way," followed by "Doo Doo Brown," and you manage to stay on the dance floor 'til the last bass drop. That's a challenge! Because your thighs are absolutely going to have to go to a whole other level of strength to withstand all three of those records in sequence. However, at the end of it, you feel like you have accomplished something. You feel like you have climbed the mountain of ratchetry to its summit! Though you may be tired, though you may be weary, you feel accomplished! (And if you're over thirty-five you feel weak in the knees!) That is what a challenge is. It's work that when done feels like a triumph rather than a depletion. Being challenged is what makes you elevate and gain strength in areas that you may have been lacking in or that you thought were unable to be further improved upon. If you're with somebody and they are not challenging you as a part of your elevation, then they, most likely, are a part of your depletion.

Dysfunction is the clashing of differences because 1) maybe the parties can't compromise, 2) maybe you simply have differences that, though valid, do not intersect in an enriching way for each other, or 3) one person thinks their values are more righteous than the other's. Guess what, your values may actually be more righteous than the other person's. Maybe you actually give a damn about the world and they, on the other hand, are out here just "doing

them." Once you recognize that, you can't cosign it. You're not compatible, it will lead to dysfunction, and there's no value in dysfunction. The whole shit is wack. It's you constantly trying, as an exercise in futility, to make two puzzle pieces come together that simply do not fit. It's you wasting your energy trying to make "fetch" happen. It's you attempting, in vain, to blend your unpressed natural with a Hawaiian Silky. It's not gonna happen. So the cycle continues because when a situation is incompatible it will continue to show you its incompatibility over and over and over again. It's never fun to always be arguing and going head to head. Yet some folks really believe "That's just part of being in a relationship." Nah, it's part of being in a dysfunctional relationship. Perhaps it didn't start out that way and your differences aligned, but people change and when they do, things can get out of line. The question becomes, is it possible to come back to the middle and are you two taking the steps to do so.

If you're reading this and a lightbulb is going off, you probably felt this way in your gut for a while but may not have had the language to identify the feeling. You can totally appreciate someone for who they are without them being the right person for you. If I'm with somebody and they're arguing with me about why Cersei should win the Iron Throne over Khaleesi, I can absolutely appreciate their shared love for the goings-on of Westeros, but if they're in defense of that evil bih Cersei, that tells me off the top that we do not belong together! But I digress, compatibility doesn't mean you don't have to consciously commit to the discipline, self-awareness, and communication necessary to make a relationship flourish, but it does provide a solid foundation upon which to do so. Some people think a relationship is constantly having to "figure it out." NO! You have enough bs going on in the world outside for you to have to *constantly* figure out how to coexist in your inner world. The bottom line is that romantic relationships, at their best, are about elevation, and you can't go upward if you're spending all of your time going at each other.

My mom always says one of the best traits of my generation is that we talk to each other and share what's going on in our lives. This helps folks to see things that they may be overlooking and can also empower folks who may feel alone in their circumstances to actually change them for the better. They say hindsight is 20/20, and when you come out of a breakup that couldn't be more true. All the red flags suddenly seem so glaringly evident, and somehow you either managed to miss or ignore them while in the midst of Lovefest 2000. I've had my fair share of red flags and breakups. So, in an effort to carry forward my mom's insight, here is a list of my own true-to-life red flags that can hopefully help you to protect your heart (three stacks)!

Though things may have started off rosy and joyful, I should have broken up with you when:

- Your sister tried to fight me because I asked her to please stop yelling and you said, "She was just trying to challenge you."
- You said, "My goal in life is to have a house with no mirrors."
- I helped you write a paper for class, and you asked if you could hand it out as a manifesto at my taping of *Def Poetry Jam*.
- You smoked ten blunts a day and said it helped you "focus."
- You were genuinely unsure if the Earth is round or flat.
- You said you were on a six-month hiatus from ejaculating because you were rewiring your mind after being addicted to porn.
- You needed money for a flat tire and without a word, went to your closet, pulled out a shoebox, bagged up some weed, went out, sold it, and came back with $50.
- You brought a gun in my house and didn't tell me.
- You asked, "Can you teach me how to DJ so we can do parties together?"
- You, a fellow artist, looked at my paintings and said, "Your pieces would sell more than mine."
- You texted me, "Good Mourning" several times, even after I corrected you.
- You asked me, "Why you gotta be going at white people so hard?"
- I told you that, on average, a migrant worker a day was dying in Qatar and you replied, "Bad shit happens everywhere."
- You bragged for weeks about how good you could eat it, and when you were down there it felt like you were trying to find out how many licks it took to get to the center of a Tootsie Roll pop.
- You *texted* me Happy Birthday.

- I was in the middle of making dinner, but you said you were so hungry that you couldn't wait. So, you decided to get some fast food to hold us over. When I ordered my Taco Bell you asked, "You good?" instead of paying for it. When I said, "You really should have got that," you said, "If this relationship is going to be about me paying for your meals it isn't going to work."
- You came to my show, and five minutes before I went on stage asked, "You gonna wear your hair like that?" (It was in a bun.)
- You loved your boys more than you loved yourself (or me for that matter).
- You lied about your age . . . by three years . . . and said you were thirty instead of thirty-three.
- You told me you couldn't bring me to climax because I "tasted funny."
- You said my work "wasn't really work."
- You had multiple Jordans and Nike Suits and no passport.
- You told me that all my Master's degree meant was that I could read books and write papers.
- You said, "My fall wardrobe is next level. I'm gonna be out here getting more compliments than you!"
- You asked if the Black Panthers were a revolutionary group.
- You said that you don't date:
    - Women who have been/are strippers
    - Women who have been sexually abused
    - Women who have been physically abused and gone back
    - Women who have had a threesome with two men
    - Women who have slept with anyone you know
    - Women who have slept with more than one dude in a friend group
- You said, "I don't care about mom approval."
- I came home off a fifteen-hour flight from Brazil and you asked, "What's for dinner?"
- I asked you to contribute since you were basically living in my apartment and did not have a home of your own and you said, "CONTRIBUTE?! I don't even like your apartment! It's too narrow."
- You asked me, "How much you think Buffy the Body would charge to hit it?"
- You wore yoga pants. Like, when you weren't doing yoga.
- You had no problem with white people saying, "Nigga."
- After hanging out with me, you said, "I'm going to head home. I haven't been productive today."
- You were living in my house and didn't wish me happy birthday.

- You told me, "If you'd ever been loved properly, you'd know that I'm not as good as you think I am."

You tell yourself the flag isn't red, it's a phase, or a moment, or your fault. You tell yourself that "it's whatever" or "not that deep." You convince yourself that this is all part of the story and no one is perfect and a bevy of other lies we come up with to prolong the inevitable. The truth is, you ignore the red flags because you don't want to admit to yourself that this person is not the right person for you. You don't want to consider that this is another failed relationship. You don't want to have to meet another person, learn another person, and try again. Because the truth is there is a piece of you, even if it is just a morsel in the back of your mind, that wonders if, for whatever reason, you would be able to find better. Know this, YOU WILL.

CHAPTER 5

People Are Weird

Handling Humans & SQUAD UP!

ALL OF US ARE ON THIS PALE BLUE DOT, and none of us are the same. Sure, we may have similarities and resemblances, but we are all unique individuals on our own journeys through space and time. Be that as it may, we come in contact with each other. We get to know each other. We learn, we love, we lie to each other. We have all types of different interactions all day long, and it seems like no matter how long we're here, we still find new kinds of people and new ways of experiencing them. Yet there is still this pseudo standard of "normal" touted like it is the bottom line upon which everything is based. When in actuality NOBODY is "normal." Some folks may be bland, or simple, or basic, but that doesn't make them normal. Normal simply means on trend, and being that everyone is different, it is perfectly normal to also be different. In terms of people and everyday life, weird IS normal!

These days, it's become cool to be weird. IT'S ABOUT TIME. The fact is, anyone denying their weirdness has been living a lie. However, there are idiosyncrasies that separate us all into different pockets on a spectrum of the expected and the unexpected. For some, being the unexpected is a way of life. Others fear being that and anyone who is that. This is where the struggle comes in. How do we all manage to be our own unique selves in the same space and time when fear is in the way? Understanding. Opening our consciousness to the fact that there are different ways that different people deal with things, and that it doesn't always mean they're coming from a bad place, just a different place. In discovering that distinction we open ourselves up to the relief and ease of not taking things personally. We also allow ourselves the grace to know that some folks just don't mesh with other folks, and that doesn't make them wack, they're just not for you.

The different circles we find ourselves in tell us a lot about ourselves. They help us to shape our world and how we want to exist in it. The curation of those spaces is integral to our happiness, stress levels, and pursuit of excellence. Your circle is your tribe. Caring about what everyone thinks is not only exhausting, it's impractical and low-key dangerous. Not everyone cares about your best interest. Not everyone should administer advice. Not everyone is who they say they are. Your tribe, whether it's just two of you or five or more (honestly, when it's more than five I always look sideways because the older you get the realer it gets, and the slimmer the number becomes!), is there to show/receive support, give/receive insight, be honest when it's time to get real, be compassionate when the realness is harsh, and encourage you to always love yourself. Seems basic enough, but it's not always cut and dry and takes time and lessons learned to truly find those who love you the way you love them and love yourself.

With the inclusion of social media in our lives, whether you have an account and an avi or you're someone who says, "Nah, I'm good on the socials," it still affects most of our lives in some way, shape, or form, and boy, it has definitely affected how people operate. It's a world within our world that has its own etiquette, operating systems, and functions. Whether it's to meet new people, watch people you don't know, or check on people you once knew (mmhmm I see you over there making sure your ex's life is still trash!), the socials serve many a productive purpose when you use them to their full potential. When not used productively, they can be a great source of anxiety and leave many in need of a course-correct on context. Humans are trying to keep up with social media's advances (them updates are like EVERY. DAY.) but the technology is changing fast, and we must continue to respond/react in order to know how to also create ways to not let it serve as a detriment instead of a device!

You simply never know who or what could come your way on a day-to-day basis. That's part of the exciting ride of life! Nonetheless, it's nothing short of interesting considering that even though we are all cut from a different cloth, we come together to form a tapestry of types that blanket the world and give it identity.

Type-A Personalities

High strung and specific
We like things just so
But must always remember
To find ways to let go.

Small Doses

TYPE-A PERSONALITY

Type-A folks are typically considered to be over-achieving, high-strung, detail-oriented, impatient, competitive perfectionists who can be neurotic, anxious, and materialistic. They are go-getters, which doesn't always translate to warmth. They are high-functioning, which doesn't always translate to empathy. They are direct, which doesn't always translate to chill. But if you want to get something done, and done well, a type-A is your person.

MISUNDERSTOOD

Common characteristics of type-A folks can very often be misunderstood as someone being mean, disconnected, or tense. When looking at the character traits individually, it's very easy to see how they can be misconstrued, but when placed in the context of the bigger picture of how and why a type-A person functions, it can reposition perspective and perhaps open the door to understanding.

- **Difficult -> detailed:** The dopeness is in the details. Though it can seem like a type-A is being nit-picky, they are simply meticulous.
- **Demanding -> intense:** The goal is the thing. It can feel like a type-A's drive is always on turbo, but they are just hyper-focused about whatever they are set on accomplishing.
- **Curt -> direct:** "Pardon the brevity, I'm corresponding on the move" is literally my email signature because, for some brief responses, it feels like a type-A is being short, but they're just all about time management and sometimes that doesn't include perfunctory pleasantries.

TYPE-As ARE OFTEN:

Nerds. They love details. They revel in minutia. They crave intricacy. To be a nerd is to truly appreciate information. Nerds aren't necessarily wise, but they are steeped with info on whatever they find interesting. They immerse themselves. They obsess. They perfect. As a type-A, being a nerd is so natural and fulfilling. Embrace your nerddom!

Leaders. They are direct. They have to be. They must deliver their messaging in a concise fashion, because it has to connect with a group of varied individuals. The direct, detail-oriented, passionate aspects of a type-A are the traits at the core of so many leaders' ability to stay the course and inspire those who follow their ideology, or who are in their employ.

Comedians. They are hyperaware. They see everything. Then they turn it over and over and over and over in their heads, looking for every grain of funny like a chicken sifting through gravel for corn. It's a tireless process, and a seemingly never complete one, but it is so worth it when you get those coveted laughs from an audience.

No. Well, sometimes. Fact is, social civility requires a certain level of amenability that a lot of type-As just consider to be extraneous. It's not that they seek to be impolite or isolated, they'd just rather use their time for things other than managing feelings. That being said: Type-As, it's on you to do the extra work to not turn that A into asshole; understand that you get what you're giving!

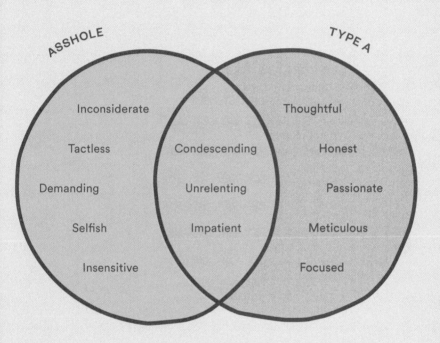

ASSHOLE

TYPE A

Inconsiderate

Tactless

Demanding

Selfish

Insensitive

Condescending

Unrelenting

Impatient

Thoughtful

Honest

Passionate

Meticulous

Focused

Overachiever
vs. Perfectionist

THERE ARE A LOT OF LAZY FOLKS IN THIS WORLD. They're out here riding coattails, sitting around waiting for life to begin, passing the buck, basically doing the exact opposite of what a type-A personality is doing, which is, typically, THE MOST. I speak from experience—us type-Aers are a special breed and not always the easiest to deal with. That can go not only for our interactions with other people, but also for conflicts within ourselves. We challenge ourselves to excellence, and if we're not careful in the process, unfortunately, we can sometimes inflict stress, anxiety, and emotional duress on ourselves during the acquisition of our dreams and goals. You start beating yourself up and next thing you know, "DOWN GOES FRAZIER! DOWN GOES FRAZIER!" with depression, frustration, and self-doubt. The overachiever and the perfectionist often get intertwined, and it's a no-bueno situation that has to be addressed and avoided at all costs! The reality is that, as cliché as it sounds, you really can only do your best. Therefore, you gotta define what your best is and truly be good with that or it's a lifetime of misery, and we ain't havin' that!

The overachiever is all about excellence as a way of life. We see a goal and we not only seek to attain that goal, we attempt to surpass it. I call this stepping into the "Genius Box." Nah, it ain't, like, an actual box that I constructed out of cardboard and Mod Podged glitter with gemstones on the side. The Genius Box is when you make the mental choice to transcend beyond the ceiling that you've hit and enter a new realm of intellectual possibility. It's when you remove all the limitations that you may have inadvertently placed on yourself in pursuit of the desired outcome, and in doing so, usher in new options, potentially ones that were never previously considered. The Genius Box is the cheat code. It's the portal to another dimension of dopeness that you can only access once you've exhausted all attempts within arm's reach. It is the tool of the overachiever because it is like the Room of Requirement in *Harry Potter and the Order of the Phoenix*. It has a designated purpose that can only be accessed by those who seek that purpose. The teacher's pets, the group project member asking for extra credit, the ones asking if they can keep the mythology book for another two weeks to do their independent study (guilty), are all overachievers who, when looked at from the outside, can come off as arrogant showoffs attempting to suck up. I'm not saying the two are mutually exclusive, but there is something to be said for not pinning those character traits on all overachievers. Because the bottom line for overachievers is always not only *how is the mission going to get done,* but also *how is the mission going to get done awesomely*. There is a momentum that we thrive on that keeps us constantly looking over the next set of trees. The thing is, if you're always looking to what's next, you never truly get a chance to examine the steps taken on the path to obtaining the goal, or to celebrate the accomplishment. It is important to do both because in examining the steps you get an opportunity to see what you did right and what you could have done better. In celebrating, you give yourself much-deserved acknowledgment, which is positive reinforcement. Even if no one else notices your accomplishments and no one else is giving you props because they're too busy looking over at their next set of trees, you still need to take the time to pat yourself on the back and say, "YASSSSSS BIIIHHHHHHHH! You did that!" As overachievers, we can get so wrapped up in the "over" that we lose sight of the "achievement." The tea is, when you take even that slight pause of stillness to meditate and give thanks, you allow for a mental download that can give you even more inspiration and invigoration as you launch into the atmosphere for your next win.

What sucks is when overachievers become perfectionists. The reality is, you can only control what you can control. As a perfectionist, you run into trouble when you aspire to a flawless outcome in a situation that involves variables . . . aka ALL SITUATIONS. You're one person. No matter how on point you are. No matter how well you've planned. No matter how ill your spreadsheets are, or whateva, you can't control everything. That goes for the other people working for you, the weather, or even the truth of the well-known proverb, "Shit happens." It does. It just does, and when it does things go sideways and it becomes a 2 + 2 = Elephant type of equation. To go into that scenario expecting a level of perfection that, due to the laws of the universe, is ultimately out of your control, will only cause you to suffer. Sometimes, this aversion to imperfection can be so overwhelming it can place folks in a state of paralysis and stasis and next thing they know, they're not doing *anything* because they feel like if they don't try, they can't fail. Don't let that happen to you. You have things to do and dopeness to share! Some of us have participated in different sports, careers, and institutions throughout our lives that demand and encourage perfection that is often unattainable. I, for instance, was a competitive gymnast. In my time, the perfect 10 was that thing! (Shout out to Nadia Comăneci!) I was very fortunate to have coaches that taught us that "perfect" is different for everyone and at different stages. For my teammate, perfect may have been sticking her handspring layout on beam. For me, however, perfect would have been for ONCE having my back leg straight in a handspring layout on beam. Even if I didn't stick it, if I was able to do that, that was a new level of personal perfection that deserved applause!

The beauty of perfection is that you can determine what it looks like for you. It doesn't have to mean that everything is exactly the way it was "supposed to be." Sometimes, perfection means you got your Legolas on and deftly managed all the slings and arrows that were attempting to derail the process. Other times, perfection means you handled *your sole* tasks up to snuff. Whatever you determine "perfect" to mean, the goal is to not let the pursuit of it dampen your diligence or your joy! Too often, as perfectionists, the hits are overshadowed by the misses, no matter how few. You're left feeling like you fell short and in creating that situation you don't give yourself the much-deserved acknowledgment of even making the attempt. Now, of course, participation ribbons aren't the goal, but you still gotta give yourself a star for getting in the game when a lot of folks are perfectly happy to sit on the sidelines.

As the great Jedi master Yoda once said, "DO or do not. There is no try." The best you can do to achieve perfection and overachievement is simply give it your all. Specifically YOUR all. You can't base that on anyone else or any metric other than that which you set for yourself. Be honest with yourself. You know when you're slacking. You know when you're not dialed in. But you also know when you did the damn thing and handled business. Make the adjustments and you make a way. Then treat yo'self! 'Cause you have more to do, and you'll need to ride that wave of winning, no matter how small the swell, in order to do it!

I was not the kid that needed an incentive to get good grades. I wanted good grades because I wanted to be my best. I wanted to be my best because it felt good to achieve. It was never about feeling validated. It was never attached to self-esteem or a sense of belonging. I simply worked hard and enjoyed the results of what that earned. Most of my teachers appreciated this about me. You remember that annoying girl in your class who asked for extra credit? That was me. Remember that chick who saw you cheating and moved her paper? Also, me. I did the damn work, why do you get to slide by on my coattails. Nah, b. Remember that one girl in the class who always raised her hand and always knew the answer?? Me and also me. I was your friendly neighborhood Hermione and I was not effin' around.

So, one day while doing research in the library (a place people would go to acquire books, and in our case to find published critiques on classic and contemporary literature. Then came Google . . .) we were asked to do a simple assignment of writing down our various sources on index cards using MLA format, a specific type of layout used to record a reference for a research paper. No sweat. I combed through my MLA format guide and recorded each source precisely as instructed. At the end of the class we each had to bring our cards to Mrs. Daly, the teacher of our gifted-level English class, for inspection and a grade.

Mrs. Daly was nice enough, I guess. She was a slight woman with a twanged Southern accent, and she took her job very seriously. One time she accused me of stealing the questions to an open-book test. Yes, you read that correctly. Her theory was that I completed my test in fifth period, then surreptitiously kept the questions, to the open book test, so that I could let my friend Julia review them during lunch so she'd have a heads up when she took the open book test in sixth period. WHAT KINDA DUMB SHIT IS THAT, Y'ALL!? Not only did she run this up the flagpole to the administrators, my friend was strip-searched to find said questions and even after I came to Mrs. Daly's classroom and explained that in the rush at the bell I had accidentally put the questions in my folder when gathering my things, this woman went BACK to the administrators and had them call me back in, at which point my mom said, "Ok now I gotta come up there and have a word with folks." Y'all, I wish you had been in that office when I said it was an open book test. Allem deans who had gathered to bust the test-question-taker case wide open had to pick their faces up off the ground. Yea, lil Mrs. Daly left that caveat out when she started this *First 48*–style investigation. SMH. My point is, she was a solid teacher but her decisions regarding students, in my experience, didn't always line up with logic/rationale.

So, imagine my frustration when I approach to have the rather mundane exchange of giving her my index cards and receiving my grade and instead I'm met with, "These are great Amanda. Perfect. But I'm giving you a B+." You know that SpongeBob meme where Patrick's world is swirling around him and he's tryna brace himself? Yea, that was me, in my platform Sketchers, choker, and skirt from Wet Seal. LADY WHAT?! Y'all, Mrs. Daly stood firm. "I've decided to give you a B+, because even though you did the assignment flawlessly I don't want you to become obsessed with perfection. I've heard of students like you, with type-A personalities, going to college and killing themselves over this so I want to nip it in the bud now." For some reason this educator thought giving me an incorrect grade for correct work would somehow help me to be less of a perfectionist. She went on, "You don't want to become too much of a perfectionist." The thing about it was, there is a difference between being a perfectionist and simply having done the work. What she failed to understand was that me wanting and enjoying credit for work I've done flawlessly is not the same as being dejected when I am unable to complete something flawlessly! My lil 4'8" flat-chested self was livid up in that library, and there was nothing I could do. She refused to give me the grade I'd earned. I, in turn, refused to let her disrupt my continued quest to excellence, and completed another set of source cards, and demanded extra credit to balance out her wackass undeserved B+.

There will always be folks who don't understand your dedication, drive, and motivation. In their attempt to make it make sense, they may try to diminish, derail, and/or distract you. Even when it's done with the best of intentions, know yourself. What Mrs. Daly proved was what so many young black women already know: I would have to work twice as hard and be twice as perfect to get the grade I deserved even when I did all the work perfect the first time. Shine on, y'all.

Da Homies

Friends, how many of us have them
Friends, ones we can depend on
A classic lyric but ain't shit changed
Family is by blood, but
Friends are the family you claim.

ARE YOU A GOOD FRIEND?

No one is perfect. We're all living our own lives and doing what we can to survive and, at best, thrive. That said, ask yourself, are you a good friend?

- Do you check in?
- Do you give encouragement?
- Do you share?

- Are you honest?
- Are you reliable?
- Are you fair?

DATING FRIENDS

They say marry your best friend, but it can be truly difficult to discern if you can date your best friend without it ruining your friendship. We like to think dating our friends would be ideal. After all, friends respect each other. Friends have shared interests. Friends are considerate. If you truly are friends and can keep those core principles, whether it works or not, your friendship will remain intact.

"HE'S LIKE MY BROTHER!"

So many people say platonic friendships aren't possible between men and women, but I don't agree. If either party isn't interested in being in a romantic relationship with the other, they can absolutely have a purely platonic friendship. Even if they HAD a romantic relationship with each other, if they are both clear on the fact that it didn't work out because that was not the best space for them, then there is no problem. Of course, boundaries should be respected when there is a significant other involved, but to expect someone to only have friends of the same gender is not only impractical, it reeks of insecurity.

"WE JUST FUCK BUDDIES"

I'm sure many would say that if you sleep together you're more than friends. I don't agree. It's really and truly about what each person wants from the other person. Not all women want a relationship with the man they're sleeping with. He may not actually be boyfriend material, but he's Vagenda worthy! We all have preferences and individual ideas about romance, love, etc. Therefore, it is no surprise that hella women can truly just like someone in their life for a specific purpose, in this case, as a friend who is respectful and considerate and can blow their back out without stress.

BORROWING MONEY

Most people don't ask for money from friends for a bevy of reasons. I get it. It can feel demeaning. It can be uncomfortable. And it can create stress where there was none. HOWEVER, it's your friend! They have ya back, right? They know you're good for it! Bottom line, I don't care who it is, when it comes to lending, get it in writing. Even if it's just an email, write your agreement down. Set a delivery date for the return. PAY BACK ON TIME. I get it, shit happens, but if they don't pay it back, you're outta pocket.

TO END OR NOT TO END

There's nothing easy about walking away from friendships. Perhaps the most difficult part is deciding when it's truly time.

- **Growing Apart:** Sometimes two plants in the same pot grow at different rates under the same sunlight, and next thing you know they can't share the space anymore. This happens all the time with friendships. It isn't beef. It isn't shade. It's just different beyond repair.
- **Why Are You Friends?:** We often find ourselves staying in relationships out of habit and not out of joy. Incompatibility is a real thing, and one that lets you know when it's time to reevaluate someone's access to your space.
- **Is It Toxic?:** Just because you call someone your friend doesn't mean they are acting in a way that meets your standard of equitable exchange. No one should willingly continue to accept negativity residing in their circle.

EXTINCTION-LEVEL EVENT

There are certain scenarios that seem to be regular sites for friend blowups. They are high pressure, high anxiety, high everything, and the shift in energy can create a rift that is so powerful it completely destabilizes the world you've both built. Before you know it you're standing on the rubble of a friendship that once was. I call those *Extinction-Level Events.* Below are some common ELEs and ideas on how to manage them:

POSSIBLE Extinction-Level Event:

- **WEDDINGS:** People get insane at weddings and legit forget who anyone is.
  Do your best to be supportive through the day of chaos and not take anything personally. After all, you'd want the same on your day!
- **DEATH:** Grief can do a lot to folks, including shift their view of their circle.
  Everyone deals with grief differently, but if you can be a shoulder to cry on, an ear to hear, and rock in a time of unrootedness, you've been there for your friend the best way you can.
- **RELATIONSHIPS:** Some people get a significant other and FORGET they had friends.
  The honeymoon phase is expected, but after that a compassionate and honest conversation is a fair move in terms of making sure your new boo understands the importance of your friendships.
- **FAME:** The height of celebrity can truly make people lose touch with their real life.
  Never become the "yes man." In a blinding sea of adoring fans, often the unwavering light of true friendship can eventually guide a lost one home.
- **WEALTH:** When you think about $ all day it's difficult to care about anyone.
  They say money lets people be who they really are.

FRIENDS TO KEEP/TO DROP

I always say every woman should have in their friend group: an OBGYN, a law-yer, and a dude who's in love with you and has nothing to lose. Lol.

The fact is your circle plays a great role in how you move through the world. Though some folks are in your life out of habit, some out of necessity, and some out of love, it is helpful to truly know where they fall on the friend scale and if they're still filling the correct compartment in your consciousness.

- **The Cheerleader:** Not to be confused with a "yes man," the cheerleader is always rooting for you and hella verbal about reminding you of your strengths. They're not a cockeyed optimist, they're just vested in you being your best and never tire of reminding you—clear eyes, full heart, can't lose!
- **The Truth-Teller:** Every space needs someone to keep it real, and your friend group is no different. Sometimes they can be harsh, but if the intention is about growth, take it for what it is. If you're the truth-teller friend in your group try asking "permission to be honest" before dropping that truth bomb. After all, the truth is typically only helpful when someone is willing to receive it.
- **The Healer:** This friend always seems to knows the words you need to get up and over whatever BS you're in. Maybe they're hella zen and willingly share their calming crystal energy with you. Maybe they're hella spiritual and can always show you a bigger reason for your slight that gives you piece of mind. Or maybe they've got jokes and can always find the funny in the fuckery. Whatever their style, they have a central line to your spirit and can give you a friendly nudge back on to your square.
- **Hi Hater:** This friend never truly is happy for you. There is always an air of jealousy, and it comes out in sprinkles of shaderade that individually don't seem imposing but when you add them up reveal someone who is insecure in themselves and is chipping away at you little by little to fill in the space of their own void.
- **Negative Nancy:** This friend always points out the negative in every damn sit-uation. It could be Harlem on a Sunday with a park full of black bodies movin' and groovin' to soulful house music living their best lives, and this friend will cross the field just to complain to you about how hot it is. Not saying you gotta drop 'em completely, but having a mood killer around is never fun.
- **"Niggas/Bitches ain't shit!":** You know this friend. You're tryna find love and their response is always to shit on any prospect. They never have any suggestions or solutions. They're above reproach. They're bitter, and in their inability to objectively look at the situation they'll only hold you back from finding the love you seek.

Friend
vs. Associate

"FRIENDS, HOW MANY OF US HAVE THEM? Friends, ones you can depend on . . ." Old school MCs Whodini been asking that since they were rocking full leather suits in the '80s, and ain't nothing changed. The circle of people around you is hella influential to how you move, how you live, and how you manage this unrelenting and unpredictable thang called LIFE. You keep shade around you, you're always gonna be in the dark. You keep light around you, you'll always find your way out of the woods. The digital age may have widened the net on who could be your friend, but it doesn't change the realities of what truly makes a friend. Though no one wants to be lonely or feel like they don't have a support squad, knowing how to properly recognize who is squad worthy, and who should stay on the outer rim, is key to keeping your circle on point and your energy preserved.

First and foremost, just because someone is always around, or because they go to the club with you on Fridays, or show up to your house parties, doesn't make them your friend. The true standard of a friend is someone you have a genuine connection with and an admiration for. I keep it this general because, as with anything, there are levels to friendship. Some friends are specific to one area. Maybe they're your workout friend. Y'all keep each other company on your quest to wellness. Or perhaps they're your work friend and y'all kee-kee and keep each other sane through the work day. Or maybe they're your good friend and cover a myriad of bases and are the family you choose. Whatever space they fall in, in order to possess the title of friend vs. homie, associate, or acquaintance, they have to be someone who has your back, who you can rely on, and who shares with you the same fundamental ethics about how to treat people. They also give you constructive criticism, support you when needed, and provide an equitable emotional exchange. They're in your world, in a real way, and you're in theirs. It's an actual relationship. As we all know, relationships have ups and downs and twists and turns and conflicts and harmony. Friends ride these inevitable waves and land back on the beach to bask in the sun and continue the kee-kee.

It is foolish to think that you and your friends will agree on everything, or do everything together, or last forever. People have differences. People have their own lives. People grow apart. Your idea of friendship will morph and evolve based on where you are in life and your experiences. You never know who you're going to connect with and why, but having friends from different walks of life only increases your consciousness of the world and yourself. Often people are afraid or unsure of whether or not they can truly connect with someone because of their differences in everything from age, race, politics, Marvel vs. DC, but even between the most random of individuals, humanity is the equalizer. That said, friendship is a cherished exchange that should not be taken lightly. Along with the fun times and phone calls comes the expectation that this is someone you regard with esteem and on a higher tier than any regular ol' Joe on the street. You show up for your friends but don't hold it over their head. You can lean on your friends but don't expect them to carry you. You ride for your friends but don't let 'em take you down the wrong road. You turn up together. You show out together. They're there to rub your back when shit goes left and to check you when you're not doing right. True friends exponentially improve your formula for life.

Things can get trippy when you start thinking anyone who shares your space in some form or fashion is your friend. We've all done it. I know I have. Mislabeled someone as friend because they always greeted you with jokes and support, they showed up to your functions, and they may have even plugged you into a good opportunity once or twice. All of that is cool, but that doesn't make them a friend as much as an acquaintance. There is nothing wrong with someone being an acquaintance. However, classifying them as such does serve as a helpful marker in keeping your boundaries and your expectations managed. You don't want to go into a situation with an acquaintance if it really calls for a friend. Next thing you know, shit has hit the fan and they're pulling a Mariah Carey "I don't know her" on you. They're right. They don't know you. Acquaintances are folks you've had interactions with and can have a laugh with but when you're down they're not on the speed dial. On the other hand, everybody wants to be liked, and being able to walk into a room and recognize individuals that you can have an exchange with is always a good feeling. There will always be more acquaintances in your life than friends because they are your network. Like markers on a map, they represent the places you've been, and can be very helpful in moving you forward to where you're going.

There's a reason your momma told you that you will eventually be able to count your friends on one hand. Because as you get older, and life gets realer, you can only give that title to the real ones. I take the word *friend* very seriously because I know what I bring to the table as a friend, and I expect the same in return. So much about friendship is understanding and compassion and simply accepting folks for who they are. In that same breath, if someone is bringing stress to your space, let them know. Friendship is not the expectation that you have to put up with everything someone does, but it is having the consideration for why they may do what they do and, based on the other positives they bring, giving them the opportunity to course-correct. Sure, you may have friends that you've kept from childhood who know you from flat-chested and annoying to busty and "outspoken." There will also be times in your life when you realize the folks you're calling friends no longer meet the definition, or maybe never did, and you'll have to reconcile that with moving forward and forging new bonds. It can be daunting, and scary, but it's a part of evolving. It also takes looking at yourself and what you're bringing to your friendships. When you get to where you're going you want people around you that aren't there for the ride, but for the journey. You party with acquaintances. You celebrate with friends. Ooh in a '90s kinda world, be glad you've got your girls.

In our quest to have friendship sometimes we mislabel folks and find ourselves disappointed when they don't show up with the way we imagined they would. The question to ask yourself is why did you consider that person a friend?

I don't know if it's because I'm an only child or because my work is so personal to me, but I have this fantasy of a work environment made up of the homies and we're like one big family that thrives and jives all while making incredible art together! I know this to be incredibly possible. However, it feels like a fantasy because it is so far from what I expected it to look like. As a leader I've experienced the good, the bad, and the ugly of working with friends. Here are some of my experiences:

THE GOOD
Especially when you're broke, friends become an essential component to elevation. Who else is gonna look out and let you shoot your music video in their apartment on a Sunday afternoon as long as you're done before *Game of Thrones* comes on?
singing "That's what friends are forrr"
Who else is gonna show up on a Saturday at 10 a.m. to shoot a party scene in your living room for a sketch that may NEVER see the light of day?
rapping "When my homies call"
Who is gonna come thru at 1 a.m. and board a downtown D train with you to be your audience as you attempt to do stand-up comedy on the train, when you've never done stand-up comedy ANYWHERE before?
screaming "THANK YOU FOR BEING A FRANNNNN!!!!"
Your friends want you to succeed and want you to win. So they'll look out for you. Don't take advantage of that. Don't take them for granted. Don't run them ragged. On the other hand, if you're working with a friend to help them realize their vision, don't hold the favor over their head. Don't half-ass the work. Don't undermine their professional values. The keys to any good relationship are communication and accountability. A working relationship is no different. The best experiences I've had working with friends have been because these two things were already ingrained in our homieship. So, in moving to the work space, it wasn't a far cry to adapt. I've worked with friends in all different capacities. The most fun is when you look around and realize, "Wow, I'm actually getting paid to hang out and make cool shit with my homies!" It's surreal, a source of pure joy, and that "I MADE IT!" feeling. Everything is clicking. The stars are aligning. Y'all are envisioning the future and driving in Benzes from the '80s through Times Square, then it happens . . .

THE BAD

Your taste changes. In this book I talk a lot about change being inevitable and within the working dynamic of your friends it is no different.
People talk a lot about "Day Ones." Drake even has a song called, "No
New Friends." Well, that's a crock of crap. Reason being, sometimes
(most of the time), your day ones don't even make it to day two, let
alone glow-up time. Even when they're your homies, even when they
love you and you love them and both of y'all want to win, as you
continue moving forward it is very common for your tastes to move in
different directions. Sometimes, it's a matter of learning. I've had the
unfortunate experience of realizing that I've surpassed my cohorts
in my education and expectations of quality and process. Once this
happens, it is VERY difficult to continue to operate cohesively. This
is because you are no longer looking to the same standard, so your
instincts on how to move, what to do, and why to do it are not going
to be aligned. This also happens when your drive and motivations

change. Sure, you all may have started working together because it was fun, but oftentimes, if you're lucky, there comes a point where the fun transforms into a career. When that happens, alterations in attitude are a must. If you become more ardent and serious and they remain in freewheeling fun-time mode, it can easily become acrimonious. So, what do you do? You elevate. NEVER stop elevating. Friends or not, if folks don't want to elevate they gotta simply stay where they're at. If you're partners, you may even have a conflict on what elevating truly means. That comes down to you all making sure you go back to how it all started. Meeting at the friend space and speaking to each other from there. Never let the business get you so far gone that you forget your friendship and how to show up.

THE UGLY

This is when it sucks. When you realize, through doing business together, that someone really is no longer your friend. Maybe they don't like the way you do business. Maybe they're no longer interested in what you're doing. Once you come to understand that they're no longer rooting for you, there is nowhere to go from there. I've seen it happen so many times. Friends work together and one or both lose sight of their friendship simply because they're in a professional space. They adopt this "It's just business" concept, which really is simply an excuse to be inconsiderate and lacking in compassion as they do some fuckshit. I remember producing a project where I cast someone I had considered a true friend. Part of my writing process is to write out the bullet points of the scene and then improv with my actors for beats and pacing. In that process it is common that funny lines may come out, and I make note of them for when I sit down to actually write the scene.

The day of the shoot, the friendtress (that's friend/actress) showed up an hour late and without her wardrobe. Already, I knew this was going to be a doozy. Were we a network production, she never would have let that happen, but because we were simply a digital series, her on-pointness was not as sharp. She grabbed some clothes from her trunk and we made it work. Following the shoot, she refused to sign the release, stating that her lawyer needed to look at it and that in order to move forward she would require a writing credit since one of the lines she had improvised in rehearsal made it into the script. Even as I write this I'm rolling my eyes. For the record, no, that's not how getting a writing credit works. Even writers who are working in writer's rooms do not get credit for writing a script simply because they gave input. As for the release, she refused to sign it several times on baseless grounds, as her concern was that there be language stating she would get more money were it to ever be sold to a network. If a show is sold to a network, you begin a brand-new contractual process and make your demands within those negotiations. She was ignorant but thought she was exerting "it's just business" professionalism. Had she approached me from the place of the friendship that got her cast in the first place, and placed more emphasis on the work that was actually being done and less on what she felt she deserved for what she hadn't done, or might possibly do, the outcome would have been far more fruitful. In the end, unfortunately, I had to simply dissolve her character and move forward. This is one of so many instances where friends switch up in a business setting and you can't go back. Because when it happens to a point where they are impeding your quest to your dream it is incredibly difficult not to take it personally.

The other doozy is when friends are not good at the job they have taken on and cannot manage your critique of their work. I consider this to typically be where the bad turns to ugly. Constructive criticism is a real thing, but some just cannot take it. No matter their infraction. No matter how you've delivered it. Some friends just cannot deal with you telling them that they're not hitting the mark. So what do you do? In the best-case scenario, you talk about it and either they step it up or they don't and you dissolve the business relationship and keep your friendship. In the ugliest cases, they get nasty and throw barbs at you for their own failures. They attempt to undermine your authority and devalue your leadership. They disrupt your process in a fashion that is irreparable to your accord. It sucks. It hurts. It frustrates. It is also super-duper common and completely avoidable. Don't work with friends. Make friends who work.

The reality is good, bad, or ugly, the people who want to be in your life will be there. If you're being transparent, and showing love, and have an open floor for them to do the same, then there should be no problems, UNLESS there is resentment, ulterior motives, or ego. In which case, there ain't shit you can do but wish them well and keep on climbin'!

Being a Realist

You keep it one hundred
So, folks think you're coming for their necks
But you're just sharp in assessment,
Straight up, and direct.

THE TRUTH HURTS

Being able to see the realities of what's what is a burden. The truth doesn't just hurt the people on the other side of it, it can hurt you to know it, and to often be expected to keep it to yourself or dole it out to an unknowing or unwelcoming party. Managing that awareness is its own beast and one that can affect many in negative ways. Try instead to look at this skill as a gift. Being able to see the truth, no matter how ugly it is, gives you the necessary tools to find resolution, elevation, justice, and more. In a world where ignorance is bliss, and facts have become "alternative," the truth is a high-value commodity that must continue to be mined and preserved, no matter how inconvenient, disruptive, or hurtful it might seem to be.

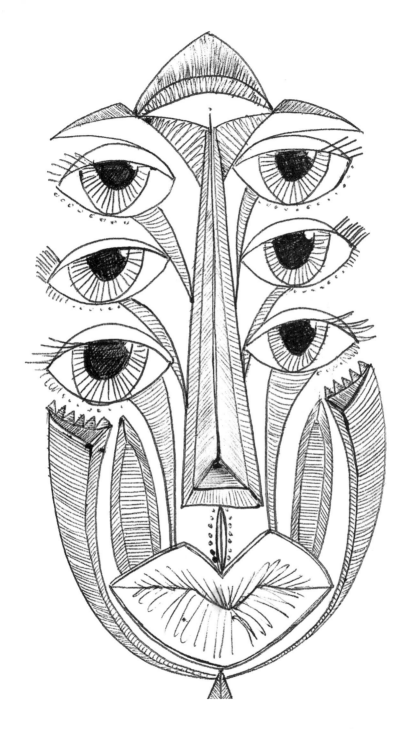

YOU'RE NOT
FOR EVERYONE

Part of being a realist is knowing that you deal in the truth, and as I just mentioned, the truth often hurts. Therefore, most folks aren't really too keen on hearing it. Nonetheless, somebody's gotta dish it, and if you're a realist, it's on you. Since that information has a tendency to cause friction, you can often get positioned as the "Bad Guy," or a "Negative Nancy" in the crew. That definitely can feel lonely and isolating and the fact is, oftentimes, NO MATTER HOW YOU DELIVER IT, folks turn truth-telling into a hostile maneuver. Trust me, I know. So, as a realist, do your best to know your role, and the realities that come with it. Some people won't like you because you reveal what they're trying to hide. Some will love you because you say what they're afraid to. Most will appreciate you because without a realist in their corner, they can never truly see the path to anything real.

READ THE ROOM

Of course, the realist is the truth-teller and, yes, the truth is necessary, but it is not always the right time to bring the real. So much of navigating being a realist is simply being real with yourself in determining, "Is this the right time to bring the facts to light?" You can figure this out in a couple of ways:

- Is what you say going to embarrass someone unnecessarily?
- Is what you point out prematurely inviting the negative into the space?
- Is where your convo headed unhelpful to the cause?

If the answer to any of these is yes, and you carry forth with your comment, you're not being a realist, you're just being an asshole.

SITUATIONS *for the* REALIST *

When it comes down to it, though some may not admit it, ya need a realist in key situations. We are the survivors. We are the planners. We are the troubleshooters. Below are some scenarios where you might feel better with an optimist, you may protect your feelings with a pessimist, but you'd thrive with a realist.

- **Starting/Running a Business:** Sure, you're riding high on hope and vision, which can get you through a lot, but the realist is going to be the key to staying afloat. When you hear people refer to *yes men*, they mean the folks who will tell you what you want to hear to either benefit themselves in some way or to simply stay in your good graces. The realist is the exact opposite. They will tell you what you need to hear to see the situation—pros and cons—for what it is so you can make a truly informed decision that best suits your needs.
- **Choosing a Prom/Wedding/Emmy/etc. Dress:** No one should even be in the room who is not a realist! I get it, you may be insecure about certain things, and you may be fragile about others, but Let's. Be. Real. The fact is, you're gonna be pissed when it's time to post pictures and no one told you that your dress has you looking like a punchline to ***insert fashion police*** jokes.
- **Lost at Sea:** The optimist is a much-needed individual here, but the realist is who's going to kick into survival mode when they do the math on just how dire the situation is. For the record, in *Titanic* neither Rose nor Jack were realists. THEY COULD'VE BOTH FIT ON THAT DOOR.

GOOD ADVICE FROM REAL PEOPLE

Some might say that you can only take advice from people who've been through what you've been through. That is a fair rule of thumb. However, realists are also great advice givers because though they may lack the experience of the situation, their brain operates objectively. Because they are removed from the emotional attachment to the situation, they can use their logic-based rationale to provide a perspective that you may not have considered.

REALISTS AND ROMANCE

You've heard the descriptor "hopeless romantic" before. They weren't talking about realists. Some realists think they'll never find love because they see too much, know too much, and are well aware of all the factors that are truly facing them in finding a match in the sea of madness that we call earth. However, be the realist you are and always look at the other side of the coin, which tells you that there are tales upon tales of folks finding each other. There are centuries-old stories of the stars aligning to actualize the hopes of a romantic, regardless of their realness. There are swipe rights that lead to legacies of love defying the transience of serial dating. A realist can absolutely be a romantic by knowing that the odds are against them, but love is 100 percent proven to have a knack for finding a way.

5 FAVE REALIST CHARACTERS

- **Yoda:** This Jedi realist was the key to making Star Wars's Luke Skywalker see the truth not only in The Force but within himself.
  Classic Realist Quote: *"Do, or do not. There is no try."*
- **Tiffany DuBois:** As *Insecure*'s resident truth-teller, Tiffany may not always have the best tact, but she does have the best intentions: to keep her friends honest with themselves about their own impediments to excellence!
  Classic Realist Quote: *"We have to do better. We can't leave it all up to Chadwick Boseman!"*
- **Lt. Commander Spock:** Everyone's favorite Vulcan with an ability to quell emotion in order to make clear decisions based on logic and rationale that kept him, Capt. James T. Kirk, and the rest of the Starship Enterprise crew alive.
  Classic Realist Quote: *"In critical moments, men sometimes see exactly what they wish to see."*
- **Hermione Granger:** The resident lady brain in the famous Hogwarts trio, Hermione's quick thinking, which is rooted in facts and intellect, played a pivotal role in helping Harry find the way to save the Wizarding World from descending into darkness.
  Classic Realist Quote: *"I mean, you could claim that any-thing's real if the only basis for believing in it is that nobody's proved it doesn't exist!"*
- **Cliff Huxtable:** It's no secret that I do not support Bill Cosby the man, but the character Cliff Huxtable was a much-needed, solid example of a father who, when it came to knowing his role in his household, regarded the importance of his wife as equal parts provider of wisdom, discipline, and income, the necessity of treating each of his children as individuals with their own ideas, identities, and intellect, and, in one scene, showed all of us the true value of money in the real world.
  Classic Realist Quote: *"No fourteen-year-old boy should have a $95 shirt unless he's on stage with his four brothers."*

Realist
vs. Pessimist

OPTIMISTS SAY, "THESE BRAIDS ARE LIVING THEIR BEST LIFE."
Pessimists say, "Them braids are tired." Realists say, "Those braids are ready to be released." Perspective is in the eye of the beholder. How you view the world starts with your childhood and can be shaped by a number of things: how you were raised, where you were raised, the amount of *Love & Hip Hop* you watched—these are all factors. Once you become an adult, and your neck is removed from under the foot of your parental figures, it's up to you how you take things in. If you are an optimist you are always looking on the bright side of things. And although this can be a beautiful trait, sometimes looking at only the bright side ain't gonna get you to the right side. That's where being a realist comes in. Realists assess the scenario, consider the facts, and determine the solution. Though their means may be less emotive and more logic-based, they are often given the unflattering distinction of being a pessimist. Nobody likes a "Negative Nancy," but the truth is sometimes the facts just don't add up to sunflowers.

For realists, the golden rule is objectivity. They operate on an "it is what it is" basis. In order to assess, to find success, realists don't look for negativity or positivity, they look for the bottom line. The bottom line can very often be an inconvenient truth that resembles negativity but is in actuality simply the way shit is. For instance, imagine you're looking to get into a club and the bouncer is out front being wild extra and giving everyone a hard time about getting in this janky lil club. A realist isn't going to say, "Eff this, let's go home." They're also not going to say, "Well, maybe he'll make an exception for us." The realist is gonna say, "Let's watch who this black crewneck T-shirt, black blazer, and shades mofo is letting in and from there determine if it's a no-go or if there's a possibility we can make shorty swing our way." In that scenario, the realist is the one who looks at all the schematics to determine the next action. Any business, friend crew, or revolution benefits by having a realist in the squad to keep emotions anchored to truth. When one person is wilding for respect, it's the realist who steps in and says, "Chill." Whether the scenario is in their favor or not, keeping it 100 is a way of life that they rely on. It's not to say that realists are any less emotional about or disappointed by possible outcomes. Keeping it real may be a figure of speech for some, but for a realist it is literal. They base their judgements, decisions, and consideration of risk on that which they can specifically account for. Therefore, the more real things are, the better they can accurately maneuver and process a situation. They call it like it is. When it comes to solution-finding, they're like that meme with the woman doing the math equation, because they look at each situation with a formulaic approach that considers all the possibilities and actualities. For realists, facts are what keep them on track. This way of thinking has a tendency to throw people off and have them hit you with the "pessimist" label.

Pessimists are an entirely different thing. You know a pessimist. It might be you, reading this book right now saying, "I don't know why she wrote all this shit, it ain't gonna help nobody." Unlike realists, who base their assessments on what's in front of them, pessimists lean to the negative regardless of what they're presented with. They're your friend that always says, "Niggas ain't shit," yet still wants a man. They're your parent that says, "I don't know why you're trying to be an artist, no one ever succeeds," but still expect you to share your journey with them. They're your business partner that says, "This movie will never sell, no one watches black movies." (Actually, they might also be racist, or just foolish. See: *Black Panther*.) The pessimist can seem like a hardened, cold person with no feelings, but beneath that tough exterior is a series of experiences that make being a pessimist "safer" than being a realist. It's often a defense mechanism against disappointment and hurt. We've all been there. There's no way you can date and not have even a lickle bit of it in ya blood. It's hard to fight the pessimism-infused cynicism of believing all people are driven by their own selfish desires when you've been shat on a number of times for that exact reason. However, you don't have to stay there. Fact is, energy is a real thing, and an overabundance of the negative associated with pessimism can truly affect your ability to get over the humps, through the obstacles, and body wave through the bullshit.

When things look like they're going left, the pessimist assumes the worst, versus the realist, who considers the worst, and begins planning on how to avoid or bounce back from it. There are times when there really is no other reality than "This is a fucked up situation." You watch a show like *The Handmaid's Tale* and you wonder, how could anyone be anything other than a pessimist in this situation? You see film from the Civil Rights movement showing dogs and hoses being launched at black people simply wanting to share a restaurant counter with white people, and you marvel at how so many of those involved managed to push forward. You think about life on Earth, and how many forces are constantly against us, whether it be the weather or each other, and you think, how can one not devolve into a well of "whatever." It is so easy to do so. But ask yourself, what is the easiest thing I can do to be a part of change? The answer is, believe in it. You can't see something through or carry it forward if you don't first believe it is even possible. The optimist is convinced of a win. The pessimist doesn't see the point in bothering. A realist identifies the possibilities and prioritizes methods of pursuit. Though we measure the expectations associated with the outcomes, we understand the bottom line. The truth is that nothing will happen if we don't at least try.

Wear my heart on my Chucks to put the right
foot forward
Trust everyone

But never sell my sword

I Be Knowin'

Nor should you
This labyrinth is filled with serpents/dementors/
and individuals
Skilled in the field of killing spirits
Distilling art of merit
And impeding people reaching for the summit

To make for better days

Inside the barrel, crabs abound sideways
They move to pull me down

but I prosper nonetheless

Stressed

THAT ONE TIME

But my pulse the inner rhythm
That tempers the cynicism
I get from living
Existing as more than just an organism

Vocalism

Never underestimate my pen
I've been known to delegate divisions of the risen.
I decimate opinions
With visions on a mission
Moving with precision
Automatic pilot
Self-driven

Cut to the chase
Incision
Bottom lines my base
No schisms
Eyes on the prize spotting the lies in the algorithms
Don't smoke the ism
Drunk on realism

Egotism?

Nah, never tripping on my own two
Grew to view this world with more eyes than two
I don't come for you,
The facts do.
If you mad
It's about you.
Folks be quick to call it hate
But it ain't shade
if it's true.
I'm a
Risk taker
Move maker
Door breaker-downer
Cliff dweller
Stellar spirit
Clown caller-outer
Shouter of the truth
Rebel with a cause
Fat lady singing on the lifespan of these frauds

Haters

They're mad at you
Cuz they're mad at themselves
So don't take it to heart
Or let it affect your wealth!

ARMS LENGTH.

DON'T READ THE COMMENTS

The comments section. You go there with the best of intentions. You've posted something you thought was funny, or dope, or interesting, etc., or maybe you read something that you feel compelled to share your thoughts on. You think, "People will feel the same way I feel about this!" Then you set foot in the comments and clutch your pearls in horror as they quickly devolve into a sea of unconstructive criticism, ignorance, and meanness right before your eyes. You thought you were posting freely, not knowing the haters were there, perched, waiting, like a New York pigeon on a streetlight, to shit all over you. Ya see, the comments section is where haters thrive! It can be a cesspool of insecurities, shade, and just good ol'-fashioned nastiness growing exponentially with each time-stamped statement. Sure, there are sprinkles of people with sense, information, and positivity, but the haters seem to go so much harder in their pursuit of pestilence. So get ya comments on but, if you're tryna dodge the haters, proceed with caution!

THE ART OF THE CLAPBACK

Haters can be anywhere, so you must remain ready to handle them. They may choose to expel unnecessary energy all day, but you don't have to. The quickest way to handle them is to ignore them or, if that's not possible, master the art of the clapback. The clapback is a quick, concise response that gathers someone so tightly, there is no room for a response. It takes a cool head and swift thinking to deliver it properly, but when you can master it, it's like finding all the Infinity Stones and having the power to turn those haters' hate instantly to dust!

- **Remove Emotion:** It is natural to feel bristled by someone coming at you unnecessarily for just living your best life, but you can't let that cloud the clarity you need to . . .
- **Find the Facts:** Sure, this person may have come for you, but hater hate is always devoid of the whole truth. Utilizing what you know of the situation, yourself, or them, identify what they have overlooked, and present it to them precisely and . . .
- **Keep It Curse-Word Free:** I know that may seem gratuitous, but as much as I love curse words, in a clapback context they can muddy the message, and insert inferred emotion where there is none.

The clapback is a cousin of the snap or the dozens. Except where those are playful exchanges of wit, the clapback is not meant to foster dialogue, but to shut it down, so you can keep it movin', hater free!

And now, some of my fave clapbacks that I reuse like grocery store plastic bags:

- Come back when you're thinking bigger about being better.
- I hope you have health insurance, because your arm can't be functioning properly after that reach.
- Be blocked and blessed.

MEAN GIRLS, CBANS, AND TROLLS

The worst is realizing your friends or your significant other are haters. At first, you may not realize it because they are not hating on you, but eventually you notice that they always have something to say about everybody else.

- *MEAN GIRLS* are notorious for rolling in a pack where they fuel one another's insecurities by collectively shading others. They will openly talk shit about folks based on nothing. You might realize they're mean girls if and when you attempt to mention an *actual* unpleasant experience you had with someone (which ain't shade if it's the truth), and they make it a point to ostracize YOU as "mean." One-on-one they may be great, but once in the pack, they assume the hater role. Know that if you're in their scope it's simply because you're super dope!
- *CBANs or Cornball-Ass Niggas* specialize in hating on successful women. Their fragile egos are supported by toxic masculinity that independent, successful, unbothered women dispel daily. In their efforts to retain their measly modicums of pride they prowl the innanets, dating apps, and your local hangout waiting for the opportunity to neg you into what they hope is self-consciousness. If you're on their mind, it's because you're getting shine!
- TROLLS were elevated when the invention of the innanets opened us all up to a whole new world of people we had no idea didn't like us. Here you were thinking it was just your neighbor, your ex's sister, and possibly your cat, but lo and behold, someone named "Getchyoish45" is taking time out of their day to let you know that not only do they not like you, they don't like whatever you're doing in your pic and think it's high time you killed yourself. Getchyoish45 is a troll. A troll is a person who gets their kicks by spreading hateration. They thrive on inserting negativity into positive spaces. They live to ruin your day, every day. However, if they're taking time to type, it's cause you're living your best life!

HATERS BE LIKE:

(ACTUAL THINGS SAID TO ME ON THE INNANETS)

- You post a pic of you and your new car on Instagram:
    "You act like you've never had anything nice before. Humble yourself."
- You get an HBO comedy special and it's announced with a photo of you in a blazer with a deep V:
    "Maybe not the best boobs to go braless . . . I'm just saying . . . zero cleavage."
- You commit your life's work to the arts and activism:
    "She's like the black Paris Hilton. Mad opinionated and famous but nobody know just exactly why you're famous or your opinion matters. lol"

Don't be a hater, witchya hatin' ass.

ARE THEY A "BLIP" OR A "BREATH"?

Your vision and your purpose are your radar. You have to determine who is a "blip," i.e., a momentary distraction, and who is a "breath," i.e., meaning they breathe life into your vision and your purpose. When the latter brings commentary your way, that may feel uncomfortable, but before you reject it, pause and take it in. It might be helpful. If it's not, release it. However, if someone is a "blip," you don't have to do alla that. Let that go right on by. Learning how to discern between the two can save you a lot of time and annoyance!

Criticism
vs. Hating

MOST OF THE TIME YOU DON'T EVEN SEE IT COMING. You're scrolling by a post and it strikes a chord. You make a comment and move on with your life. Next thing you know, your notifications are blowing up. "Damn, did I just become Rihanna?" You check, and instead of an abundance of likes, you scroll through a litany of comments where everyone is calling you a hater and telling you to "Quit hating!" and asking "Why so much hate???" Someone even went so far as to say, "Kill yo'self!" You're confused. All you did was say that you're tired of folks supporting a known woman beater, and people want you to die?! It was just a simple comment, and a factual one at that, right?! No boo, you said something outside of praise, that folks are not feeling, and the innanets have come for you because the distinction between hate and criticism is very blurred. The other reason they came for you is because the innanets as a medium are very blurred. Whether it's an IG pic, a twitter thread, a tumblr post, etc., the www's is a giant forum of perspectives and opinions that find their way to each other. It's both a gift and a curse. People can speak freely, but often without any sort of monitoring. Therefore, you never know who you're really talking to or where they're coming from. So in order to determine whether something that seems like criticism is really just hating, you first have to take a step back and consider the context. Regardless, we all gotta manage ourselves and what we bring to the conversation, so even if you can't determine the difference in what someone else has voiced, you can at least be clear on the difference for your own digital diatribes.

Constructive criticism is necessary. It's necessary because, guess what, we don't have all the answers for how to make things work, how to improve, or how to move. We can't have all the answers because we can't see through everyone's eyes in order to have all perspectives. What makes criticism constructive is when it allows us to actually build on what we've already created or are already doing. It involves information exchange, includes thoughtful

insight, and looks at the work at hand from both a micro and macro perspective. A key to ensuring that the criticism you're providing is constructive is not getting stuck on what someone should have or could have done but staying focused on what they can do *now*. Lemme say that one more time, for the folks in the back: the key is talking about what someone *can do now*. If your homegirl just got dumped by a dude you knew was trash and you come in post-dumpage to make mention of all of the wackness you noticed while they were together that you never spoke on, that's not constructive! It's just annoying. If, instead, you spoke on how to prevent the previous bad decisions from continuing, that is constructive criticism.

To clarify, a correction is not a criticism. Correcting someone delivering incorrect information or using clearly defined hate speech is not criticism.

The internet didn't give birth to haters, but it absolutely gave them a platform for hate that's unlike anything before. Once upon a time, the only way you really knew a person's opinions about you was if you actually knew them! Now, literally anyone, anywhere can not only feel all types of ways about you but they can also let you know. Next thing you know, you're online in a proverbial boxing ring taking proverbial blows from someone with a cow smoking a cigarette as their avi, and a profile that reads like they choose to go hunting instead of to English class. A hater is someone who simply chooses to insert negativity where there is no need for it. They are the person in the comments telling you to be humble when you celebrate buying a new car. They're the person under a picture of a woman in a dress, bringing up how another woman wore that dress better. They insert shade where there is none. They are jealous. They are petty. They are in the way. When haters enter the conversation, they don't push it forward, they obstruct it. With all of that being said, the key is to remember that their input is opinion-based, and not based on valid information, therefore it's not constructive. Trolls are folks who make a lifestyle out of this.

In the case of these innanets, It's important to make the distinction between commenting in a forum and commenting on someone's personal page. If it's in a forum, criticism can often be misnomered as hate. Especially if it breaks from the status quo of the post. When you call out an inconvenient truth or call attention to an issue that the comments en masse are clearly ignoring in favor of applause, you will undoubtedly be labeled a hater. However, if it is pushing the conversation forward and elevating the engagement, it is absolutely not hate, it is critical commentary, which is something we as a society are painfully lacking. However, on a someone's personal page, no matter how constructive you think your criticism is, if it is not solicited, it is not necessary to share, and probably won't be welcomed. I know that may seem antithetical to my previous point, because yes, constructive criticism is

valuable! However, in the case of the internet it is pretty much impossible to constructively give unsolicited criticism to someone who you don't even know outside of the digital space. So often folks are shocked when they share their criticism (constructive or not) of and with a stranger and it's not met with open arms and a deep discussion. This is because these innanets have created a false sense of access and connection. Folks forget that even if you are a fan, follow someone on a platform, and have seen their breakfast, their cat, and a cute dress that they got on sale, it doesn't mean that you know them. It sure as hell doesn't mean that they owe you an explanation or a conversation simply because you chose to engage. So many seem to think that just because they support someone's work or their persona, that their criticism, which is simply just an opinion, should be met with acceptance, regard, and merit. When it is not, they feel they have been dismissed or disrespected. Stop it. Being a fan of someone does not entitle you to them. They are not an object, they are a person. Celebrity does not make courtesy and consideration any less expected.

In these Wi-Fi times, being conscious of how we interact with each other is far too often met without etiquette or concern. Thoughtlessness has been born from the disconnect of humanity due to the shift to connections made digitally. You can leave a comment that seems innocuous to you, and completely ruin someone's entire day while never having to actually have an exchange with them. It has now spilled over and affected how we interact outside of the web and must be considered in our everyday life as well. When engaging, think to yourself, "Would I be cool with someone saying this to me?" When determining if your input is constructive criticism or hate ask yourself, "Does this comment elevate, or just distract?" The old adage "if you have nothing kind to say, say nothing at all" is often a solid ethos to stick to when scrolling. You of course are entitled to your own opinion, you just don't always have to share it with the person you've got an opinion about. In my case, if I don't know you, and I'm not hurting you, I mean this from the bottom of my heart, don't @ me. I genuinely don't care what you think about what I'm doing if it ain't in support of it. Namaste.

Nonetheless, when it is solicited, being able to give valid, helpful criticism is a useful skill that everyone should have and that folks around you, especially those that strive for excellence, will truly appreciate.

Once upon a time, I aspired to be a rapper. In doing so I did what all rappers do and every so often would freestyle over beats that were buzzin'. My rapper name was Amanda Diva. So, it was only natural that when Beyoncé dropped "I'm a Diva" I hopped on the record with some bars about my own Diva status. I had no idea it would almost take me out the game.

Whenever I would do a freestyle or had a new song, I would service the hip-hop blogs of note and, along with the MP3 of the record, I would include a promo pic as artwork to post along with the bars. In this particular case I sent along with the MP3 a pic of me in my usual uniform, spandex & kicks. One blog in particular decided that they would not be using my provided pic and instead opted to use one they found in a Google search. The pic was from the Black Lily festival in Philly where I had performed with The Roots in red heels, a black-and-white strapless romper, and—surprise—a red Kangol. None of that sounds too crazy, right? Well, what was crazy was that the pic had been taken from an angle that was rather suggestive, aka it was by someone standing in the press pit and pointing up toward me, their camera lens aimed directly toward my vaginal beyond. All it took was some imagination and you could see right through those two layers of cotton. Imagination is a beautiful thing. So is time, when you use it wisely. You know who has a lot of imagination and a seemingly endless amount of useless time? Internet trolls. They are a legion of angry, insufficient pricks, forging through the innanets, like Gollum looking for the ring, to find someone's day to ruin. That day was my day.

I won't even tell y'all the name of the site, because I refuse to give it any more play than it has already gotten. The (bitch-ass) owner of the site, along with choosing to post the suggestive photo, placed with it a caption that read, "Amanda Diva versus the comment section." I'm over here, tryna rap, and this dude, who I've never had any interaction with, let alone an acrimonious one, is using me to incite his legion of losers to attack, and like the men and women of the Starship Enterprise, when he said, "Engage," they went to warp speed with the wackness. It began basic enough, with negative comments about my rhyming abilities, which is par for the course. However, it quickly spiraled into sexual explicitness. I didn't even know it was happening until I got a text from a friend asking if I was okay. Incredulous, I asked why, and he sent me the link. I was blown away. Comment after comment demeaning me in any way possible. I remember one that read, "Amanda's hair looks like pretzels and cum,"

and another, morbid and grotesque, that read, "I wanna take her eye-balls out and nut in her eye sockets." It was shocking and disturbing to read, to say the least. They didn't even care about the music, they were focused on nuclear-level hating and it was an extinction-level event. Scrolling, I was clutching my pearls when I got to a post from the actual owner of the site. In the midst of madness he could have taken the post down. He could have steered the convo in a different direction, but no. This man, again, whom I had NEVER met before, who ran one of the biggest hip-hop blogs out there, for some reason, had a vendetta against me and was gonna see it through. He quipped, "Y'all done with Amanda or can I put up the next post?" and they responded by going even more ham in their inhumanity. Needless to say, I went from disturbed, to LIVID.

I hit the Twitters. I contacted dude directly and publicly, asking why he would encourage his commenters to come for me and his callow reply was, "I will not censor my forum." Here's the thing y'all: it's one thing to censor your forum, it's another thing to embolden them. That night I went to see *Precious* (hey, Gabs!) and I remember, while in the theater, getting texts from folks saying I shouldn't have said anything to dude because, THE INTERNETS. "You can't beat him." "He has too much clout." The overlying commentary being, "If you want to be an artist you have to deal with this." Now, yes, as an artist you have to deal with haters. Folks hating on your music. Folks hating on your comeup. Folks hating on your kneecaps and saying they look like Patrick Ewing, tho??? Yes, that is hilarious, but NO, that's not a part of the "Mama, I made it!" package! Furthermore, blogs planting the seeds of your destruction without any real cause? What part of the game is that!? We all know the internet is the wild wild west, and EVERYONE knows, "Never read the comments" but this was over the line because it became a verbally, sexually explicit attack on my body. As a woman, that's not about hating, it's all about sexism, patriarchy, and plain old disrespect. While they were typing, their bum ass's moms prolly came downstairs and asked if they wanted a sandwich. NO. I was not going to remain silent. No, I was not gonna just, "let it blow over," because this was not about folks not liking my music or thinking I can't rap, this was about a blogmaster purposefully posting a sexually suggestive photo of me, a woman, to drive traffic to his blog and using my likeness as chum to feed the sharks circling the drain of his shit bowl excuse for a digital publication.

I gathered myself, defied everyone's advice, contacted Ms. Info, and asked if I could post an open letter to the innanets on her blog.

She obliged. Here it is from 2009:

The homie Amanda Diva has been in the hot seat this week and sent this letter over to address said hot seat and the folks who turned up the burners. I am running out to an appt but I wanted to get this up before I did, because this week, the debate on sexism and censorship lead to some terse Twitter moments, a biting Complex poll, and some interesting thoughts on both ends. So I'll check back in a few.

Amanda writes:

*Well I pretty much got mollywhopped by the internet this week and labeled "emo," "emotional," "triflin'," essentially, "a pussy punk bitch" for speaking out against the ill treatment of women in regards to a blog post on the popular **insert trash blog here.** I thought it would dissolve but after day two of being internet murked I decided to take a shot at clearing up a couple things.*

*When I first read the comments on **insert bum blog here** I wrongly read them as being written to myself. Normally, were they simply referring to my music, I would've said "fuck 'em" and kept it moving. But there was something so personal, at first, about the sexually explicit nature of the comments that they really hit me. In reading more of the foulness I then took it as an affront to women in the game in general. Real talk, we put up with SO much BS from dudes simply based on, "I mean, niggas will be niggas. You know the game," but fuck that! It doesn't have to be that way and the disrespect should NOT be accepted . . .*

*Viewing the comments like "I wanna f— her raw in her c—," and "She looks like she takes n– in her face," (ewww nasty) etc. and the blogger's indifference of them honestly made me feel like, "dag here we go with another forum for dudes to objectify and completely demean us." It wasn't about me wanting respect as an emcee but more so me wanting at least the minimum as a woman. So, I approached (not attacked as some have been insinuating) **insert bitch-made blog owner here** because I felt a "way" about his handling of it. In the end however, I felt like he understood my point and have no ill feelings toward him whatsoever. There was no "twitter fight" of any sort. What I look like fighting on twitter?! Gimme SOME credit y'all, lol.*

Then the epiphany. A friend of mine pulled a Mobb Deep and dropped a gem on me. He said, "Listen Deev, the commenters aren't talking to you, or women. They're talking amongst themselves about their IMAGE of you and other women. They see you and other chicks and they see a target to get their frustration off on, their jokes off of, etc. They think hey, "They put themselves out there so we're entitled to get at 'em! They don't care! They're off in the fun land of showbiz!"(<–he really said that word, haha)

You know what though? They're right! Normally I wouldn't care. Normally I would've laughed and went right back to recording, but I admittedly stepped off my square for a second and forgot these facts:

1. The blogs don't love you but I nonetheless love the blogs and do appreciate their support of independent artists and personalities like myself.
2. The commenters on a lot of blogs are just bored, angry, resentful, etc. and wallow in it with each other at the expense of whoever's face is posted, regardless of how nice, talented, smart they are because for some reason it makes them feel better.
3. Artists, especially broads, ain't allowed to EVER have a sensitive moment without being considered "pansies" and getting written about! (Ask Kanye! LOL)*
4. Not all bloggers/tastemakers feel it is their job to influence their readers. They call it censorship. I call it responsibility. Tom'ay'to, tom'ah'to.

Of all those facts though, there is one thing that I, every other woman in this biz, and most importantly all bloggers and commenters know and must never forget:

Them same folks talking all that mess would NEVER say a word of that to our faces . . . let alone get a chance to nut in 'em!!! HAHAHA!
So yo, let's move on and have a great '09 folks! I hope you enjoy Q-Tip & my video for "ManWomanBoogie" droppin tomorrow, and Tuesday finally begins the Obama era :)

---

* It was 2009 pre-MAGA hat.

Woohoo!!!
Deev

In hindsight, I let him and the whole situation off easy. Why? Because I felt like my only option was to have grace and poise where others didn't. That's the nature of these innanets, constant commentary being hurled at you along with commentary on your commentary. All you can do is live your truth. My truth is that I am a person. Somehow people think that intelligence makes folks unable to make mistakes, that being considered "pretty" alleviates insecurities, and that celebrity makes folks impervious to criticism, to hate, and to disrespect. It doesn't, and in the case of being a celebrity, along with praise and support you're also receiving all the above in BIG. ASS. QUANTITIES. Regardless of your social status, be conscious of what you put out there into the interwebs. Life went on. I later ran into dude from the site and he scampered away like that viral vermin he was/is. I later transitioned out of music, and via Instagram my introspective videos served as fodder for fools. Nonetheless, I remember coming to the conclusion that regardless of the opponent, were it a person, or the whole world wide web, I would not entertain anyone's suggestion I be afraid to speak on injustice and unfairness whether it was directed at me or others. These innanets are not to be feared but be to be utilized.

CHAPTER 6

Glow On

Affirming Your Excellence & Shinin' on These Hoes

GETTING ONE'S "GLOW ON" IS EASIER SAID THAN DONE.
This ain't the glow you have cuz you just passed your driving test or
cashed that paycheck you'd been waiting on, or that morning-after
luster when your crush lived up to the hype! No. When I say "glow on," I'm
talking about a luminescence that comes from way down deep in the
depths of you, past your skin and bones, beyond your gut, ascending
through your heart, out from your soul. You know the tune "This lil light
of mine/I'm gonna let it shine"? That's the glow I'm talking about. Your
light, and how you let it shine. Yet, though all of us have it, not all of us
are aware of, ready for, or know how to change the ways we are dim-
ming our glow's glimmer.

In a world that's become obsessed with "likes" and "RTs," the
superficial has become a landing site for a lot of folks' self-exploration.
I'm not saying don't use your assets—if you got it, flaunt it! But why stop
there? If you're really trying to make the most of your time here by being
your best self, wouldn't it seem natural that you'd have to know your full
self in order to do so?

See, that's the part that gets people shook. Contrary to popular
belief, no matter who you are, or what walk of life you come from, in this
lifetime we all go through a lot of shit, and instead of facing it head on, a
lot of us simply do what we can to actively ignore it and keep it moving.
Some folks try to sex it away, or dissolve it in liquor, or smoke it into
a cloud. Some attempt to run from it by moving, by flying around the
world and masking it with new experiences, or by literally trying to run it
off like it's that pesky freshman 15. Others don't even acknowledge the
trials they've faced. They treat struggling like an unwanted child wizard
and hide it in a cabinet under the stairs, wash their hands of it, and go
about their daily life.

However, inevitably, it outgrows the cabinet, it's at the bottom of
the bottle, or it's right there at the finish line, meeting you face to face.
If you're not ready it can take you clear off your feet, knocking the wind
and the glow out of you in one fell swoop, and have you flat on the grass
like you just asked D-Bo for your bike back. Nobody wants that. Instead,
I say choose to adventure into your own unknown. It's easier said than
done, but find ways to explore the parts of you that confound you,
confront the elements that frighten you, and redefine the beliefs that no
longer serve you. Sure, you may find some memories that need dusting
off and dealing with, you may even stumble upon a demon or two that
was lurking around with a battle axe chipping away at your security, but

the reward is that in doing the work, you'll find strength and courage and resolve that you didn't know you had, and that is the fuel you'll need to get your glow glowing.

I believe that everybody has a candle within to guide them. Some people seem born with theirs aflame. It's lit! Yours may take a few attempts. Just know that the person you follow on Instagram that *always* seems #blessed has trouble keeping their glow burning just like the rest of us. It's understandable, all sorts of things can get in the way: insecurity, the Saturn Return, that full set of baggage you need to unpack in therapy, and the arduous path to Living in Your Truth, to name a few. Though getting your Gandalf on and duking it out with your demons can seem daunting, be encouraged, because the power is all within you. You don't need anyone else's approval, or any achievement of success, or any level of privilege to get to work on clearing the way for your candle to do its thing, thus enabling you to do your thing! Deciding to do the work is your choice, and with choice comes freedom! Whether spoken in the prose of Shakespeare, "This above all: to thine own self be true," or spit in the verse of Rakim, "It ain't where you're from, it's where you're at," to glow on is to emanate self-love from within and let your light be a beacon of boldness that lets the Universe know I'M HERE.

Insecurity

They come in all forms
To have them is the norm
But trust in what you know
And don't them dull your glow.

FEAR FACTORS

For the most part, insecurity is rooted in fear. Fear of acceptance. Fear of failure. Fear of success. There is a plethora of reasons. The first step to challenging your own insecurity is to identify what you're afraid of and find a way to conquer that shit.

"INTERFERENCE!"

ten our insecurities are created and exacerbated by outside sources. It
ms like there's a never-ending stream of assholes just waiting to find
thing about you and trick you into hating it. These, of course, are
In fairy tales they guard bridges, and in life they're no different.
and at the bridge past your self-doubt spewing misinformation,
etimes just straight-up hateration (yup, even outside of the dan-
an effort to keep you in it and prevent you from moving past it,
across the bridge, and getting over it! Don't let other people's
et in the way of you loving yourself.

SELF-SABOTAGE
ISSA SELF-SABOTAGE!

Why let insecurity obstruct a good time? Too often I've seen folks let their own insecurities get in the way of the flourishment of a fly situation. You've seen it, too!

- Ending a relationship before it starts because of self-imposed limitations.
- Creating obstacles and conflicts to offset shortcomings.
- Undermining others' achievements whey they seem to en-croach upon your own.

Nobody has time for any of this. Practice flexibility, dispose of sabotaging, and check your jealousy. It's in the way of your joy.

YOU'RE NOT
for EVERYONE

Not everyone is going to like you. It can be a really a tough pill to swallow, but they simply aren't, and you do yourself a disservice trying to get them to in order to feed your self-esteem. The reality is some people just ain't your people and that's kool and the gang. As my mom always told me, "Attend to who is at the party, don't worry about who didn't show up!"

Rock with people intrigued by your differences, not intimidated by them. Stop seeking approval from people who see your strengths as flaws. Because insecurity is fueled by fear, instead of attempting to learn how you move in the world, far too many folks will attempt to diminish your uniqueness under a blanket of mediocrity that makes them more com-fortable. Don't listen to them. The teacher that tries to simplify your name because she's afraid of the foreign nature of your culture and revealing her lack of knowledge on it—make her say that name, LOUD!

TODAY IS THE GREATEST

Things most people are insecure about that you can change TODAY:

- **Having food stuck in your teeth:** Finding out you have food stuck in your teeth after you've been talking to hella people is such a gut punch. You feel like you've been looking crazy and no one said anything. Here's the thing, food gets stuck in teeth. It's happened to LITERALLY EVERYONE. Anyone who's judging you based on that ain't worth your clean teeth anyway!
- **Your boyfriend/girlfriend:** Listen, if you have concerns with your significant other based on insecurities developed from past relationships, that needs to be addressed and supported, within reason. Whether travel-size or big enough to be checked and stowed below the plane, everyone has baggage they carry with them and the other person in the relationship has to take it or leave it when it comes to working through unfolding the fears neatly packed away. You do this by demonstrating your character through acts of consistency, and by giving your partner the space and the chance to do the same.
- **The money sicheeashun:** Ok, so you don't have your dollars right, YET. Keep it real with yourself and your process. You may not be where you want to be just yet, but in the meantime, explore ways to still enjoy life to the fullest even with the lack of $$$ access. Nature, food fairs, free day at the museum, picnics, Groupon trips, a library card, the Zara end of summer/winter sales—we all have interests that bring us joy. Don't let a couple dollaz get in the way of 'em.

People have to be able to tell you their feelings in a rational way without you getting defensive. Don't get me wrong, defense mechanisms are understandable and human. That clapback reflex that you feel is you coming face to face with the uncomfortable possibility that you could be wrong or disliked for being wrong. However, arrogance thrives if unchecked. So, if you're truly 'bout it 'bout it, let them speak their truth, then you can decide if you should shift or nah.

VIEWS FROM THE MIDST

Insecurity is all about perspective. Change your approach, and you change your response to it. When you face the triggers that bring up your insecurities, you become more skilled at not only recognizing them, and knowing how to curtail them, but also how to dissolve them. Doing so opens the door to using your energy toward things/people that serve you, receiving the constructive criticism that helps you grow, and evolving the insight that will continue to push you toward excellence.

WOBBLEDY WOBBLEDY DROP IT LIKE IT'S HOT

Don't try to find stability on some wobbly shit. If someone doesn't believe in themselves it is difficult to consider that they could truly believe in you.

BULLSHITTO NON GRATA

People will pass you their BS. PASS IT BACK. What I mean is, pay attention to what people show you about their own insecurities and how those can affect you. You'll be busy taking something personally, not even realizing whoever you're talking to is actually just deflecting their own insecurity back onto you. Get your ninja skills ready and *Last Dragon* them vibes to the left.

KNOW YOUR RIGHTS

Don't ever let anyone make you feel insecure about demanding they treat you right. When folks find your weak spot, that place where you're most vulnerable, they may be inclined to flip it on you as a reason why you don't deserve what you are demanding. You've heard the sentiment before, "She ain't cute enough to be acting like that." "How you poor but want to look nice?" etc. Your desire to excel and to be treated to a standard consistent with how you treat others is your right.

Confidence
vs. Arrogance

NO MATTER HOW WE'RE STEPPING OUT IN THE WORLD, we should all aspire to put our best foot forward. Insecurity, however, has a way of sneaking in and turning that step into a tiptoe, a shuffle, or even a Stanky Leg. It makes you second-guess yourself, doubt your moves, and can go so far as to force you into paralysis—if you let it! Everyone deals with the presence of insecurity differently. Some lean on facts, by either exploring what they know to be true internally or by seeking out information to strengthen their solidity on the subject (think: doing extra prep before a big job interview so you're armed with not only facts about you, but also about the business). Others attempt to mask insecurity with false assurances, usually resembling overcompensation in some form or fashion (think: the 45th president, who's always accusing everyone of lying or having no class to divert from the fact that he has no qualifications). The former exemplifies confidence, the latter describes arrogance. Because they both appear to be positions of strength, they can easily be mistaken for one another.

Confidence is rarely won without incident. Meaning it cannot truly be accomplished in a vacuum. For instance, yes, you can belt out SWV's "Weak" in the privacy of your shower all damn day, but until you've actually stood in front of people and flawlessly done them Flo Jo runs up and down the record like Coko did, you aren't truly confident in your ability to sing the song. You can read all the Game of Thrones books and feel secure in your knowledge of Westeros, but until you've debated whether or not House Stark really is superior to House Targaryen, do you truly have a handle on the topic? You can take Spanish classes all day, but until you're in Cuba and this fine-ass papi is trying to speak to you and your ability to properly converse is the determining factor in whether you leave the club alone or with a Havana boo, you don't truly know if you've mastered the language. This is because confidence is developed not just by learning, but by living with what you've learned and providing empirical proof that you are not an imposter but someone with a true grasp on what you seek to demonstrate knowledge of.

Ask yourself, what am I confident about? The majority of your answers will be related to things you've been committed to and seen various sides of at various levels of experience. A couple things I'm confident in: public speaking, frying plantains, and giving head. All three were born from a genuine interest, developed through practice, and honed with precision resulting in positive responses from my delivery of each. The confidence therein comes from not just how well I can do them, but how experienced I am at doing them. That is why repetition is a vital part of the process for actors, athletes, pilots, etc. Not just because of the muscle memory you gain, but also because of the mental security of knowing, for a fact, that you have given your consistent attention to this skill and earned its ease. The best pep talks don't require much more than simply reminding yourself of the certainty that you've done this shit before, you're gonna do it again, and, having examined your missteps, this time it will be better. The confidence comes from acknowledging not only what you feel, but what you know. When I find myself feeling insecure and nervous or doubting my ability to do something, I go to those facts. Confidence is quiet and peaceful, drawn from a reservoir of assurance that you cultivate from within.

Arrogance is loud. It's what happens when instead of settling insecurity with fact, one tries to silence it with ego. It comes from a place of distraction and denial. It is a mask of fraudulence that the wearer dons in an attempt to prevent themselves and others from seeing the truth of their own human condition, which inherently includes fear and vulnerability. In other words, it's a really annoying self-defense mechanism. You've seen arrogance before. It's always the ones saying TOO. MUCH. while actually doing THE. LEAST. Throwing their bravado all over the damn place like when rappers screw up your hair by spraying the crowd with champagne. NOBODY LIKES THAT. Insecurities will always find their way into the light through arrogance. It's the mean girl who always has something to say about somebody because in actuality she doesn't like herself. It's the dude who brags about how good he is in bed when really he's a "fast pumper" and instead of doing the work to create intimacy with you, he's more interested in beating up your box. (My vagina is not the face of the girl-bully who stole your chicken nuggets every day of seventh grade!) It's the person who isolates themselves by saying, "I didn't come here to make friends," when they're simply just scared they won't make friends. The barrier created by arrogance gets in the way of true connections and constructive criticism, both of which are needed to continue to elevate our self-awareness and the attainment of our desires.

The thing is, in this growing world of daily digital demonstrations, it can be increasingly difficult to tell who's arrogant and who's confident. The truth is in the foundation of someone's presentation. For instance, a person can approach you for a date and express confidence in themselves and their ability to speak to you, their romantic interest. The arrogance shows when the approach is done in such a way that assumes that you'd be foolish to say no. The arrogance that says, *anyone who doesn't respond in kind is flawed* is an insecurity-based shroud used to protect them from rejection. The thing is, when we're experiencing our own lows beneath the weight of self-doubt, the boastfulness associated with arrogance can seem empowering. Fake it 'til you make it, right?! Different situations call for different tactics, but when it comes down to it, you will inevitably have to show up and show out, so better to root your footing in what you know than in a pretense that only makes it seem like you know.

Too often confidence is mislabeled as arrogance by those intimidated by someone who is self-assured. "You think you're all that," has been echoed by many a girl in a schoolyard to another girl who she feels is vibrating way too high for the comfort of her and her surrounding prepubescents. Society is so fear-riddled and hierarchical that many feel only certain types of folks deserve confidence. When that hierarchy of who is "deserving" is disrupted, and someone who is seen as undeserving dares to exude confidence, the instinctive thing for many to do is to try to test that person or dismantle their self-worth by attempting to trigger their insecurity. When I told my third grade teacher that I wanted to be "the first black female president of the United States of America," she guffawed and wrote a note home saying I was "overconfident." As a young black child in an Orlando, Florida, school, she felt I did not have the right to set my sights so high, and she therefore sought to suppress my belief in myself. Sixteen years later I found myself in a meeting with a very high-profile television producer who, baffled at the clear and intellectual answers I had to his myriad of professional (and unprofessional) questions, told me he found me "overconfident." I pointed out to him that to say I'm overconfident suggested that I was overreaching regarding my ability to deliver on what I was promising. However, I was speaking based on what I know I can do, because I've done it. In both cases, the absence of fear and the presence of assurance was a threat that they felt they needed to smite out, which only served to reveal their own arrogance. Had I demonstrated insecurity, they would have considered me easier to manipulate.

Not today, devil. Don't let anyone gas your arrogance, and don't let anyone undermine your confidence by saying you're immodest. Confidence does not negate humility. In fact, it breathes it. It is the humility in your confidence that allows for growth and learning for which arrogance does not allow space.

Everyone is insecure about something, but you can find confidence in simply knowing your insecurities and facing them. I call it "*8 Mile*-ing" à la Eminem's character in the film of the same name and his tactic to call out his own issues before allowing someone else to belittle him with them. In a nutshell, confidence is knowing that whatever way the wind blows, you got this. Arrogance is believing that you're beyond the reach of the wind. Truth be told, no one is. Anyone who thinks they are is lying to themselves. Don't let 'em sell that lie to you.

I don't send nude pics. Never been my thing. I could claim that it's because I refuse to objectify myself before the male gaze, or because I exercise a high level of discretion and am too responsible to allow for images of my body to make their way to the masses. You'd believe me if I said either of those. But if I'm being honest, the true reason I don't send nudes is because I'm insecure about how my boobs look in photos!

Listen, blame it on me being an overachiever, or plain old fear, but if I'm going to send a topless pic I want it to look Louvre-worthy: a masterpiece of areolic proportions, a tit-ular triumph, so to speak! However, only once have I been able to attain a pic even remotely resembling that. Otherwise all attempts have been off-kilter captures with one boob perky and in place, looking dead on, damned near smizing into the lens and the other looking off to the left like it hears its phone in the other room. No matter the angle, this always happens. Both boobs are photogenic in their own right, but they can't seem to get on the same page at the same time! My left breast is like that one girl in your friend group who has to Beyoncé every situation and stand out from the crowd, "I know we all said we were wearing white, but red is my color!" It simply wants to do its own thing and in turn makes any photos look like I'm doing performance art of a surrealist piece aptly titled, "Melting THOT." Therefore, I have yet to snap and send.

Imagine if I did. Imagine if I dug into the facts and said, "Amanda! This is silly! It is incredibly common for dem tiddaysss to operate on individual agendas. Also, let's be real, guys don't give a damn. They're just happy you didn't send them a dissertation text that they're going to have to decipher! Your breasts are beautiful, no matter what!" All truths! Then, imagine if, now confident in what I can lean on as reality, I toss my insecurity to the wayside, like an evil underwire bra after eight-plus hours of confinement, muster up the moxie, snap a selfie, and send it on through. Imagine if, on the receiving end of said selfie, the receiver opens his phone, takes the image in, in its full glory, and replies with a thumbs-up emoji? A THUMBS-UP EMOJI?!?! I WOULD COMPLETELY LOSE MY MIND. Alarms would sound, whistles would blow, animals would begin behaving strangely as if they can sense a shift in seismic waves or the (inevitable) arrival of extraterrestrial beings! Because, were I to surmount this insecurity over the photo-graphing and sharing of my unwieldy mammary glands and follow through with a digital delivery, I would require a grand-gesture level of appreciation! For instance, a reply involving a rhyming pattern of some sort, akin to Shakespeare or Shabba Ranks that went something like:

Titties so round
Titties so brown
Make me wanna
Lick you up and down

It's only right!
That said, since I have yet to achieve that jedi level of security in the hooters department, I've archived the one shot I managed to snare and will eventually share it with one who is deserving. Until then, I keep my titty cards close to my chest, literally.

Individualism

There is only one you
Combined of bold hues
Define yourself
Based on your own truths.

NAY CRAY

The world is made up of billions of people, yet so many find it odd that you would have the audacity to be different. That's how "witches" got burned at the stake. It's why there needs to be an LGBTQ community. It's why that one girl in your high school who always wore Renaissance dresses to class was considered a "weirdo" instead of an "innovator." So many folks are afraid of anyone who doesn't look/think/act like them. You're not an alien. Don't let them make you feel crazy. Let their fear empower you to be fearless.

SOLO DOLO

Walking your own path is not for the faint of heart. Literally, if you have a faint heart, you need a buddy, because life is hard, even when walking the paths most trodden. When you are "marching to the beat of your own drum" you are cutting the bush from the path yourself. It can wear you out. Be fair to yourself. Take breaks. Rest your mind. So that when you get back to it you can work smarter, not harder, to get to where you want to go.

CHECK YASELF, BEFORE YOU *WRECK* YASELF

DON'T LET OTHER PEOPLE'S WACKNESS DIMINISH YOUR DECENCY. No really though, often we allow the poor judgement, limited consideration, and pure shade of others to make us think that it's okay to return those sentiments. Don't get me wrong, sometimes even when it ain't ok, it just feels good. I get it. But the whole "being the bigger person" thing is really about not letting someone else's behavior influence you into acting beneath your character.

IT'S ALL RELATIVE

DRASTIC MOVES CREATE DRASTIC CHANGE. Think of it like New-ton's third law of motion: for every action there is an equal and opposite reaction. When you find yourself stuck or static, it can be the perfect time for a shake-up. Whether that means diving deeper into a complexity that scares you or a simplicity that seems like regression, an intentional move in a pointed direction can often be the action that gives you the reposi-tioned perspective you need to see your new path.

BISH GET OFF ME!

Don't let yourself become ensnared in other people's limitations. Your vision is bigger than their moment. So often folks deliver advice based on their terms. Too often folks make predictions based on their own experi-ences. Hella often folks react to their own fears, not to your truth. Learn to tell the difference. This is the art of choosing the battle. The finesse of dodging the distraction. The foresight to overcome the obstacle. On your path, people will be all of these things and will cause all of these things based on nothing having to do with you. Rise above them by remaining so rooted in your goal that they only shake some leaves from the tree, but never topple its growth.

BENZ OR BEAMER?

You're only high-maintenance to those unprepared for high quality. The only people I've ever had tell me I'm "high-maintenance" are those who think little of themselves. Your circle is a reflection of who you are as an individual. If they don't get it, it's not for them.

IT'S YOURS

Your story isn't less valid because you haven't seen tragedy, nor is it tainted because you have. We're all here trying to get through this thing called life, and everything is relative. Yes, some have more privilege than others, some have seen more tragedy than others, and we should all be aware and compassionate to the unique experiences around us. However, everybody's experience is theirs, and your story, though perhaps seemingly trite to someone else, is authentically your experience to acknowledge.

LIST IT!

WHAT ARE SOME ASPECTS OF YOURSELF THAT YOU CONSIDER TO BE UNIQUE?

Some of mine are:

- I am a fearless speaker. I'll say whatever needs to be said, in any room.
- I am able to reference resources across a wide spectrum, from pop culture to sports to Shakespeare to history and beyond!
- I have a seemingly endless ability to bounce back from heart-ache and still believe in romantic love.

There are various factions in this world that seek to control people by unifying them under a banner of sameness. Religion, race, class—all have been used to diminish individual thought in order to enforce mass messaging that doesn't always serve the many and usually empowers the few. Even if you are religious, identify as a race, and have been relegated to a class, ask questions. Identify what gives you peace, and what gives you pause. Consider the fact that things are how they are because they were made that way, and if they can be better, it's on us to make that change.

Normal does not mean better.

Weird does not mean strange.

Simple does not mean stupid.

Different does not mean odd.

Individual does not mean alone.

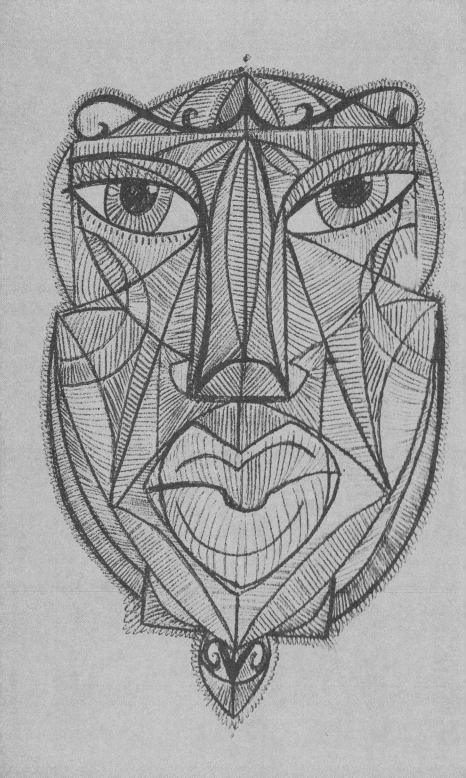

Selfish
vs. Self-Aware

WHEN YOU WATCH THE SAFETY VIDEO at the beginning of any flight they always say the same thing: "Secure your own mask before helping others." At first listen it's like, "Dammmnn that's cold-blooded!" What if there's a crying baby next to you? Or a bilateral-below-the-elbow amputee? Or a passed-out passenger who had one too many vodka tonics? Is it shitty to not look out for them before looking out for yourself? From a certain angle some might say, "Hell yes!," but to my understanding of the ethical logic, and the FAA's logic, the idea is that if you take care of your own mask, and make sure your oxygen is flowing, then you're much better equipped to help others. That's an example of being self-aware. Now, if your mask isn't working, and you take the baby's mask without sharing, that's an example of being selfish (and also, evil—it's a BABY!). There is absolutely nothing wrong with being self-aware about your needs so you can be your best self, but lately the term *selfish* has been misused as a course-correction for someone taking control of their lives, getting focused, or "doin' bad all by themselves," and it needs to get cleared up! Selfish is knowing yourself and making self-serving or harmful-to-others decisions in spite of that knowledge. Self-aware is knowing yourself and making informed decisions based on that knowledge.

I'm not sure when it happened. Maybe it was post–*Waiting to Exhale* or pre–*Eat, Pray, Love*, like, around the time on *The Hills* when LC's boss told her, "You'll always be known as the girl that didn't go to Paris" because she made the lame decision to stay in LA for the summer with her bum BF, but the whole "I'm selfish" movement really took off. At some point, saying "I'm selfish" became all the rage. It seemed like everywhere I turned someone was taking ownership of their selfishness as a declaration of their dedication to focus on career, decide not to have children, break up with you (I literally had a guy tell me, "I'm in love with you but you can't be a priority right now. I need to be obsessed with myself"), you name it! The phrase has become more common than a pair of Timbs on a New York 2 train, and it's never sat right with me. I'm all for the reclaiming of words, but in this case it isn't actually a reclaiming of anything. In fact, as far as I can tell, it's simply a new way to excuse bad behavior, which, btw, is still problematic, whether you claim it unapologetically or not. It's like when people say, "Well, at least I was honest," after saying some egregiously shitty shit. You don't get points for the honesty because the honesty doesn't unshit the shittiness! "I'm selfish" is in the same boat.

Selfishness is wack. It's all about caring about yourself, but its root is in doing so *regardless* of how that makes that others feel. Here's the thing: No one exists in a vacuum. We're all here together. Yes, there are situations when you have to narrow your focus and diminish all distractions, but that can be done in a way that doesn't hurt others. When you encounter a selfish person, be aware that they only want you to thrive if it is best for them.

Unlike *selfish, self-aware* is not used enough. You can claim to be selfish all day, but that doesn't mean you know yourself. In comes self-awareness. Self-awareness is how you know when you're ready to date again after a bad breakup. Self-awareness is knowing that when you drink too much you cry and ruin the party, so you just babysit a glass of champagne all night 'cause no self-aware person wants to be all *"Terms of Endearment* Tammy" in the corner. Self-awareness is knowing that as an artist, you can sometimes be *a lot*, and respecting that not all spaces have enough "room" for that. Self-awareness is great. Not enough of our society has gotten rooted in it. Folks are so caught up with owning their raggedy "selfishess" that they fail to see the value in self-awareness. Its beauty lies in the fact that though it is completely about you, it does not diminish the value you place on others. Though the word *self* implies that it is solely individually focused, the addition of *awareness* broadens the scope to one of responsibility and accountability.

A classic example of selfish: the person who is not emotionally available yet will still date and pursue romantic partners, even though they have no intention of being in a romantic relationship. This is emotionally manipulative and downright inconsiderate, aka selfish. An example of being self-aware: to be in the same situation, but either letting your soon-to-be significant other know your emotional state from the jump, or simply not walking through that gate at all until you have equity to bring to the table. I hear people say, "I've decided not to have kids, I'm too selfish." Well, are you? Or do your interests simply lie in a different place than the behemoth task of raising a human to adulthood, and thinking, in the event of an emergency, about putting your mask on first? Because if it's the latter, you're simply self-aware of what speaks to you and what interests you, and you have every right to feel that way without it being positioned as selfish. Selfish would be bringing a person into this world for a purpose that serves you (i.e., to futilely try to save your marriage [does this move *ever* work?], to get press as an irrelevant celeb, to have someone to force your ideals on, to make you feel purposeful) yet detracts from the child getting the attention, love, and time they need to thrive. The self-awareness of being about your shit has nothing to do with the selfishness of being about *only* your shit.

Listen, we all have at least a modicum of selfishness. You can't think about everybody all the time. With so much trouble in the world, sometimes you simply have to put the blinders on regardless of people's feelings in order to self-protect, to heal, or to quell outside distractions—but making it a way of life is no bueno. Self-awareness demonstrates growth. It informs you to be able to make responsible decisions. It is what you have when you are clear on who you are as a person in a room, a city, a country, the Earth, the Solar System, the Universe, the mind of God.

UNTITLED

BY
LEAH HAPPI HAMILTON

I can't remember the catalyst, but one day, my homegirl Leah casually penned this and sent it my way. It spoke so clearly and so succinctly to the space I inhabit that it has now been on the wall of three different homes I've lived in. May her words be the mantra for you that they have always been for me!

i mix my neon with my pastels
my zen with my most high
tequila with my vin du bougie
flip my daily codes and designs
intensity levels go up
every time i change my mind . . .
they have a choice to stay put or fly
i don't regret it, they don't forget it
FUCK EM DEEV
keep the spirit and stay AMPLIFIED!

Therapy

Goodbye

It gets a bad rap as being
for the "crazy" or weak
But that couldn't be any less true.
It takes courage and strength
To go to a therapist and commit
to working on YOU.

WHAT IS THERAPY?

Therapy is a massage for the brain. Everybody has issues. Therapy is about learning how to manage them and, in the best case, move past them. A lot of people think of therapy as lying on a couch while someone with a notebook sits beside you and answers your questions with more questions. Though that is a form of therapy, there are many different kinds—cognitive behavioral therapy, psychoanalysis, art therapy, etc. It's important to explore the difference in styles and goals attached to the different types of therapy, to find out which is right for you right now. You may not find the right therapist out the gate. You may grow out of your therapist. It can be tedious, but it's worth the effort to find someone who makes sense for your specific wellness journey. Regardless of whether or not you ENJOY it, therapy (of any kind), like eating healthy, meditating, reading, and travel, is good for you and deserves a place in your regimen.

ONLY YOU CAN SAVE YOU!

Going to a therapist is not about them telling you what to do or making decisions for you. It's about them helping you learn how to make the best decisions for yourself. That is an ongoing process that you may never perfect but, as with anything, when you put time toward it you get better at it.

"THERAPY IS
for CRAZY PEOPLE"

Crazy = irrational. Though there are mental disorders that can affect one's ability to make rational decisions, there is nothing irrational about wanting to speak to a professional about how to better function in your skin and in society.

JESUS IS NOT A THERAPIST

Religion and spiritual spaces are a great resource for community, gathering and shared experiences, and some also provide counseling. However, they are not the same as the individual interaction between you and the objective party of a licensed therapist. You may feel more willing to be open and honest with someone who is not a part of your community and your personal space, whereas others feel safer speaking to someone who, as a pillar of their community, has presented themselves as a reliable resource for guidance. Different strokes work for different folks, but it is important to know and acknowledge these differences in order to manage your expectations and get the best outcome.

ACTIN' BRAND-NEW

Like finally growing out that perm, therapy leads to a whole lotta new growth when the roots of your issues are revealed. In order to truly do the work, try your best to keep your mind malleable and flexible, open to change and new techniques, belief systems, and practices toward self-improvement. Some may say, "You switched up." Nah, you wised up. Know that in this process you will hopefully evolve but that not everyone will evolve with you or at your same pace. Creating space from them doesn't make you mean, it just makes you conscious of the fact that not everyone can breathe the air in your new climate.

You are your partner's:
- Friend
- Companion
- Teammate
- Lover
- ~~Therapist~~

You are your friends':
- Confidante
- Road dawg
- Wing (wo)man
- Sounding board
- ATM
- Friend
- Teammate
- ~~Therapist~~

Just because they are your family members does not mean your family members are your:
- Responsibility

Sometimes you gotta just body roll your way through the wackness.

BREAKIN' DOWN THE BREAKDOWN

Mental health does not mean you are happy all the time. It does not mean that you are always at peace and serene. It does not mean that nothing bothers you. What it does mean is that you are able to be in touch mentally and emotionally with life's ebb and flow, without becoming a victim of it. That is easier for some than others and easier at certain times than others. Be kind to yourself and be patient in understanding the unique idiosyncrasies and triggers you're managing daily in order to manage life.

Dear black folks across the diaspora,

It is on us to address the ways in which our pasts, presents, and futures have, are, and will be affected by our unique place in society as black people. Contrary to popular belief, therapy is not "for White People." It was simply reserved for those who had the means and for far too long white people preserved the means and the benefits only for themselves. We, as black folks, have endured so much and passed down so much pain yet, far too often, we continue to overlook the value of mental health as an asset in stopping this cycle. We misnomer its work as an exercise of insanity when in actuality it's a journey to self-discovery.

   Never forget, the oppressor did not want you to read. They did not want you to write. They did not want you to have your own name. They did not want you to sing your songs or dance your dances. They did not want you to own property, or raise your own children, or have your own community, language, religion. They have never wanted you to truly know the extent of yourself, and what you possess, because once you know, you will fight for it. Not only is going to therapy and facing your issues one of the bravest things someone can do, it is revolutionary.

Amandafalrs

Steady
vs. Balance

YOU HEAR IT ALL THE TIME: "You must have balance to have peace." On many levels, I get it. There is value to the thought process that suggests that when things are out of balance they create disruption and chaos. That leaning too much in any direction weighs one down and can get you off your square. It's with this in mind that you set forth to do all you can to make sure nothing in your atmosphere is getting more attention than other things and that all elements of your life are working in harmony and then you're like, "Wow, this balance shit is harder than I thought." You beat yourself up. You question your path. You come back to the middle. Lather, Rinse, Repeat. At some point it dawns on you, "There must be another option!" There is: steady.

When I thought of the big B, I imagined this serene place where all paths converged in an oasis of clarity. I'd read self-help books and listened to people talk about finding a synergy with their worlds and like Liz Lemon I thought, "I want to go to there." It felt like if I could just figure out how to get everything I am doing, and everything I want to do to line up, precisely and with equal purpose, I would no longer be stressed. The notion is so appealing, and at a glance doesn't seem like some crazy accomplishment. After you've taken out a full head of twists that took two days to put in, balance seems like a goal within reach. We all give measure to things. Relationships, career, hobbies, health, etc. all have their own place in our galaxies. Balance suggests that each receives an amount of attention that doesn't prevent the other from receiving its own fair share of attention. However, when you look at your life and attempt to deconstruct each aspect of it with the same meticulousness of removing a braid extension so as not to damage the hair hidden within it, you realize that there simply are aspects of it that not only require more attention than others but that these levels are constantly fluctuating. How are you to handle that? The inconsistency can be overwhelming because life is unpredictable and balancing that is taxing. So, perhaps the idea of balance could be better represented through the concept of remaining steady.

I write this because in my own quest to try to attain balance I became imbalanced! It essentially gave me anxiety that I could not manage to sustain all the things in my life in an equally harmonious way. A deadline would be around the corner and in trying not to stress about it I would stress even more about it. I realized, however, that balance is all about what's outside of me, and I needed to instead work on steadying my inner self. Steadiness is all about maintaining your own balance within, as opposed to balancing the things that you're trying to maintain. When the elements of your world become out of whack, and they absolutely will, how do you remain rooted and not dragged behind them like shoelaces on a dirty bathroom floor? It's just the nature of life. No matter how hard you work to keep things in order, there are outside factors that will always have an effect. When that happens, the hardest thing can be trying to manage the notion of control.

Imagine that you go out to a gorgeous field on a clear day. You get out your colorful, beautiful kite and let the wind take it up in the air. You're just out there enjoying your life, minding your own business, when along comes a windstorm, whipping your kite around, reaching down and tugging aggressively on your arms, nearly pulling them out of their sockets. Pulling the kite in might seem like a daunting task. Sometimes you simply have to run after the kite as it whips around. If that happens, how do you stay on your feet to pull the kite in? In fitness you always hear about the strengthening of the core muscles as the foundation of the body's sturdiness. That same strengthening happens when your mind is steady. Steady is figuring out where your mental and emotional sturdiness lies in order to handle the imbalance that is inevitable in a world full of variables. It is attaining the ability to juggle the rise and fall of the many planets in your solar system and still retain the rotation of your axis. Meditation, deep breathing, and the many other methods associated with stress relief and calming the mind aid in increasing your inner steadiness, which affords you the ability to plant your feet and pull the kite in to a point where you can gain control.

When I was a gymnast, up on the four-foot-high-by-four-inch-wide balance beam, balance was key. Without it, I would fall. However, it was being steady that allowed me to not merely stay on it, but to thrive on it. The steadiness was the solid feeling that even if I lost my balance, I had the fortitude to recover from it without falling. None of this is easy, and it requires time and patience, trial and error, to truly uncover. The takeaway is to explore what works best for you; the concept of balance or the study of how to remain steady. Either way, there is more than one way to look at how to manage moving in this world and not letting its madness drive you mad!

Therapy

If I'm lying to myself, I say I started going to therapy because I was moving to LA and wanted to be ahead of the curve in preparing for the stress that moving naturally creates. If I'm being real with myself, I admit that I started going to therapy because three "friends" too many told me, "People don't like you," and it was officially getting to me. Also, if indeed I was unlikable, I wasn't really tryna move across an entire country to have a whole new city not like me either! So, I asked around and I found a black female therapist, which, unfortunately, even in a city as diverse and populated as NYC was like tryna find a flat-top fade at the Country Music Awards. They simply aren't in abundance (yet). For some people, it really doesn't matter the ethnic background, race, and/or gender of their therapist. Because, for them, their ethnic background, race, and gender don't inform their everyday movements and emotional and mental developments. For me, however, it's a large part of my makeup and makes up a large part of my work, which in turn makes up a large part of how I move through the world and how I react to that which I encounter. That said, I was very fortunate to find a match in my therapist, and we dug in.

To me, the most eye-opening part of this first run with a therapist was how much I didn't know about what you even do with a therapist. Our first visit I remember saying, "I'm not even really sure how this works or what I'm supposed to do or if I even need therapy." She told me that it was a place to talk through interactions, thoughts, desires, failures—really anything that I felt was added baggage to my person. I started with what prompted me to seek her out in the first place, and began talking about my difficulties with certain people and what they voiced as their issues with me. Over time we addressed these issues and basically determined how much of it was bullshit and how much of it was real shit that was in my way. Which brought us to my real true concern: Am I in my own way? When people were telling me that some people don't like me, it wasn't so much that I truly cared if they liked me or nah, but rather, I wondered if by not being compatible with them I was hindering the forward movement of my craft. There were traits about me that were consistently called into question. "You're difficult!" "You're condescending!" "You're too direct," among others, were the hit tunes on the album, *Unlikeable: No, Really, People Don't Like You.* But perhaps the biggest epiphany was realizing how much I had internalized their words and had reached a point where I didn't like myself! My own dag-on self, y'all!

Even though it was 2015, and I was thirty-four, I was moving, and I didn't truly feel like I knew what my purpose was. Yes, I knew

I needed to get out of New York, and I was loving my new path in comedy, but at the time I began therapy I hadn't truly actualized it as my skeleton key.* What I didn't know then but know now is that before I could get to that I had to unpack the baggage that had piled up on my path. Instead of just attempting to debunk what people had said about me and either agreeing with or denying it, we took the approach of exploring each instance and finding out what had caused the comment. We looked at how much of it was construed properly, how much of it was the other person deflecting their own shit, and what I could do to manage the situation in either case. My guided self-exploration with my therapist gave me my self-love back, heightened my self-awareness, and raised my self-esteem. I became able to determine which behaviors I needed to work on and which practices simply required a different audience. Most of all, I got comfortable with the fact that errybody ain't gone like me and thasalright. This is a big huge world, and thriving in it is not only about continuing to work on your own improvement but also finding your tribe—people who inspire, acknowledge, and appreciate the work you're doing!

Therapy is a constant journey that twists and turns and sometimes feels like a plateau. I personally don't feel it's necessary for everybody to always be in therapy. You figure out what works for you. For some, life is always a state of chaos that requires regular attentiveness to keep the good in clear view. Sometimes life is peachy, so you take your board to work and ride the wave. Other times life hits you in your face so hard you need extra help to get your (common) senses back. THAT'S OK. Last I checked, nobody is an X-men out here and yet, in my opinion, Jean Grey woulda done well with a weekly talk on the couch!

PS: I do think it's imperative to go into therapy with a goal and a direction for both you and your therapist to pursue. It has been very helpful for me in determining if a therapist and I are a match and measuring progress.

---

* See Side Effects of Being a Multihyphenate (page 140).

Living in Your Truth

Keeping it real in this
oh so fake world

Is no easy feat

But you need to know
who you are, and face
where you've been

To become who you want to be.

YOU HAVE REACHED YOUR DESTINATION

When you are living in your truth, it does not mean that you are living without obstacles or challenges. It does, however, mean that your willingness and enthusiasm to conquer those obstacles and challenges is seemingly boundless. It provides a thesis statement of self for you to go back to whenever you're lost or bewildered on the path. It serves as a heading for others to know where you're coming from so they know how they should best step to you.

MICHELANGELO IT UP!

Your truth is the colors outside the lines that you define as your masterpiece. Meaning, it is what you say it is. To be clear, you will be challenged on it. Whether by the Universe, by individuals around you, or by these innanets, when you define your truth, you will inevitably be forced to demonstrate it/support it/define it/explain it. Be aware that what you may deem your truth, others may consider a lie, and it is your choice on how, or if, you want to address it.

YOU ALREADY KNOW

I get so many DMs from people asking for advice on how to handle a breakup, or if they should leave a job, or what they should say to that friend who is not really behaving like a friend. Though I don't have time to answer most messages, when I do, I find that most people already know, in their hearts, the next prudent step to take, they just want someone they trust to cosign that it's the right idea. Truth is, the best advice I can give you is to trust your gut, because so often we don't, and our intuition is the truthiest truth of them all! When you work on letting all the doubt fade, silencing all the outside noise, and tapping into that voice inside, it combines with facts you've gathered intellectually and lets you know exactly what you need to do to change the course of your life and live in your truths.

INTUITION INSHMUITION

The question is what's keeping you from doing it? What is keeping you from doing the thing your intuition is telling you to do? It's fear 99.9 percent of the time. It may be a real, viable, understandable fear, but it is fear nonetheless. So the first step toward tackling what's in the way of getting to your truth is acknowledging the fear at your feet and figuring out how to stomp it out. Face that, and you'll see results.

OHMMMMMM

Mediation has become all the rage in recent years, but it is nothing new. I think a lot of us consider it something foreign, or for a specific type of person, or simply too still and silent for our taste. The truth is that meditation comes in many forms, and you may already be doing it in your own way. In the most basic sense, meditation is a practice of calming your mind and body from the distractions and dissonance around it. The practice pursues the power of finding peace from within and carrying it through your daily life to limit stress on your mind, body, and soul. The typical image of meditation may be someone sitting cross-legged with their eyes closed, but there are other forms. When we pray, we are meditating. For some, lying still in bed, eyes closed yet awake, and actively taking in the stillness before facing the day can be considered meditation. Simply stopping, taking deep breaths, and clearing your head before making a big decision is also a form of meditation. The power of it is found in the ritual of making it a consistent part of your life, so it can positively affect all parts of your life. Afterall, inner peace is the only weapon against outer fuckery.

WHAT IS YOUR PURPOSE?

My purpose is: _____. The importance of finding purpose is without limit but, in a nutshell, for many its ability to give clear definition to how we use our time on earth helps to provide a sense of grounding in a life path that is so often out of our hands. It is that groundedness that serves as a cornerstone of contentment for many of us and a springboard off which we leap into living. We are beings made of atoms banging up against each other all day, giving off emissions, radiating light, and constantly combusting. In essence, we are energy. When all that energy lacks intention, it can feel chaotic, depressing, diminishing, and many other harmful feelings. In intentionally pursuing purpose it focuses that energy. In identifying purpose, it refines that energy. Purpose can change; it can shift and morph and does not have to remain static, but the journey to identifying it can't begin until you first ask yourself, What is my purpose?

FROM NEGATIVE *to* POSITIVE AND IT'S ALL GOOD . . .

Give the negative things in your life positive function. Pain makes us feel powerless. There are things that happen to us that can range from annoying to terrible. There are people who happen to us who can range from a being a nuisance to being a devil. In some cases it feels like there is no healing, or liberation, or release from the negative impacts in our lives. A source of power can come from trying, whenever possible, to give positive function to these negatives.

- **Shifty coworker?** Let someone's attempts to undermine your hard work encourage you to find other outlets to display your skills.
- **Injured?** Use the downtime to work on something you never would have taken on were you at full mobility, i.e., reading, writing, binging all eight seasons of *Game of Thrones*, etc.
- **Broken up about a breakup?** Explore some new exercise options to get those endorphins going and up your good vibes.
- **Fired?** Apply for new jobs in your field and maybe explore other options outside of your comfort zone that could open new doors of possibility/experiences.
- **Stalker?** Take a self-defense class and elevate not only your Jason Bourne–level hand-to-hand combat skills, but gain some piece of mind.

WHEN KEEPING IT *REAL* GOES RIGHT!

Living in your truth does not have to mean that you have only one way of expressing your truth. Honesty has a way of getting misused as tactlessness very easily if not carefully considered. There is no shame in curating your truth to serve the situation best. You might feel that if you do so you're "being fake nice" or "being phony," but you aren't at all. The truth comes in many forms. It ain't about being nice, it's about finding a new way to be real.

"DID I DO THAT??"

Don't forget your role in your outcomes. You can't expect people to be positive about the negative situations YOU create. In living in your truth, you must always look within at how you affected a situation. You may not like what you see, but it is key to identifying if there is any opportunity for you to take accountability, and, at the very least, learn from it, to not repeat your role in wrongness in the future!

INTUITION

I legit have an inner voice that is my ancestors. It is a direct line to knowledge that comes from deep deep deep deeep deeeeeeeppp within. It's what many people refer to as instinct. I've worked over the last ten years to perfect the ability to instantaneously shut everything off and speed-dial it for the REAL. But I got there from applying to also really just believing in the truth that our souls are connected to something much wiser and driven by something much stronger than our earthly bodies/brains can truly comprehend. And, no bullshit, this realization came from an episode of *Avatar*. But I think some people that we label as "crazy" aren't really crazy, they're just in touch with their intuition in ways that we can't see. I believe that intuition is the collective wisdom of all the lives you've lived guiding you through this one. Those "crazy" people are listening to that guidance, and I'm listening to mine. Some would say that's crazy, but it keeps me sane.

HELLA DEEP

You never stop learning, BUT at some point, searching gets in the way. How do you know when it's in the way? Some tells:

- When you're so entrenched in self-exploration that you are no longer *living* in the present but always *examining* it.
- When you've become one of those people who is concerned only with learning but not about actually applying the lessons.
- When your self-exploration devolves into self-involvement.

It's admirable to boldly delve into the depths of the black hole that is you. However, it's easy to swim so deep you forget which way is up and which is corny. You think you sound deep. You actually sound lost. Make sure to come up for air, interact with those around you, and as the saying goes, "don't get gassed" from breathing your own hot air from staying down there too long. Come on back!

Be Nice
vs. Be Kind

ONCE UPON A TIME, BEING *NICE* AND BEING *KIND* were kinda the same thing. They pretty much meant you had a pleasant disposition and didn't piss people off for no reason. However, as serious threats like plagues, world wars, and Jheri curls have died out, political correctness and passive aggression have swelled to commonplace status. And, since everyone's politics are different, people have gotten a lot easier to piss off and offend. Which has, in effect, changed the meaning of what it is to "be nice." These days, *nice* looks a lot more like being understanding of bullshit, pretending you're unbothered, and being accepting of mediocrity so that everyone can feel calm, untriggered, and at ease in any and all scenarios.

Growing up in the '90s, the message was "Keep It Real." It was the only goal. I mean, is there anything realer than the video of the beating of Rodney King, the "Mammie" episode of *A Different World*, or Tupac as "Bishop" in *Juice*, or hell, Tupac just as a human being?!? From the clothes to the music to the movies, throughout my youth there was a constant surge of honesty that wholly shaped the way I viewed the world. However, since then, *real* has gotten a bad rap while *nice* has been lifted up. In my opinion *nice* is overvalued in comparison to the shit you can't fake, which is being kind.

"Be nice." You hear it all the time, but at this point, what does that even mean? I'll tell you. The expectation has become that, regardless of the situation, you're always supposed to be smiling, and sweet, and cool, which sounds to me like *nice* is really about how you appear to react to what someone is saying and not so much about the contents of what they're actually saying. Where does telling someone who is ABSOLUTELY full of shit that they're full of shit fall on the "be nice" spectrum? These days, it doesn't even make it on the spectrum because, to hella folks, "be nice" really means "be fake," so just plain saying the truth is a nonstarter. When it comes to women, this is nothing new. "Be nice" has always landed in the bosom of "make all men feel like they are special." That was the mark of a lady—a woman who knew her place (read: when to shut up) and knew her purpose (read: to shut up and serve). Well, thank GOD many of us have gotten past that *Mad Men*–style madness, and although there are guys who love to see us living out our hard-fought right to tenacity, in general, there is still the underlying expectation that a "nice" woman is one who smiles and says, "OK."

In the case of black women, this concept runs deep, as the "angry black woman" trope continues to rear its ugly weave over every one of us who attempts to stand up and be heard. It's like a sista can't say "Happy Birthday" without someone saying, "Whoa, I don't like your attitude." We should be able to speak our minds honestly, without this added expectation to soothe with our speech. On the other hand, for guys of all races, the whole *nice* thing has gotten out of hand. Take the tired-ass saying, "Nice guys finish last," or "Women like jerks." Wrong. It's not that we don't like "nice" guys, it's that we don't like boring guys. We don't like SIMPS who don't have anything exciting or funny or intellectual to add to the conversation. Hear me on this, men: BEING NICE IS NOT ENOUGH. The standard has gotten so twisted that somehow being "nice," which should be a basic requirement, became the only requirement. Now, dudes think that just because they're not douchebags, they deserve entrance into Shangrilina. No, sir. Can we raise the bar and stop getting so hype for men doing basic shit that many women are expected to and would do for them in the blink of an eye? You gotta do more! WE ALL

HAVE TO DO MORE. That's where "be kind" comes in. Unlike being *nice*, kindness is not about what you're portraying, but what you're doing. It's about how you are using, like for real applying, actual love to make the world a better place. Sure, you may smile nicely at the old woman on the bus, but kindness is what makes you give up your seat for her. Yea, you might nicely say hello to the baby on the flight seated next to you, but kindness is what makes you have empathy instead of annoyance when it's crying because its ears won't pop. Ok, you may think it's nice not to point out the food in someone's teeth because you don't want to embarrass them. But let's be real. You just don't want to feel uncomfortable telling them. Kindness is getting over your fear and giving them the heads-up so they don't continue to walk around looking like they just feasted on a carcass.

Niceness is cosmetic. Kindness is kinetic. It is the act of. It is the application to. It is the implementation within. It can be difficult. It can be exhausting. However, contrary to this whole "be nice" thing, kindness is absolutely about being real. It requires truth and principles, two things this world could use a lot more of these days. Make no mistake, just because someone is nice does not mean they're kind. What do you always hear after someone shot up a school, or some man chained three women to a rusty radiator in a basement, "But he was so niiiiicccceeee." Niceness is a mask many folks can wear because that is simply a part of being in a society. You want things done? You can't expect it if you're a prick. You want friends? They're hard to acquire if you're a cold-hearted Scrooge. You want to get ahead? People have to like you! So, niceness is necessary. However, it is not a fair expectation for every situation. It is not fair to expect others to be nice about your unexplained shitty attitude. It's not cool to expect others to be positive about the negative situations you create. Expecting folks to be silent about your mistreatment of them or others? Where they do that at?! Folks will disrespect your time, disrespect your livelihood, disrespect your home, and expect you to serve up a response with sugar on top just so they don't have to feel uncomfortable, guilty, or ashamed. They want you to "be nice!" aka passive.

Now listen, I'm not saying, SCREW NICENESS!!! As I said, regarding the original definition of *nice*, there is a place for it. We live on this rock together. Being *nice* is an active part of being *civil*. That's why I work on it. OG *nice* can require added effort because of its use of extra words, extra thought, and extra patience to make people feel at ease. As a straight-to-the-point, high-brain functioning, type-A personality, only child, few-fucks-given kinda person, sometimes my shortness gets mistaken for meanness, when it's not meant to hurt, it just wasn't nestled in *nice*. I do little things to help along the process: 1) My email signature says, "Pardon the brevity, I'm corresponding on the move :)" I started doing this after a business transaction stalled because the other party felt I was being short with my responses. Of course, I was simply answering his questions, but because in my directness I didn't use extra words of cordiality and niceness it came off short and disinterested when on my end it was simply concise and succinct. 2) I speak in a higher register on the phone with customer service so my deep voice doesn't get misread as abrasive or "over it!" I try, really, truly try, to smile through folks' fuckshit and their attempts to get it past me. I call it, "emoji speaking." It's the live and in-color version of texting someone, "You're full of shit. 💩"

I am a daily work in progress. I will admit that kindness comes naturally to me, but the "old" nice can be tiring and the "new" nice I won't even entertain. The saying goes, you catch more flies with honey than with vinegar, but the question is, how fast are you trying to catch the flies? The pretend politeness of niceness can get in the way of tactful honesty and constructive critique that can be essential to advancing people and projects to a higher plane. As I've gotten older, I've learned that being "nice" about something can save you conflict, but often, being real about it can save you time. You just gotta learn when, where, and how to apply your realness. Nonetheless kind always has a place in the game, even if it's just being kind to yourself. My point is, we gotta challenge the new status quo. Regardless of if you're "nice" based on its old or new definition or nah, not everybody is gonna like you. Not everybody is gonna rock with you, and you know full well why you don't rock with them. All you can do is try your best to be yourself and make a practice of being kind.

In 2013 Barack Obama was inaugurated into his second term in office, I mounted my one-woman show, *It's Complicated: Hilarical Answers to Serious Questions on Love*, and everyone was rumbling about the film *12 Years a Slave*, which was soon to be released in theaters. Two years prior, I had a series of epiphanies that led me to change my name from Amanda Diva back to its original form, Amanda Seales. This was a part of my decision to leave the music business and my pursuit of being a recording artist, and to instead place my attention on finding my way back to TV from the digital space. It was tumultuous, to say the least, and classic Saturn Return behavior.

Sure, I was an artist, and yes, I was a woman, and of course, I identified loud and proud as a black woman, held a master's in African American studies, and was a legit hip-hop head, but then what? When I looked around at my peers blowing up (which you should never do), I knew that I was missing something. I didn't truly know the direction I was going in, because I hadn't truly figured out where I was coming from! The advice I kept getting was, "You need to be more crossover" or "You need to be an 'it' girl" or "You gotta get the whites to like you." But, how? The answer seemed to be: By toning down all that hip-hop-African-American-studies-"Who-you-callin'-a-bitch?!" stuff and fitting in. I wrote blog posts on pop culture that shied away from social commentary and topics in the African American zeitgeist. I tried to go to the "right" parties, which pretty much had a Taylor Swift, Katy Perry playlist and invite list, so I was often one of only a handful of people of color in the room. I also attempted to define myself simply as a "personality"—WTH does that even mean? It was all so contrived. Nonetheless, it seemed like if I wanted the success of being recognized as a notable voice and talent, this was the only option. And maybe I'd have to front or fake a lil bit, but it'd be worth it, because eventually I'd have the clout to do what I wanted to do and define the rules myself. I continued on the path to pop culture maven, resolute that this was the way, on up to the fall of 2013.

It was October and *12 Years a Slave* was set to drop. There were rumblings within the black community about whether a film like this was "needed." Did it unnecessarily continue the already exhaustive narrative of black folks as slaves? Did it bring anything uniquely creative? Was it a responsible choice of work? All valid questions, none of which stopped me from going to see it.* I'm not quite sure why, but I ended up going to a movie theater in New York City's Lincoln Center. Literally the hotbed of upper-class geriatrics who serve as patrons to the various performing arts venues surrounding the area. These were the liberal elite, who are often more white savior than white ally (we covered that in "Race Realities" [see page 45]), and although they may use their funds for foundations and providing shoes for a generically Latin-named child in some Central American nation, they, themselves, don't do much mingling with the "others." This was painfully apparent when my mom, a Swedish girl who was AirBnBing at my apartment, and I sat down in our seats at the theater. It was winter and my trademark curly fro was serving as an effective head warmer, glistening in all its glory, when I felt a finger tap my right shoulder. I turned around and was met face-to-face with a woman who seemed to share the age of Downton Abbey's Dowager Countess and the style of *Vogue*'s Anna Wintour. Without even so much as a morsel of irony she asked in an unassuming manner, "Can you please put your hair away?" Y'all, I nearly climbed over that seat!!!! However, I remained calm and told her, through gritted teeth, "Sure, I'll tuck my ethnicity in for you," and turned, back to face the screen. No sooner was the Swede asking me what happened when another Dowager Countess to my left sent a sharp "Shhh" my way. Already triggered, I turned to her and said, "This is not the film you want to be giving me orders at." Without a word, she faced forward. The lights dimmed. The movie began.

The film was unwavering in its honesty and its portrayal of the characters as individuals trying to thrive through their strained and suppressed existence, instead of simply as black characters representing a tragic tale. It was not a Hollywood interpretation of an era that many know about but that few speak about candidly. It told the story of these Black lives and was vivid and bold and earnest and sharp and unapologetic and visceral and real and done with grace. I left the theater quickly, skootching past DC2, leaving my companions behind, and climbing the stairs to the fresh air of 66th and Broadway, a well of emotion overflowing. Angry at the history that came before me, frustrated with the present, and motivated for the future, I stood on the sidewalk and cried that single silent tear that Denzel did in *Glory*, or like my best friend in college said she did when she had her first orgasm. Seeing such a daring depiction of this individual's previously untold story steadied my rudder. It made me look at my own

---

* I still look sideways at black folks who haven't seen this film. It truly is an artful piece of work worthy of anyone's time. Also, Steve McQueen is from Grenada. BIG UP!

path as a creative and as a descendent of those who were enslaved, and it gave me courage. In that moment a calm came over me and I had an epiphany. It was time to abandon the false narrative and discard the misplaced ideal. It was time to stop looking outside of myself for acceptance, but instead to start digging deeper to plant my purpose in authenticity. It was there on that curb, surrounded by a bunch of rich old white folks, after seeing this masterpiece of black storytelling, that I decided I would no longer try to cross over, I would commit to breaking through, and do so being as black as I wanted to be.

Glow On

#ImOut

This may be the end of this book, but it's far from the end of its evolution. If I wrote it right I'll come back in three years, laugh at how much I've learned, and hit y'all with a volume 2! May your journey to self-awareness continue and flourish into social impact.

Love,